IN PURSUIT OF QUALITY

David Hutchins

David Hutchins Associates Limited, Ascot

Pitman

Pitman Publishing
128 Long Acre, London WC2E 9AN

A Division of Longman Group UK Limited

First published by Longman Group UK Ltd 1990
Reprinted 1991

© David Hutchins 1990

British Library Cataloguing in Publication Data
Hutchins, David
  In pursuit of quality–2nd. ed.
  1. Quality circles
  I. Title II. Hutchins, David. Quality circles handbook
  658.4

ISBN 0 273 03231 3

Typeset, printed and bound in Great Britain

CONTENTS

PREFACE

In the time which has elapsed since the publication of the first edition of this book under the title *Quality Circles Handbook* much has changed on the industrial scene. The track record of Quality Circles in British and other Western countries has not been impressive, and many industrialists have become disillusioned and dismissive of the concept. This is not only unfortunate, it is disastrous for Western industry, because without this concept, or something very similar, it is impossible to compete with Japanese companies on a one-to-one basis.

Since 1979, when the author introduced British industry to the concept of Quality Circles at the London Conference entitled 'The Japanese Approach to Product Quality Management', we have virtually wasted ten precious years of development. Although many companies have introduced Quality Circles during that time, it is likely that around 90% of all attempts have failed totally; of the remainder, none have reached anything like the levels of performance of their Japanese counterparts.

The principal reason for this failure is the fact that most executives, managers, and probably Trade Unionists also, do not understand the overall objectives of the concept, cannot relate it to management style and direction, and most fundamental of all, have no idea as to the dynamic power of Total Quality, of which Quality Circles form a vital part.

This edition is intended not to focus simply on Quality Circles, which was the purpose of the previous edition, but instead to provide an insight into the power and dynamics of Total Quality.

The reader will be taken through each step from the creation of corporate vision to corporate mission, to the creation of business plans and goals aimed at making their company the best in its business. The book offers a competitive strategy which aims to harness the resources of all of an organisation's people to enable it to rank among the top companies in the world.

From plans and goals, the reader will be helped to identify a structure for total involvement of all levels, layer by layer, from the top to the bottom. The philosophy is carefully explained, and all of the ideas presented are already in operation in successful companies: no theory is included which has not been demonstrated to be effective.

Ultimately the reader is taken into the concept of voluntary improvement activities and reintroduced to Quality Circles. There is no detailed coverage of any statistical processes or techniques since it was felt that these could be learned from many other sources. However, it is recommended that when the application of such techniques is to be included in Total Quality, the maxim 'keep it simple' must always be uppermost in the minds of trainers.

This applies as much to the literature as it does to the techniques. If good text material cannot be found from Western sources, then look to Japan where a veritable abundance of good material can be obtained from the Japanese Union of Scientists and Engineers (JUSE), the Asian Organisation for Technical Scholarship, and others – and fortunately much of this is written in English. In the words of Dr Juran, a world pioneer in the field of Quality – 'Good Luck'.

David Hutchins

PREFACE

TO THE *QUALITY CIRCLES HANDBOOK*

In the late 1960s America's Dr J.M. Juran commented: 'The Quality Control Circle movement is a tremendous one which no other country seems able to imitate. Through the development of this movement Japan will be swept to world leadership in Quality.'

In June 1966 the European Organisation for Quality Control held an extended conference session at its conference in Stockholm to discuss the phenomenon of QC Circles, and by that time the majority of Western leaders in the field of Quality Control were aware of the concept. I know I was aware of Circles as long ago as 1969 because I have an examination paper that I prepared in that year with a question asking students to compare Quality Circles with zero defects – a concept quite popular in the West at that time. However, my impression of Circles then was little different from that of others acquainted with the concept. Quality Circles were Japanese, and all I then knew of the Japanese was that they supposedly sang the Company Song each morning, participated in physical jerks at intervals during the day, and punched effigies of their bosses at break times. It never occurred either to me or to others that there was anything the Japanese were doing that could be practically transferred to our society and culture. However, as we came into and through the 1970s I became increasingly concerned about two major problems in our industrial society, both of which prompted me to take a closer look at Quality Circles.

1. I formed the belief that Western approaches to Quality Control based entirely on Quality Assurance were fundamentally wrong and
2. Whilst there has been a widespread awareness of the need for greater worker involvement or participation, we have never been able to find a satisfactory vehicle that is attractive to all levels and groups within an organisation, and to society in general.

By the mid 1970s my concern for both of these problems, combined with a greater understanding of the Quality Circle concept, led me to believe that, first of all there was nothing inherently Japanese in Quality Circles at all; it simply represented another way of treating people. Second, it provided a form of worker involvement which could not only overcome my misgivings about Western Quality Control, but if properly understood would be extremely attractive, both to management and workpeople alike.

At that time, unfortunately, I lacked a suitable platform to convey my ideas to others in a position to accept the challenge that such an approach offered. But, later, when speaking to Tony Shaw of Ashridge Management College in 1977, I commented that if only I could bring a prominent Japanese specialist to the UK to explain this concept, perhaps we could encourage a number of companies to start these activities. Tony Shaw replied: 'Professor Sasaki from Sophia University in Tokyo comes here regularly, perhaps you would like to discuss your ideas with him.' Professor Sasaki then put me in touch with Professor Ishikawa, the father figure of Quality Circles in Japan. Apart from sending me a considerable quantity of material on the subject, Professor Ishikawa offered to come to the UK. I then organised a three-day conference in London at the Institute of Directors in September 1979 and Professor Ishikawa spoke for the whole of the first day.

Whilst organising the conference I learned that Rolls Royce at Derby had already started a similar programme which they referred to as 'Quality Control Groups'. Frank Nixon, a Director of Rolls Royce, had been to Japan in 1969 with Harry Drew, Director General of the Defence Quality Assurance Board, and returned with a quantity of training material which was subsequently adapted. The programme at Rolls Royce was organised by Jim Rooney, who has since become very well known in the field. I asked Rolls Royce if Jim Rooney could participate in the conference, to which they agreed. I shall be eternally grateful both to Rolls Royce and to Jim Rooney for that co-operation. The fact that we were able to show a well-known British company already established with an adaptation of Quality Circles must have given considerable confidence to the 120 participants.

Professor Ishikawa said to me at the conference: 'Don't expect too much. If you are able to encourage just two companies to take up the concept within a year, you will be doing very well.' Twelve months later, having established my own training company, I had in fact trained over fifteen companies, and at the time of writing (1984) the number has grown to over one hundred firms trained in the UK, besides others in Belgium, France, Ireland, Switzerland, Hungary and Germany. I have also been to and lectured several times in Japan, have visited over 40 Japanese companies and met many Japanese visitors to the UK.

This book is based upon these experiences and those of my friends and colleagues with whom it has been a pleasure to work. Whilst there are far too many to mention by name, I am particularly grateful to my Japanese friends, especially Professor Ishikawa*, President of JUSE, Mr Jongi Noguchi, General Manager of JUSE, my good friend Naoto Sasaki of Sophia University, Mr Miyauchi and many directors and managers of Japanese companies who have been so helpful in my acquisition of knowledge. I should also like to give special thanks to Dr W.R. Thoday*, a past President of the European Organisation for Quality Control, who has given me great help and encouragement over many years. Jeff Beardsley of Beardsley & Associates Inc., whose advice, based upon practical experience in the implementation of Quality Circles in the USA, has proved invaluable, as has also his friendship. I am likewise greatly indebted to the many facilitators from companies trained by David

---

* Unfortunately, both Dr William Thoday and Professor Kaoru Ishikawa passed away in 1989. They will be sorely missed in the Quality world.

Hutchins Associates, and especially to Dick Fletcher from Wedgwood, who is doing so much to further the Circle Movement through the National Society for Quality Circles, and to Frank Glenister, Ted Jowett and Brian Tilley of David Hutchins Associates who have all contributed materially from their own experiences to this book. Most of all, I owe a grat debt of gratitude to my wife Margaret, without whose steadfast support I could never have had the opportunity to develop my work.

This book is written in the hope that in its own small way it will add a further dimensions to this most exciting new concept, which I am sure will soon affect the lives of us all.

David Hutchins

CHAPTER 1

INTRODUCTION

In around 1750 Great Britain began a period of explosive growth so dynamic that, one hundred years later, it dominated virtually every market in the world. Its naval might was awe-inspiring. The organisation of its armies was subsequently copied by every nation on earth.

Blast furnaces in its Northern towns poured out quality steel at such a pace that in one short ten-year period from 1840 to 1850 its railway lines reached every corner of its shores. Never in the history of mankind had the creative forces of an entire nation been so galvanised to success. Risk-taking, entre-preneurial drive, and creativity moved at an almost unbelievable pace.

The power and force of that period carried the country for a further hundred years, but never with the energy of those early days. During those 200 years Britain passed through the same classic cycle experienced by all great Empires: spectacular growth – followed shortly by complacency and a degree of arrogance, followed by decline and then eventually loss of confidence, and an ultimate re-submergence with other nations, with retention only of tra-ditions and memories of past glories.

Almost exactly two hundred years later, a near replica of that explosive dynamism is occurring. Not in Europe, but on diametrically the opposite side of the world, in Japan, where only two or three decades ago it would have seemed inconceivable that such a thing could happen. There are of course many important differences between the rise of Japan and the rise of the UK, but there are also some striking similarities. The most important one from our point of view is the dominance of world markets.

The period of Britain's explosive growth also saw the rise and comparative decline of several other great nations. The growth periods of both the United States and Germany came during the first half of the twentieth century, and the decline of the United States has been gradual ever since the end of the 1960s.

A key question now presents itself: 'Must decline be inevitable?' History would seem to indicate that this is the case: the Chinese, Egyptians, Greeks, and Romans, all dominated part or all of the civilised world at different times in history, and all have subsequently faded into oblivion.

So, little encouragement can be gained from looking at history if the USA and Europe hope to respond to what has been described as the Japanese Challenge. Moreover, the performance of the Western world compared with Japan and the Pacific basin over the past two decades has been that of a tired society, quite unable to compete with these newly risen countries which are brimming with enthusiasm and confidence and currently swathing through world markets.

Despite all the lessons of history, however, I do not believe that failure is inevitable and decline irreversible. (Already the Americans seem to be fighting back. In the late 1980s, there is considerable evidence of a dramatic renaissance of many of the American giants, the effect of the Malcolm Baldrige National Quality Improvement Act of 1987. Public Law 100–107, passed in 1987, established an annual United States National Quality award, which parallels the famous Deming Award in Japan and is having a phenomenal effect on US quality.)

This book is founded upon that belief. All of the failures of past civilisations occurred before the existence of cultural and organisational analysis. They occurred before the existence of mass media, at a time when the only civilisation that was known was their own. Today it is different. Macro-economy means global economy. Now, as never before, we have the means to study cultures, past and present, and organisational growth and decline, and to learn from them. We are no longer victims of unknown and unseen forces. We have the means of analysis and the opportunity to fight back. So we could almost say that destiny is now totally in our own hands. It is we as individuals, as an organisation, or even as a country, who can determine our own success – or failure. If we have the drive, and the belief in our own ability to succeed, then anything becomes possible.

This book suggests how Western companies can fight back and win. It is about competition. There is a well-known phrase in boxing and tennis circles: 'They never come back'. This may be true for individual sports, but it is less true for teams. In Association Football, there are many teams which have descended from the top of Division 1 to virtually the bottom of Division 4, and back to the top again. It is happening all the time, and is what makes football such a fascinating game. The reason is that, unlike individual sports where people get older and tired, a team can remain the same age and be constantly rejuvenated.

As with teams, so with countries and so with companies. Every so often, the team loses direction, management becomes fragmented, the team spirit is lost, failures begin and a vicious circle is set up. Failure brings loss of confidence, loss of confidence causes failure, and so on. For some teams this circle is broken and they make it back. Invariably this recovery is precipitated by a change of manager, directors, and sometimes, but not always, a change in team members. In fact, it is quite remarkable how often a team comprising players of only average individual ability can often out-perform a star-studded cast. This happens every year in the FA Cup when, match after match, a group of no-hopers embarrass teams composed of individual players each at the top of their profession.

As with football teams, so with countries, and so with companies. The characteristics of a people do not change; not perceptibly, anyway. What does become lost are the forces and energies which drove them to the top in the first place. If these can be rediscovered and the fires rekindled, then success again becomes possible. This is the belief upon which this book is based and the energy source to put the ideas into words.

A company is a team, or should be. All winning teams have certain commonalities, as do the failures. This book is intended to rediscover the commonalities of success, to put them together as a cohesive, co-ordinated whole through which any company, in any country, can galvanise the resources of all of its people to work towards achieving ultimate, and continued, success.

The decline of British industry

In the 1950s 60 per cent or so of young people in Britain left school at the age of fifteen without a qualification of any kind, or for that matter an examination success. Yet even against that unimpressive background of achievement, the world could still have been their oyster if they had wanted it to be so. Within weeks of leaving school, many such people would be signed up for apprenticeships in such well-known companies as De Haviland, Fairey Aviation, BOAC, and so forth. All but the least capable could grasp such opportunities.

Of those who had failed the selection process into Grammar or Technical Schools, many took the evening classes route to success. In September each year enrolment at evening classes was such as to fill not only the Colleges themselves but most of the available classrooms in local schools as well. From a standing start at the age of 15 many motivated young people had achieved a degree-equivalent qualification by the time they had entered their 20s.

Nowadays few if any such opportunities exist.

At that time, industry was throbbing, people were prosperous, and prospects looked good. Politically, though, things were different; the Empire was slipping inevitably away. In one short decade the spirit of the people switched from the feeling of intense pride and Churchillian 'We'll fight them on the beaches', 'fortress-UK' mentality to one of smallness and vulnerability, compared to the super powers today.

The political decline preceded industrial decline, and perhaps that was inevitable. Whilst economic success might be achieved in a political vacuum, it must require great vision and strength of will to do so. Of course, this has happened in many cases, and explains the continued successes of companies such as Marks & Spencer, ICI, and a limited number of others. Without the vision, foresight, and direction, many have inevitably succumbed to the energy-sapping demoralisation of a perceived loss of international standing.

But, there is a lesson here. Why have some survived when so many have failed? What is the real difference between, say, Marks & Spencer on the one hand and companies such as McMichaels, Sobel, BSA, Bush, Ultra, Triumph, Frances Barnett, Fairey, De Haviland, etc., on the other? Certainly they are in different industries, but there is nothing wrong with the industries concerned, and for all the companies listed above, the markets have grown rather than declined. The causes of failure lie elsewhere.

To find the reasons for the decline we should look back, much further, to the days of McAdam, Telford, Brunel, Newcomen, Watt, Wedgwood, and their contemporaries. If these men had been alive in the 1950s and 1960s, would our industrial decline have been prevented? The chances are no. At that time, it is doubtful that their talents would ever have been allowed to emerge, and even if they did, it is unlikely that they would have been given the opportunity to develop their ideas and attract the resources necessary to do their work. There are probably hundreds of would-be Brunels, and Newcomens and Watts walking our streets today, whose creativity will never see the light of day because our society is not in a state where such entrepreneurial drive is encouraged or given the opportunity to develop. Why? Well, this is part of the decline process. To understand this we shall look at the cycle which companies pass through from development to decay.

Life cycle of companies

It is a well-known organisational development concept that businesses may pass through three identifiable phases in their life. They may not survive all three, and they may not experience each of them. It is conceivable that industrial countries may also pass through similar phases in their life cycle.

The first phase may be described as the **entrepreneurial** phase. In the case of an industrial company, this usually begins with the founder as the entrepreneur. Generally such people are visionaries, and enter the commercial world in order to exploit an idea or some skills which they believe give them an advantage over others. Growth during this phase can sometimes be spectacular; typically risk-taking is high, market exploitation aggressive, and organisation often poor to non-existent.

After a period of dramatic growth and high earnings a succession of crises frequently hits such companies. The lack of organisation leads to unfulfilled promises and tensions, cover-ups emerge and finances become unstable. The failure of companies in this phase can be as spectacular as their earlier successes, and is often catastrophic. In other cases, the disillusionment of the entrepreneur, who was probably ill-equipped to handle this type of situation, is such that the business passes into the hands of others, whereupon it enters the second phase.

This is referred to as the **mechanistic** phase. The new owners lack the entrepreneur's original vision and passion for the product. They see a valuable asset with high earnings but even higher costs. They know how to deal with this, and gradually the business is brought under control. The organisation becomes established, financial controls are developed, and a period of stability is achieved. Unfortunately, however, the very means by which the business was saved begin to suffocate it. The loss of entrepreneurial drive and vision result in a loss of market leadership. There follows a regression from being market-minded to being product-minded. Instead of leading, the company begins to follow, always being one step behind the leading competitors and becoming reactive rather than proactive. Lacking drive and inspiration, bureaucracy begins to develop. Revenue declines and overheads creep up. Eventually, the company becomes totally finance driven, and all risk is avoided. This vicious circle continues until eventually market forces put the company in trouble.

If it is lucky, and with the right sort of help, this is the time when the company may enter the third phase. Unfortunately for many companies no such help is forthcoming. These companies are either sold and their assets stripped, or they may be absorbed into some larger organisation – which itself may be still in the mechanistic phase. This would be the case with Triumph, Wolsely, Morris, and Austin, which are now absorbed into the Rover Group. Any one of these famous names could, if they had been managed differently, be standing today alongside Toyota, Nissan, Matsushita and others – or might even have prevented their emergence.

The third phase is the **dynamic** phase. The ailing, mechanistic company may, if it is lucky, fall into the hands of those who possess entrepreneurial vision, and who are capable of revitalising the company and putting it firmly back on its feet. Such people possess a delicate blend of an understanding of organisational values with the need to be market leaders; they are able to take any company, whether it possesses assets or not, and step by step mould it into the world beaters of tomorrow.

Who, only twenty years ago, could have anticipated that Komatsu would outsmart the giant Caterpillar company, or that Canon would squash Xerox? That Digital would come from nowhere to breathe down the neck of the giant IBM, and, more recently, that Toyota, Nissan, and Honda would exploit the markets of Mercedes Benz, BMW, and Porsche?

All of these companies and the many others who now dominate the world scene have one essential element in common: all of them possess corporate beliefs, vision, and mission. Their stated objectives are without exception world domination of their selected markets. These objectives are shared by the entire payroll and everyone, from the top to the bottom, is clear as to their own place in the grand design. Such organisations take risks, and can change direction to outwit their competitors so quickly and effectively that they are unable to be beaten.

As with companies, so with countries. It is an interesting idea to think of a country as a company, and then to identify where it may be in the three phases of development.

The entrepreneurial phase for Britain would have been the period from 1750 to around 1850. During this time, all of the features of entrepreneurial management can be identified: vision, high risk, astronomical successes, and shattering failures, but overall the spectacular growth which gave Britain the label 'workshop to the world'.

Slowly, the vision disappeared and the mechanistic phase developed. Some of the companies formed by the great entrepreneurs of that age survive to today. Wedgwood, the pottery created by Josiah Wedgwood, is still impressive on the world stage, but what of its motivation? How many ideas have emerged following the inheritance of his abundance of revolutionary ideas which transformed that industry? With the exception of Rolls Royce, which itself was kept alive thanks to government intervention a decade or so ago, how many other such companies now survive other than by being absorbed into one or other corporation, many of which have also required state intervention?

The likelihood is that Britain is now in the death throes of the mechanistic period. The present government may well have arrested the seemingly inevitable march of bureaucracy, and all that it brings in its wake, but has that really done anything other than slow down the inevitable finality of failure? Where are the vision, the drive, the desire and motivation to become, once again, a world leader?

The Japanese progression to world domination continues unchallenged, even as this book is being written, industry after industry is falling under the scythe of the unprecedented and relentless competitive advance of companies such as Toyota, Nissan, Toshiba, and Sony.

Who is doing anything to arrest the tide; where is the dramatic response? Why do we still revere the captains of our industries whose only skills seem to be to get out while the going is good – to acquire, and to asset strip? Where are our global leaders about whom history books will be written? Where are today's Wedgwoods, Brunels, McAdams, Watts, and the others whose inheritance we have plundered? If our decline began in the 1940s and 1950s it is near terminal now. Our school leavers may be better educated than the children of the 1950s, but where can they go? Not for them the De Havilands, the Faireys, or the other once famous companies. If they are lucky, they may wield a screwdriver for a foreign-named company, but they will never own the business.

How can this downward trend be reversed? How can the companies of Britain and Europe regain their former confidence and stand alongside their major competitors?

To find the answer, we should take a leaf from the books of dynamic companies. The stated objective of Kamatsu is to 'encircle Caterpillar'. The stated objective of Canon is to 'beat Xerox'. Every employee on the payroll of these companies knows what these objectives mean to their future security and prosperity. These are dynamic objectives, and go far beyond mere survival. Unless we can compete with such determination, unless we can develop counter-strategies and follow them through, failure is inevitable.

Discussions relating to the cause of our malaise frequently gravitate towards workers, the Unions, or middle-band management. It will be interesting to look briefly at each of these groups to see if they can really be to blame.

It has been said that companies get the Unions they deserve. This must be true. Why is it that on a single industrial estate some companies have many industrial disputes, walk-outs, etc., whilst others, often in similar industries, have none and yet pay between the two groups may be nearly identical?

If criticism is not directed towards the Unions, there is an underlying belief amongst the middle classes that the workers collectively are lazy, indolent, and don't want to work. It is doubtful whether those who share such beliefs have ever acquired much first-hand experience of the British worker, who can equal any in the world if he is put in the right environment. There is plenty of evidence, from companies such as Nissan in Washington, Sony and Yuasa Batteries in South Wales, etc., that, properly managed, the British worker can equal his counterparts in Japan or elsewhere.

The third group to come under fire are the much maligned middle-band managers. Referred to variously as 'the frozen layer', or 'the concrete layer', these people are invariably blamed for resistance to change when new initiatives are contemplated. I have lived in their world for enough years to know that they are more often victims of their circumstance than the architects.

In reality, the fault lies squarely at the level of top management, and in particular, British top management. In my mind it is no coincidence that the companies which are currently attempting to counter Japanese competition are in the main either American owned (Hewlett Packard, IBM, Rank Xerox, Cabot Carbon, Caterpillar, H. J. Heinz, Honeywell, etc.) or mainland European owned (Philips, Thompson, Peugot, etc.) or joint – for example Unilever, which is British and Dutch. One reason for this of course is the fact that Japanese competition impacted the United States before it hit Europe. The US response has been a renaissance of some of its industries, which of course puts further pressure on European industries. The Malcolm Baldrige Award in the USA is now making a significant impact on the Quality performance of many American companies.

How many purely British owned companies are really responding to the challenge? In my view JCB, Tioxide, ICI, ICL, Rylands Whitecross, and a handful of others, including a small group of laundries under the name of Paragon, in the South West, represent a distressingly small number. Most of the rest are at best playing with the concepts necessary to survive, and many will be swallowed up by predators before they even move from square one. It is top management, in the form of the captains of industry, who are the only people who can change what will otherwise be inevitable. They, together with the professional institutions, must obtain a clarity of vision as to how to bring about the recovery of our industries. If we continue to allow their asset-stripping mentality, which may suit them personally and make them appear as heroes due to their personal wealth and power, to dominate our industries, we will wake up too late to the fact that these people, for no other reason than personal gain, have plundered our heritage.

Hopefully, the European Foundation for Quality Management which was recently formed and which has made an impressive start, will soon begin to influence European industry in a strong and positive direction.

The economic argument

Ever since the start of the terminal decline of many of our industries in the 1950's, there has been a persistent cry that successive governments have failed to invest in industry. In the late 1970s there was a storm over Sir Kenneth Corfield's report which rejected the argument put forward by the now defunct machine tool industry and much of the motor industry, that its problems were due to lack of government funding for new designs; other claims have been made for government investment in new plant and machinery. Other excuses include 'high rate of value of currency', 'high interest rates', and 'inflation'. All of these are symptoms; none is a cause. If governments had invested in new designs or plant, they would have been pouring water down the drain. The money would have sunk without a trace, and the problems would probably have been worse rather than better. What have we achieved from the discovery of North Sea Oil other than a slowing down of the inevitable? The problems confronting British industry have virtually nothing to do with investment and almost everything to do with attitude and a clear understanding of the means by which our competitors are beating us in the market place.

With regard to the value of currency, in 1960 there were 11DM to the £ sterling, now there are less than 3DM to the £. As recently as 1980 there were ¥552 to the £; in 1990 it was down to ¥270 to the £. If differential currency values were the only factor to consider, we should be able to sell our products so cheaply in Germany, Japan, and elsewhere as to be accused of dumping at that difference in rates, and German or Japanese products would be priced beyond reach. The same applies to the dollar. In the early years after the war £1 sterling acquired between $3 and $4. Imagine the protests from industry if such rates returned today!

Throughout the 1980s, the biggest economic problem facing Western organisations has been inflation. In the United Kingdom, inflation has become almost uncontrollable since the mid 1980s. In the period immediately prior to that, it was brought seemingly under control through massive cuts in public expenditure and tightening of money in circulation. The initial cost-trimming carried out by industry, achieved mainly by stock reduction, gave the impression that control was possible. This is, however, not the case because the underlying problems had not been addressed, and never have been, not since the end of the Second World War.

Over the years, due to the continued and unhindered decline of British manufacturing industry, the opportunity for consumers to purchase British designed and British manufactured products has slowly but surely diminished.

The first to disappear was the British motor bike; the British television followed, then British machine tools, and all of the associated supplier industries.

Nowadays, there are no British television or video manufacturers, and most white and brown goods available in showrooms sport foreign-sounding names. Such as Bosch and Zanussi.

As soon as tight financial controls improve the economy, and the Chancellor lets out some slack, the consumer buys foreign products because in many cases he has no option. There follows a balance of payments deficit followed by a run on the pound, followed by an increase in interest rates, followed by a rise in inflation. This sequence cannot be prevented without the ability to produce at home the products we wish to own. Encouraging foreign investment may appear to be an attractive solution, but not if we become a screwdriver economy as a result. It is we who should be strong enough to buy overseas, not the other way round. In any case, the profits go overseas.

Even when the products are available, why should the consumer select home-produced products if they are of inferior quality to foreign goods, or if the service support is inadequate? Surely it is the responsibility of the manufacturer to produce products which people wish to buy rather than expect an undeserved loyalty to a company which attempts to rely on patriotism to remain in business.

Another excuse is the widely held myth that our problems are in some way due to the Japanese refusing to accept our exports. Whether this is true or not, do people really believe that if our manufacturers had unlimited access to the Japanese home market, it would actually make one scrap of difference?

Japan is only one market out of an entire world, and even without controls, unless our products can compete in Japan on quality, price, and delivery, then there is no law on Earth which will force the Japanese consumer to actually buy them. Protectionist rings can be put around the home market but never around the export market. There, only the best will survive.

Ten years ago British Leyland had 23 per cent of the Norwegian market and an extensive dealership network. Norway does not produce its own cars and so therefore has no special allegiance to any country's products. Today, Nissan and Toyota are more familiar names to Norwegians than Austin Rover.

Foreign investment

In the face of the alarming decline in British Industry, and the lack of any clear and coherent remedy being offered either by industry itself or by the government, recent governments have, in apparent despertion, encouraged foreign investment in Britain, mostly from Japan and the United States. Ministers of Trade and Industry, and the Prime Minister herself, have fallen over themselves to encourage such investment in a desperate attempt to create jobs. Are they really aware of what they are doing to the country in the long run? Do they realise what they are saying when they encourage such investments? What they are actually saying is, 'We do not know how to run a plant, or manufacture goods, but our people are OK at making them'. Brunel and our forefathers would be greatly saddened if they knew we had reached this sorry plight.

Is it likely that these foreign investors will ever bring the technology to design and develop the products we hope they will allow us to make, back to these shores? Will they invest in the re-creation of our technical colleges and universities, in order to improve the stock of our people — thereby potentially creating competitors to those organisations? Of course not. Every foreign factory which sets up in our society represents one step further away from self-dependency, and one step further into someone else's hands.

What of the future?

Do we have the chance to reverse this tide? Can we, at this late stage, set the wheels in motion to make a come-back? The answer is a resounding 'Yes', but the assignment is going to be one of the toughest we have ever faced. To my mind, it serves no useful purpose whatever to hide from the sheer magnitude of this task — provided we are prepared to gain the resolve to win.

It is hoped that this book will provide some insight into what must be done, to help rediscover the pride, self respect, and respect for others that can only come from pride in one's own achievement.

Towards Total Quality

This book is about quality. Its objective is to help the reader to discover the means by which any organisation, large or small, manufacturing or service, can harness the creativity and resources of all of its people to work towards making that organisation the best in its particular field.

This concept is referred to throughout the book as Total Quality. The term is free from any restrictive nouns such as 'management' or 'control', as in 'Total Quality Management', or 'Total Quality Control', since Total Quality embraces all of these specific concepts. Total Quality is the name given in this book to the concept of total involvement of executives, Managers, and the managed. It also embraces the entire range of Quality-related concepts such as 'Just in Time', statistical process control, quality systems and procedures as outlined in publications such as British Standard 5750, International Standards Organisation 9000, etc., and the fundamentally important concepts of such groups as Quality Circles (referred to, as Quality Control Circles in Japan) and suggestion scheme approaches.

In essence, Total Quality is the term used to describe the way an organisation operates in its markets. It also repesents a social industrial revolution, which in twenty to thirty years' time will be regarded as of at least equal importance to the introduction of the factory system in the mid 1700s, and the advent of scientific management as defined by Fredrick W. Taylor at the turn of the twentieth century.

CHAPTER 2

WINNING THROUGH VISION

It is probably true to say that no one ever achieved anything without first of all being possessed of a dream or vision.

There is nothing wrong with dreaming. The principal difference between dreamers and high achievers is that high achievers attempt to turn dreams into reality, the dreamer is content simply to dream.

A small child may achieve limited success simply because it perceives the need to meet the social norms of its peer group. No one, particularly a child, wants to appear different. At this stage, its dreams or objectives may be no higher than to equal or surpass the achievements of the social group of which it is a member. Minor goals may be to obtain the favour of the parent or teacher. As the child gets older it will, if it is become an achiever, set its sights higher: 'Head of School', 'Four As at A-level', 'First Class Honours Degree', 'Captain of the Football or Rugby Team', and so on. It is doubtful whether anyone in history has ever achieved any of these attainments without having first of all dreamed and wished for such a result.

For the achiever, this wish must be supported by a high level of *desire to achieve*, to provide the necessary motivation. The reasons supporting such a desire may be many, and lie deep in human psychology. However, the reader might at this point stop reading and reflect on some of his or her own achievements, and recall the original drives and thoughts which motivated efforts to reach them. Analysis of one's own experience is always the most convincing approach to testing any new idea.

Subsequent progression through life for the achiever thereafter becomes a succession of vision – strategy – achievement. Often the achievement of a high-order goal may be obtained through a series of lesser, more realistic goals. For example, whilst a 20 year-old may dream of being Prime Minister some day, he or she would be unlikely to share that dream with anyone at a job interview. Such a goal would be regarded as fantasy and unrealistic. No one knows what may have been going on in the minds of Margaret Thatcher, Ted Heath, or Harold Wilson at that age, but it is likely that to become Prime Minister one day became a drive many years before the actual time of achievement. However, it is unlikely that this passion would be shared with even the closest confidant until it becomes an obviously attainable goal.

In addition to dreams and vision are reasoning and logic. These activities are carried on in the left-hand side of the brain, whilst dreaming and vision are most definitely activities of the right-hand side. There is much evidence to suggest that the world's greatest achievers have acquired a good balance between the activities of the two hemispheres. Many would assume that Albert Einstein was a left-brained, logical thinking person, and yet it is well known that he deliberately allocated time every day to meditation in order to stimulate right-brained thinking. He also encouraged his students to do this. (It is said that it was during a period of meditation that he first identified this theory that the universe is a continuous loop.)

Consider any number of famous people who have achieved greatness through their own efforts: if they had been merely left-brained, it is doubtful whether they would ever have set their goals in the first place, let alone achieved them.

Can one imagine any intelligent person at the age of 20 saying that they intend one day to be Prime Minister, using only their powers of logical reasoning? The first point of rejection of such an idea would derive from the laws of probability. Mathematically, the probability of such success is so low, given the level of competition, that pure logic would almost certainly reject such a proposal. However, a right-brained thinker would pay virtually no attention to this, but rather would look for all the ways to cut the odds and to increase the opportunities.

It is this attitude which is essential to dynamic management, namely – the determination to win against all odds. It is the mentality which enabled Drake to take on the might of the Spanish Armada, which, even with the forces of nature on his side, was still a formidable task.

It is almost certainly this visionary mentality which drove Brunel and our other famous forebears to achieve greatness.

And today, this drive to win against all odds is what spurred Komatsu, Canon, and others, to take on the giants such as Caterpillar, and Xerox.

The reverse of visionary leadership, with no goals or positive beliefs, is characterised by the feeling of hopelessness derived from a sense of the inevitability of decline and failure in the face of seemingly impossible odds. Such an attitude is almost without exception self-fulfilling, since without vision and direction, failure is inevitable. The problems we have in most of our manufacturing companies, and nowadays in increasing numbers of service-based organisations, are almost entirely due to lack of vision and belief.

To emphasise the point: the single factor which separates successful people, successful businesses, and successful countries, from the rest is vision, and the will to achieve.

A business is driven by vision in the entrepreneurial or dynamic phase which were described in Chapter 1, but not when in the mechanistic phase. It is the contention of this book that British and perhaps many other Western businesses have become entrenched in the mechanistic phase and are hence prey to any competitor which intends to pick them off in the marketplace. A few, such as Jaguar cars, have made some attempts to introduce vision-led management with partial success, but they have failed to obtain the full commitment of their people, and they have also failed to use the vital powerful tools and techniques. Consequently they are still at the mercy of their foreign competitors. Jaguar seek a weak pound to increase their competitiveness in US markets. The Japanese succeed even with an over-strong currency because they know how to achieve the ultimate in competitive performance.

Few of our organisations have any idea as to what they must achieve to counter this level of competition. One thing is for sure, they have to do considerably more than they are doing at the moment.

Features of the dynamic phase

Unique features of the dynamic phase include:

- a market-based strategy
- people building
- sense of community within the company
- winning team mentality
- individuals being allowed to take controlled risks as part of their personal development
- development of company-mindedness rather than departmental-mindedness
- identification of common enemies – usually competitors
- clear but very flexible organisation
- financial planning used to monitor decisions, not as a basis for making decisions
- lack of obvious status symbols, eg. single status eating areas

and most important of all:

- 'Managers don't make decisions; managers make sure that good decisions are being made'

However, 'vision' is not all that is required. Many people or competing organisations may have similar visions and goals which are mutually exclusive. The winner will then be the one with the superior strategy and tactics. One thing is certain: without vision there is no chance of winning.

We have already seen that dynamic and entrepreneurial management are vision led. How then can vision be created where none exists?

Road blocks to vision creation

For organisations entrenched in the mechanistic phase, the creation of vision will probably be the most traumatic experience ever carried out by the management team as a group. For privatised, publicly owned companies it may be virtually impossible for the existing management team to make the transition to the world of competition. The transmission of the vision downwards through the organisation will be equally traumatic.

Creating vision

To be effective, the corporate vision must satisfy three fundamental criteria:

1. It must be stretching at all levels.
2. It must be stated in such a way that everyone will believe in it.
3. It must be aggressive and growth-orientated.

In some organisations, particularly those with a powerful and charismatic leader, it is sufficient for the leader to project his vision into the organisation, and gain acceptance through drive and enthusiasm. This will work in the short term (or in the case of Japan in the long term), but for Western organisations, with a greater mobility of top and senior executives, it will bring about a succession of different vision statements. This results in confusion, cynicism, and resistance through lack of belief that the message is serious.

The alternative is to create a collective vision based upon the individual goals and ambitions of the management team. The advantage of such a collective vision is that, whilst individual executives may change, the overall group remains essentially the same. Another advantage is the fact that if all members of the team participated in the creation of the vision, they are far more likely to work towards its achievement. Collective goals become individual goals. The concept of taking ownership down to the lowest level is fundamental to the concept of Total Quality.

The negative features of companies in the mechanistic phase which will prevent the establishment of a clear vision include:

- lack of clear leadership from the top
- spirit of departmental- or specialism-mindedness rather than company-mindedness (less true in public utilities)
- 'tough' managers and 'tough' shop stewards
- low morale and significant levels of demarcation
- members of the management team are defensive, aggressive, and operate a 'blame culture'.
- 'blame' culture extends downwards right through the organisation
- product-mindedness rather than market-mindedness

State-owned organisations all display characteristics associated with the mechanistic phase, and cannot by their very nature be described as either entrepreneurial or dynamic. In addition, they suffer from the fact that they have had virtually no competition at any time since their institution. Without competition, a certain vagueness often exists as to the precise nature of the business. Whilst such organisations remain in the public domain, this presents no problem other than the fact that they are probably the most inefficient organisations in existence. Being protected by government decree, and not being exposed to market forces, such organisations become sprawling, aimless bodies, suffocated by bureaucracy to a degree which would be impossible for a privately owned company to sustain and still remain economically viable.

When such organisations are privatised, the very process of becoming market-orientated may be beyond the ability of those who have spent a lifetime protected from such considerations.

Mechanistic-style management

Mechanistic-style top management exhibits some unique and disadvantageous features which will never be found in dynamic management. One of these is status-consciousness, which rapidly leads to remoteness.

Remoteness

The chief excutive of such an organisation will only be known personally by a handful of senior executives. He is unlikely ever to visit the departments of the organisation. In one such organisation, a fairly senior member of staff exclaimed that the only time the chief executive ever visited his department was when he was looking for his own office!

His style will be distinguished by deliberate remoteness in order to avoid involvement or contact with the lower orders of the organisation. To achieve this, such an executive will often encourage his own direct subordinates to develop similar characteristics, and hence to create a select or exclusive group at the top. Such strategies very quickly ripple down through the hierarchy to create very structured organisations.

In the worst examples each layer of organisation will have its own eating and relaxation facilities, separate car parks, and a clear distinction in terms of office furniture, carpeting, and other perk-related factors.

Experience indicates that organisations such as this will find it virtually impossible to change to dynamic management, however much it may be recognised as necessary. There are too many counter-strategies and entrenched positions involved to achieve change, without the very toughest of personalities at the top. Such executives must have a crystal-clear vision of what they are attempting to achieve, coupled with a knowledge of the behavioural under-currents which could only be acquired from having lived in the organisation at all levels. The likelihood of such personalities already being present in the organisation is remote.

Perhaps the biggest barrier to change is the fact that every executive and senior person in the organisation will be very much aware that, whilst they may theoretically support the proposed change of style, they achieved their own existing status under the previous regime. How do they know that they will maintain that status under a different style of leadership? It is this fear which more than anything will prevent them from supporting change.

'Blame' culture

Fighting for position is yet another characteristic of this style of management. Status breeds jealousy and the development of a blame culture. A typical example of blame culture can be found in the following scenario.

Consider a manufacturing company which produces product X. The delivery is late, causing a reaction from a major customer. At a management meeting the managing director presses the production manager for an explanation. The production manager provides a long list of 'reasons':

- Plant or equipment breakdowns – a problem for the maintenance department.
- Lack of staff – personnel problem.
- Wrong drawings and specifications, design changes, etc. – a problem for the design department.
- Poor supply quality – purchasing department.
- Problems with jigs, fixtures and tooling, etc.

All of these 'reasons' will be intended to put the 'blame' on the shoulders of others. The maintenance manager may react to the suggestion that the plant is in poor repair with the remark 'If you got your people to look after the equipment better, it wouldn't break down so often. Anyway, if I had another fitter and two more electricians then I would have been able to fix his machines'. Similar counter-arguments will almost certainly be used by the other personnel subjected to criticism. Most of these counter-arguments will be defensive reactions, and whilst there may be a grain of truth in all of them, it is unlikely that any one of them will be the real answer.

Typically, it will be the manager who puts up the least convincing defence who will in the end carry the blame. This may provide relief to the other managers, but it does not solve the problem, because it is unlikely that they will have found the true cause even if the problem is in the hands of the manager concerned. For one thing, he will be the least convinced that he is to blame. He will develop a strong sense of grievance, and in all probability the only effect will be that he will be determined to put up a better defence the next time such a problem occurs.

Whilst this type of scenario is all too common, it is also futile, and downright destructive. By seeking to apportion 'blame', the organisation is actually suggesting that the manager in question was either negligent or that be deliberately caused the problem. In the main, both suggestions are unlikely.

Within the concept of Total Quality, it is assumed that the vast majority of personnel who go to work do so with the intention of doing a quality job. If this is true, then it follows that if there is an 'unquality' outcome, the apportionment of blame serves no useful purpose. In a Total Quality company, the assumption should be that if there is an 'unquality' factor then the real causes are likely to be in the categories of:

- inadequate or unreliable processes

- unclear, imprecise or inadequate specifications
- poor systems
- cross-functional misunderstanding, etc.

If it transpires that a 'person' caused the problems, then it is likely that that person has been poorly trained to perform the task in question, or that he was provided with misleading information.

It is only when problems are addressed at this level that real improvement and real progress can be made.

Companies which have experienced this type of blame culture for decades will probably find it most difficult to transfer to a Total Quality environment. Managers within such companies will see themselves as survivors. Every manager has a fence around himself, a pile of dirt, and a shovel. He sees his job as shovelling the dirt over the fence into someone else's area. It is the manager with the biggest shovel who will be most likely to progress.

In severe cases, managers will feel so insecure as to be afraid even to take holidays for fear of what may be on their desks when they return to the office. In some cases, the desk may be occupied by another. On a recent industrial study tour to Japan, one participant was so afflicted with this style of management that he phoned his company at least four times every night, and then in the end returned home early. In contrast, a team of Japanese managers could easily take a world tour in the happy knowledge that their colleagues and subordinates could adequately address any problems which were likely to arise during their absence.

In a Total Quality organisation, problems such as these would almost certainly be dealt with by a cross-functional project team. Whereas individuals, in a blame culture organisation, would generally be looking to blame each other; with a cross-functional teamwork approach, the responsibility for the problem would lie collectively within the team as a group.

Whilst each of the team members may have theories as to the possible causes, these theories often conflict with each other. Therefore, it is the responsibility of the team to test these theories. This will usually involve the collection and analysis of data, and use of other problem-solving skills, in order to find the true cause, or causes. It is this cross-functional teamwork approach which in the early stages of development of a Total Quality organisation is the essence of Total Quality.

Related to the problem of 'blame' culture is the establishment of 'professional' management in Western organisations. This is also present in Japanese management to some extent, but it has long since been recognised as being antagonistic to good management, and most leading organisations take active steps to reduce its effects.

Professionalism

'Professional' management derives from so-called 'scientific' management which was originated at the turn of the century by F.W. Taylor and his contemporaries. Basically, Taylor suggested that the execution of tasks should be separated from the planning and checking, i.e. management manages and people do. This was distinct from the then European approach whereby management or owners were dependent on a largely craftsman-based labour force: managers or owners simply provided the resources for the foreman and his team of craftsmen to determine how and when to perform the necessary operations to produce the company's products.

Under the Taylor system, management would make these decisions and send instructions to the workforce. This subject will be developed further in a later chapter.

It soon became evident that line management could not individually possess all of the skills necessary to control a complex plant. Hence the introduction of specialists such as 'production engineers', 'industrial engineers', and 'personnel'. This compartmentalisation continued until sufficient scientific knowledge was acquired under each of these classifications to warrant the use of terms such as 'professional engineer'. From the point of view of progression of scientific knowledge, this was a beneficial process, and at university level enabled the research and development of new and better methods for use in industry.

At the industrial level however, process, whilst bringing benefits in the form of specialist expertise, also contained powerful destructive elements. Perhaps one of the most important of these is the tendency for such a specialist to view himself as a member of his chosen profession first, and an employee

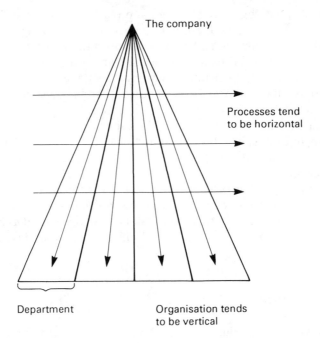

Fig. 2.1

of his company second. Another equally important problem is the tendency for career progression to take place solely within that or other very closely related and overlapping functions. For example, a production-based work study engineer may progress upwards solely within work study, or he may move between this, industrial relations, production engineering, and sometimes line management. It is unlikely, unless he personally makes a dramatic change in his career path, that he would switch to design, sales, or finance.

The result is that designers talk to designers, production people to production, finance to finance, sales to sales, and so forth. Consequently, organisations develop very strong vertical fibres of organisation, but very weak horizontal fibres. Since processes are mainly horizontal, cutting across function by function, the result is that no one owns the process. It is not surprising therefore that blame culture related problems may abound. Often these are attributable to nothing more than a breakdown in communication between related functions in the same organisation which never speak to each other.

In addition to cross-functional project teams suggested earlier, there are other ways to address this problem. One such alternative is to organise career development on a rotational basis. For example, young graduates joining a company, regardless of their chosen degree specialisation, are required to work progressively in all other functions of the company. In many Japanese organisations this is carried out on a structured basis right up to the age of around 35. By this time, the individual will not only have a good understanding of the activities of all functions, but will also appreciate the interrelationship with other internal functions which act as suppliers or customers to that function. Furthermore, they have developed friendships and acquaintances with people in those departments, and this progression helps the formation of a common company language.

Experiment

In order to test out the importance of the internal customer/supplier relationship concept, and the problems which Western professionalism can bring to an organisation, an experiment was conducted in a company in the electronics industry employing some 6,000 people.

A group of five people from the finance department and and another of five from research and development were selected. The two groups of five were then sent to two separate syndicate rooms and asked to conduct a brainstorming session to identify all the tasks they performed as suppliers to the other function. Following this, each group was then required to brainstorm all of the services they received from the other function.

Theoretically, in an ideal situation, both the customer/supplier lists would have been identical. In reality this is unlikely, although some commonality could be expected. In the event, all four lists contained some twenty to thirty items, and so both groups were asked to select ten from each list which they thought were the most important, and then to rank these in order.

Following this exercise, both teams were brought together and required to present their results to each other. Before describing what happened, it is necessary to explain one important process which took place in the company.

The flow diagram in Figure 2.2 shows what were thought to be the key steps in the design, development, manufacture, sales and distribution of the company's products. It can be seen that at the appropriate time in the design cycle, cost estimates were produced in order to validate the design, and to

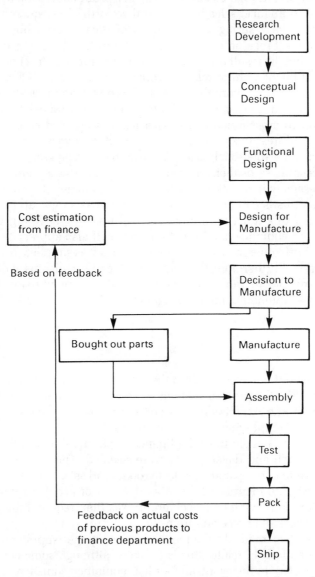

Fig. 2.2 Key steps in the design, development, manufacture, sales and distribution of a company's products

estimate selling price, profit levels, and so on. According to the diagram, this information was obtained from the finance department, as a supplier to research and development.

When the research and development group presented the results of their syndicate, however, not only did this service not appear on the short list, it was not on the full brainstormed list either. Whilst this information was being presented, it was noted that one of the members of the finance group was looking decidedly unwell. At the end of the presentation, he asked why this feature was not included. He then described the form used to provide the information in more detail. Suddenly one of the research and development group said, 'I know what you mean – that form, we don't use it'. 'Why not?' inquired the man from finance. 'Because we don't understand it', came the reply. 'How then do you validate designs?' came back the question. 'We use estimates' was the response. The man from finance then exclaimed, 'I have worked in this company for over 27 years, this is the first time I have ever sat in the same room as anyone from R & D before, and I had no idea this was a problem for them'. Guess what his job had been for those 27 years, and it will be understood why he had appeared so unwell during this session!

On paper, the company appeared to have a good system. Costs were estimated, then after activities had taken place it became possible to compare actual costs with estimates, and then in the future to improve on the estimates by learning. Because the loop was not closed through use of this information, no use could be made of the learning, and so consequently the company probably made a profit largely by luck.

The shock of this and other revelations caused the company to conduct similar sessions between all functions. Similar situations appeared in all cases. The result was that the company set up cross-functional project teams to look specifically at this type of problem, to find remedies and create a 'company language'.

The problem of process ownership is one which must be resolved if Western companies are to compete successfully on a global scale. Organisations simply cannot afford the luxury of this major deficiency in the future. Like it or not, the problem must be addressed. This again challanges American-style 'scientific management', or 'Taylorism', as the Japanese refer to it.

Product-mindedness

Perhaps the most striking difference between an organisation competing from the basis of Total Quality, and its more traditional counterparts entrenched in the mechanistic phase, is attitude to the market. The Total Quality organisation is characterised by the ability to change direction at astonishing speed if it perceives a change in market requirements or if it sees a weakness which it can exploit in a competitor's strategy. The product is almost but not totally irrelevant. The Total Quality company is always seeking to increase its share of market and to open up new markets.

For example, traditional companies or those in the mechanistic phase will usually make investment appraisal decisions on the basis of 'payback', internal rate of return, or some such measure. The Total Quality company will generally give a higher importance to the question 'Which of the competing proposals is most likely to take market share from our competitors?' on the basis that once they have secured the additional market share they will get the costs in order later. Obviously there are limits to this strategy, but it is the principle which is important. How many typical Western companies would even ask the question?

There are many indicators of a product-minded organisation, the most common being a 'take it or leave it' attitude to the customer: 'We are the specialists, if you want it come and get it.' Most of us suffer the misfortune of experiencing this attitude in our everyday lives, at the local garage, at the specialist DIY shop, in hotels, and so on.

In Japan, if an individual requires some attention to be given to his motor car, he will normally pick up the Japanese equivalent of the *Yellow Pages* and phone a garage. In less than one hour the garage will have come to the address and taken the car to the garage, and will then later return it to the owner. This is because of competition between garages.

In the West, and certainly in parts of the UK, it will be necessary for the owner to make an appointment with the garage, often some time later (in the case of the author, frequently two to three weeks later). He will then usually be required to take the vehicle to the garage, sometimes at considerable inconvenience, and then hope that it will be ready when promised, and in a satisfactory condition. Apart from all the possible outcomes of this experience, and even if everything technical is dealt with satisfactorily, it will still take about three days to readjust the seat angles to a comfortable position!

This example strikingly shows the difference between a product and a marketing mentality. In the case of the former, the provider of the product or service uses the excess of demand over supply to have an advantage over the customer. In such cases the attitude towards the customer may range from polite to indifferent – the latter being most in evidence in organisations which are not directly involved in any form of competition, such as government departments, local authorities, and state-run organisations. Airport hotels which can be sure of full booking often exhibit similar characteristics.

A more graphic example can be found in the car industry in the 1950s and 1960s. It is also largely responsible for the demise of the motor cycle industry. In these cases, the industry used the excess of demand over supply to provide the customer with an indifferent product whether he wanted it or not, even though, in most cases, the technology existed even in those days to produce vehicles which could have been considerably more reliable than was being achieved.

Despite massive public criticism, almost without exception the industry refused to rust-proof their products, with a 'We know best' attitude. When you can sell everything you can make, this seems to be a practical strategy. Of course, it is not something that a manufacturer would openly admit. It is necessary from sales and marketing viewpoints to dress this up to make it more palatable for the consumer – hence the creation of terms such as 'throw-away society'. The argument being, 'Of course we can rust-proof, but that would be uneconomic. It is better that we make cheap, throw-away products. That gives the advantage of high volume production, and a cheaper product to the user'! This policy is OK for the manufacturer for as long as his competitors operate similar policies, but of course it is not OK for the customer. At the time Western manufacturers felt safe because they could see no one in the world who was likely to break ranks. They did not even consider the possibility of a threat from Japan in those days, because no one could have guessed that Japan was about to explode upon the world in the way that it did.

In Japan, the entire situation is and was different. Taking the case of the local garage to illustrate the point. In any given location in Japan, if an excess of demand over supply existed, garages would expand their facilities to take up the excess. Then, out of competition with other garages, they would probably use door-to-door selling to offer services which outsmart their rivals. Consequently, even at the lowest level, competition is very severe in Japan, and business failures are high. Any company which can survive this and grow will be fiercely competitive. If such a company becomes large enough to compete on an international basis, then it is almost like taking candy from a baby when it comes to head-on competition with Western rivals who have never experienced such agressive market-mindedness.

It is not surprising therefore that when Nissan, under the name of Datsun, first attacked the European market there was virtually no response to the fact that the marketing was directed at the user; that, for example, radios were supplied as standard, whereas British Leyland, being product-oriented, were attempting to get the non-mechanically minded would-be purchasers of its products excited about the wonderful merits of 'hydrolastic suspension', 'transverse mounted engines', and other such wonders of modern science.

Conclusion

Modern organisations which wish to survive in the future will only do so through vision-led, dynamic management. They must harness the resources of their people to a degree never before considered. They must create a sense of community within the organisation, totally market-oriented, and growth minded. The organisation must move quickly from the mechanistic phase, build its people, and allow them to take risks.

In the next chapter, the theme will be the translation of vision into corporate reality through Total Quality.

CHAPTER 3

WHAT IS TOTAL QUALITY?

So far we have made frequent references to Total Quality, but now it is necessary to look at the concept in some detail.

It has already been stated that Total Quality represents a competitive strategy. 'Quality', in terms of 'Total Quality', is everything an organisation does in the eyes of its customers, which will determine whether they buy from this company or from its competitor. Total Quality therefore is as much concerned with confidence and the 'overall impression' of the market as it is with specific measurable or quantifiable characteristics. Sometimes, the customer is adversely influenced by some quality deficiency which may even work in his favour. For example, if a supplier forgets to invoice his customer, this is clearly to the latter's advantages, but even so, the effect on him will almost certainly be negative. It may well occur to the customer that if his supplier is poorly organised in this respect, then he may also be weak in other areas. His confidence will be lowered and it is quite likely that he may put future business elsewhere, particularly when the service to be purchased is critical to the customer in some way.

Principal objectives

A Total Quality organisation must have four principal objectives. which are common to any organisation. A given organisation may also have many additional specific goals.

1. Continuous improvement of the organisation, which must be equal to or greater than that of any competitor.
2. Continuous and relentless cost reduction.
3. Continuous and relentless quality improvement.
4. To create an organisation whereby everyone is working towards making *their* organisation the best in its business, and to capitalise on the sense of achievement and working in a world-class organisation.

Let us look at each of these goals in turn.

1. *Continuous improvement ...*

Many organisations take a natural pride in their progressive improvement

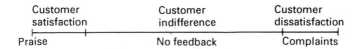

Fig. 3.1

activities, which is laudable and to be encouraged. It is amazing, however, to discover how few organisations have any idea as to how they are actually perceived in comparison with their competitors in the marketplace.

Many people mistakenly think that if you are not achieving customer satisfaction, you are causing its opposite, i.e. customer dissatisfaction. By so doing, they forget the most important and dangerous situation of all: customer indifference!

It has been said that to be successful in business it is necessary to be better than your competitor at at least something. Nowadays, even that may not be enough. We must be better than our competitor in every possible way. Just 'meeting the requirements of the customer' is not sufficient.

Consider a restaurant as an example. Typically, the manager or head waiter will ask his customers whether or not they enjoyed their meal. In most cases, the response will be affirmative. Only occasionally do people complain, and then only when they are quite upset. Only occasionally do we give praise, and then only when we are very pleased. So in most cases, we do not provide feedback for the services we have received. It is easy to see how the restaurateur can be deceived. We told him the service was OK, and yet we probably will not go back. The service meets the specification, but some competitor does it better. Just meeting the requirements of the customer does not provide feedback for the services we have received. It is easy to see how not meet the exacting requirements of Total Quality.

On many occasions at seminars, we in DHA ask the audience, 'How many of you think that your company is good at what it does?'. Usually about 60 per cent of the participants will put up their hands. Very few can answer the subsequent question, 'How do you *know*? What information do you have to support your belief?', except to say, 'We get very few complaints'. For most, this is an indication that they are probably in the 'indifferent zone'. It is amazing how many companies in the same business think that they individually have over a 50 per cent share of the market!

Even when we do know our market share, and even if we find out that, yes, we are the best, and yes, we have the lion's share, there is no cast-iron guarantee that things will not change. Even as the reader is reading this book, there is some organisation out there conspiring to take away his livelihood – because that is what modern competition on a global scale is all about.

The graph in Figure 3.2 shows the well-known comparison of the Japanese and Western automobile industries as devised by Dr Juran, which we can use as an example.

Dr Juran claimed that the Japanese automobile industry overtook its

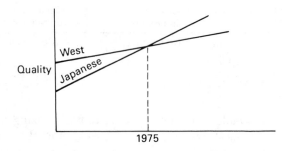

Fig. 3.2

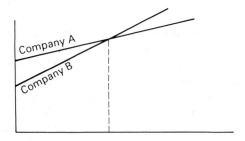

Fig. 3.3

Western competitors around 1975. Substituting Company A and B in the example, as in Figure 3.3, we see that for a long time, Company A has the biggest share of the market and the best reputation. However, Company B introduces an aggressive Total Quality programme with the express intention of taking pride of place from Company A. In the words of Dr Juran, 'The gap narrows until it closes. A time of trouble besets Company A'.

Generally speaking, the warning signals do not reach Company A until after the lines have converged. It is only when faced with plummeting market share and the onset of serious cash flow crises that Company A begins to realise that it is in trouble. In many cases, the realisation comes too late for the company to be able to respond – the patient is too weak to withstand the operation!

That is what happened to companies such as McMichael, Sobell, Murphy, Decca, Bush, Ultra, HMV, Pye, and so on, in the domestic television market. In that example, the rate of closing the gap between those companies and their executioners (Sony, Hitachi, Toshiba, Panasonic, JVC, etc.) was so rapid that a response was virtually impossible. Only Philips and a handful of other European competitors had the will and the expertise to survive.

Even if Company A can respond in time, if it has waited until after convergence it will be forced to improve at an even more rapid rate than Company

B if it is ever to regain its place in the market. Otherwise, all it can hope for is to progress at a parallel rate.

The lessons to be learnt from this are:

1. we must react before convergence, if there is still time left;
2. it is our rate of improvement *relative to competitors* which is important, not simply the fact that we are getting better;
3. we must obtain the information from the marketplace to know where we stand in relation to the competition, and monitor this continuously.

With regard to point 3 above, the majority of Japanese companies operate what they often refer to as 'Green Groups', which consist of key company personnel and selected leading customers. These groups are regarded as an extremely important part of a company's business strategy.

The groups meet on a regular basis to discuss the future plans of the business, progress with existing developments, and to solicit from the customers their thoughts and attitudes towards these developments, and their perceptions as to competitive advantages and disadvantages in the marketplace. Unfortunately, such activities are not commonplace in Western organisations, mainly due to a product-oriented mentality.

2. and 3. *Continuous and relentless cost reduction and quality improvement*

Depending on individual perceptions of the meaning of the word 'quality', these two points may seem to be in conflict with each other. Certainly, it is possible by reducing cost to cheapen a product or service, and of course, regretfully, this often happens. The laudable concepts of value analysis and value engineering were brought into disrepute in the West (but not in Japan!) for this reason.

The confusion is due to different interpretations of the word 'quality'; to some people the term refers merely to the specification of a product or service, and not necessarily to the processes which take place to achieve that requirement.

Consider the widespread advertisements for 'Quality Homes'. The intention of such advertisements is to convey to the would-be purchaser that he will be getting something out of the ordinary in terms of the specification: for example, brass fittings, panelled doors, primary double glazing, and so forth. Whilst these items are clearly 'quality', the decision to produce homes to this higher specification is a marketing decision aimed to attract a particular type of customer. At the other extreme, it is an equally reasonable 'quality' decision to produce the most basic homes at the most ecnomical price in order to attract the first-time buyer. Of course, in both cases it is necessary to identify very carefully the requirements of the intended customer, and then seek to provide that requirement. That would be a 'quality' decision, and a major element of business strategic thinking consistent with earlier comments in this book. It would also include the notion of pinpointing weaknesses in a competitor's strategy and exploiting a 'quality' advantage to the full for as long as it lasts.

For the purposes of this chapter and much of the rest of the book, we will be looking at quality from a different point of view. Namely, the quality of the *processes*, and not the quality of the specification.

Imagine the perfect company that never did anything wrong. Perfect raw materials or supplier support come in at one end; perfect processes take place such that there are no hold-ups, hiccups, or redoing things because they were wrong or inadequate the first time. Everyone is properly trained and does their job well. There are no misunderstandings or inquests, and there is perfect provision of the product or service to the customer at the other end. In our perfect world, there are no customer complaints, no warranty claims, and our reputation is second to none. In this situation we get the best of both worlds: better quality for the user, and lower cost for ourselves. In the context of points 2 and 3 this is the aspect of quality referred to. It can be seen that cost reduction, and improved quality in terms of the process, are totally interrelated.

4. An organisation in which everyone is working to make it the best in the business...

This is the behavioural aspect of quality upon which most of the rest of the book is based.

Quality concepts can be separated into two distinct categories: hard or logical, and behavioural. The 'hard' or logical aspects of quality include 'systems', 'process control', 'problem solving skills', and other organisational aspects. The majority of quality practitioners are likely to be basically left-brained thinkers. It is their attraction to logic, systems, procedures, organisation, measurements, calculations, problem-solving tools, etc., which drew them into the subject in the first place. Without balancing right-brained thinking, it is unlikely that such people would show much interest in the behavioural aspects of the subject, which are very much right-brained. On the other hand, the behavioural scientist is likely to be almost exactly the opposite. He will shrink away from what he regards as the mechanistic aspects, and will want to concentrate on the purely people-related features. Neither of these groups on their own can possibly get Total Quality into perspective, since Total Quality requires an equal appreciation and understanding of both aspects.

In Western society such gifted people are not much in evidence in the field of Total Quality. That is not to say that they do not exist; the author of this book has conducted no research in this area, but it would be very useful if this was looked into. However, there is a distinct possibility that in Japanese management circles, a better balance exists. Such theories have been put forward in recent years, and one explanatory hypothesis is that Japanese written characters, which are pictorial, encourage right-brained thinking.

It is clear that, whatever the characteristics of the key decision-makers and opinion influencers in any particular organisation, the benefits of Total Quality cannot be achieved purely through the introduction of techniques and skills. The high failure rate of Total Quality programmes in Western organisations is almost entirely due to a failure to understand the people factors, and virtually nothing to do with understanding the intricacies of the statistical method, BS 5750, or any such mechanical concept.

Whenever discussions take place regarding failures of such programmes, it is almost always the much-maligned middle manager whom we hold to be responsible. On other occasions it may be 'lack of top management commitment' or 'union resistance', etc. It is doubtful whether anyone has ever suggested that it is due to the inappropriate use of any of the techniques.

How can middle managers be collectively to blame? Much as some people may wish to argue otherwise, the middle manager is not genetically different from any other group of people. If he behaves in a certain way then it is the culture which is responsible. To blame any particular class or group of people provides no answer to the problem. If they behave in a certain way, then that must be a symptom, not the cause.

It is doubtful whether any one behaves in a negative way because he wants to. Most people want to feel good about themselves and towards the society in which they live. If they became negative, then it is invariably due to either a real or a perceived threat. If middle managers are seen collectively or individually to be working against the will of the organisation then it may safely be assumed that they perceive their security or enjoyment of working life to be at risk in some way.

When studies of many organisations' approach to Total Quality or Quality Circles are analysed, it is not usually difficult to see why one group or another is behaving in a negative, unco-operative way. More of this later. For now, we will consider how a positive approach will benefit an organisation.

Total Quality is founded on the belief that people produce their best results when they enjoy what they are doing; enjoy the relationship they have with their colleagues; like, trust and respect those in higher positions; have belief in their organisation; and see in their jobs an opportunity for continuous self-development, and the feeling that their company is better for them being there. In the ultimate, people should feel on a Sunday night, 'Oh good, it's Monday tomorrow!' instead of the usual, 'Oh God, it's Monday tomorrow, and I have to grind through a whole week to pick up a pay cheque'. We spend a significant part of our lives at work, and in terms of our social standing our job is very important to us. It seems fundamentally wrong that this should be a painful experience for so many. Is it their fault, or does the collective blame lie with society? We cannot change society on our own, but we can change the organisation in which we work and live. The upper managers in any organisation can, within limits, create any culture they wish, provided of course that people are prepared to suffer at the worst end of the spectrum.

In the Total Quality organisation, everyone is working towards making their company the best in its business.

Let's take a sporting example. Consider two 16-year-old boys, each of whom would like to be a professional footballer. One attends a trial at, say, Liverpool, who are top of Division 1 in the English league more often than not, and the other attends a trial at a fourth division club. Both are successful. The boy who is accepted at Liverpool will probably run home to tell his parents; the other may walk home, and still not be certain whether football is the right choice of career.

If the boy at Liverpool ever gets the opportunity to run through the tunnel onto the field for a Division 1 game, with the roar of 40,000 Anfield supporters, he will probably run his legs off, because he will be thinking all the way through the game, 'I don't want to let my mates down', every one of whom will have been his hero only a year or so before. He will want to play up to their standards, and they will support him, because that is what teamwork is all about.

That example is directly analogous to the ideal Quality company. Any organisation which world class can, as a bonus, cream off the top of the universities, technical colleges, and local society because everyone wants to work for the 'best' company. Such companies hardly ever need to advertise for jobs because if they did, they would not be able to cope with the number of replies.

Those who work for such companies will give their best efforts because they will not wish to let their colleagues or their company down. Hence the organisation gets the best of all possibilities, better quality work people and better quality performance.

A Total Quality policy is also probably one of the best forms of protection against head hunting ('Don't develop our own people – just steal from others').

Remember, in Total Quality *managers don't make decisions, they make sure that good decisions are being made.*

Economic justification of Total Quality

So far we have focused on the business strategic reasons for the introduction of Total Quality. It has been implied that the process can also be justified on the basis of cost reduction, and this is what must now be considered.

Figure 3.4 describes a simple model based on our perfect company described earlier. The diagram shows that not only does the perfect company operate at lower cost than its competitors, but it can command premium prices in the marketplace due to its reputation.

Most people will pay extra for something if they know it will be good. Even where this is not the case, and where products and services are sold purely on lowest tender, it will be the most efficient organisation which will be able to undercut the price of its competitors.

In addition to this, if the perfect company decides that it wants to increase its share of the market, and brings its selling price down below the cost of

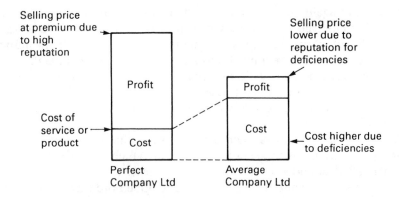

Fig. 3.4

manufacture of its competitors, the result may be 'exit Company Average from the market'. This is in fact what has happened with many of the Western companies which have failed to meet Japanese competition in the past three decades.

The cynical reply to the above argument would be, 'Well, all this assumes two things:

1. that the cost difference between perfect and average is sufficiently large to make a difference, and
2. that significant reductions in total cost are possible to avoid a situation where the cure costs more than the disease.'

In the first case, of course it is not possible through the pages of a book to identify the actual quality-related costs of any organisation. However, there is sufficient evidence to suggest the minimum such costs are likely to be in any organisation which has never before embarked on a programme to reduce these costs.

It is a fairly safe assumption that these costs will be at least 20 per cent of the turnover or sales revenue of any company, regardless of industry. In other words, we are paying at least 20p in every pound we spend for the internal inefficiencies of our supplier.

Many companies find it hard to believe it is possible for such costs to exist in their organisations and not already have been picked up in the accounting system.

In one large high-volume food manufacturing company, the author was challenged on this point by the Finance Director, who said, 'I don't know what companies you have worked in, Mr Hutchins, but they were not in the food industry. If we had figures like that, we would have poisoned half the population by now, and we would be out of business. It is more like 1½ per cent'. Fortunately, my continued involvement with that company did not rest with him, otherwise the rest of the story would be lost. About four weeks later, we met again, after having both done some work on the topic. The Finance Director said, 'You were wrong about that 20 per cent'. When asked what he thought it was he replied, 'It's more like 35 per cent'. In the author's experience this would be a much more common and normal figure.

The question then is why did he originally think 1½ per cent, only to discover so soon afterwards that it was as high as 35 per cent? This was a highly educated, highly articulate man who knew his job well, and who was at the height of his profession.

The answer is that very few companies separate the consequential costs of poor quality from other accounting figures, which are usually lumped together as ledger coded overheads or direct costs.

His 1½ per cent would have consisted of scrapped products, some rework but not by any means all, warranty claims, etc. However, each of these quality deficiencies, when they occur, create many other costs, often orders of magnitude higher than that which is accounted for. For example, most companies are aware of the value of stock, work in progress, and so forth. Very few companies indeed will know how much of this tied-up capital is due to quality-related deficiencies.

In Western organisations, if a breakdown in plant or a process occurs, it is normal to keep upstream processes running. Could one imagine a typical company closing down its entire production line because one of the final assembly operations had broken down? Usually, what happens is that all upstream operations continue to supply their output, with everything converging at the point of breakdown like a log jam. Of course, in a typical organisation there are multiple mini log jams occurring almost all the time. These create 'work in progress' – which is a curious term since most of it isn't progressing at all. The same applies to 'working capital': all too little of this is actually working either.

A non-production example of quality-related costs which are not classified as such involves the R & D and Design departments of a well-known British company. In this case, the consultant was called in to conduct a company-wide quality audit prior to assessment by a major customer. The company was aware that it had quality-related problems but it did not know what or where.

The audit indicated that in terms of manufacturing organisation, all appeared to be well. The same applied to supply quality. However, the company had altogether too many recorded customer complaints for such an apparently well-ordered organisation, and it was also losing market share rapidly.

The customer complaints were analysed by using a matrix as shown in Figure 3.5. A team comprising the consultant and three senior company personnel then identified which of the various functions was primarily responsible. If it was difficult to be certain, then ticks were put in the most likely areas, as shown against complaint number 7.

When all the complaints had been analysed in this way, the consequential cost for each was determined and assigned, and thus the proportion of quality-related cost could be estimated for each function. The results showed

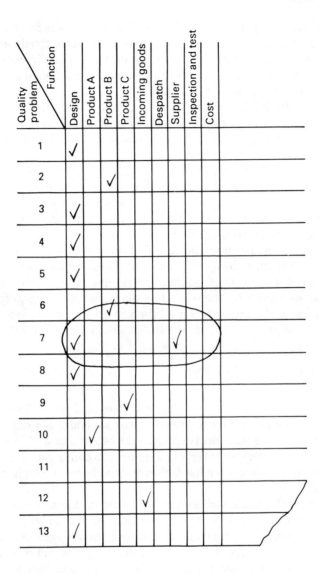

Fig. 3.5 Customer complaint matrix

that over 80 per cent of the cost of poor quality in this case originated in the design department.

Quite naturally, the engineering director responsible for the design function reacted to the results. He was then asked how many of his 28 design staff were, at that time, actually engaged in creative work on new designs, and how many of them were doing reactive re-design of existing products for no other reason than that there was a known quality deficiency which should not have been there in the first place. He did not know the answer, but as it turned out, every single employee in that department was so engaged. How many companies, or finance personnel, would ever have considered putting the entire salaries of the design department down as a quality-related failure cost? Perhaps this was an extreme example, but the likelihood is that similar situations are all too common.

In Dr Meredith Belbin's famous paper 'Quality Calamities', published by the British Institute of Management, based upon research in the 1960s, he quotes very similar statistics. It appears that little has changed since those days.

The cases quoted above are of course taken from manufacturing companies. It is conceivable that none of this may apply to service-based companies, but there is every indication to suggest that such companies are no better placed than their manufacturing counterparts. Anyone who wishes to test this out can do so quite simply.

Using a flow diagram, draw the organisation as it is now. Then repeat the exercise, but this time draw only those activities which add value to the service, and assume no errors, so therefore do not allow for any checking or monitoring; then compare the two! How many people are required in each case, and what is the lead time for all the activities in each case?

How then can an organisation identify its quality-related costs? There are two possible approaches:

1. expand the accountancy system
2. use estimates

All of the experience of DHA consultants advises against the first option. We have tried it and it doesn't work. We have seen several organisations attempt to do this. Some have used British Standard 6143 as a basis. These attempts usually fail before they are ever implemented because generally, the total cost of such programmes stretches far beyond the benefits which are likely to be achieved.

The reason is that quality-related costs are not uniform, and in fact follow the 80/20 or 'Pareto principle'. Under this principle about 80 per cent of the cost of poor quality will generally be incurred by only 20 per cent of the problems. Conversely, over 80 per cent of the problems incurs a total of less than 20 per cent of the cost. Expanding the accountancy base to capture all quality-related costs will mean that the cost of collecting some data will generally be greater than the problem itself. It is far more sensible to concentrate on the important few than to attempt to include the trivial many. Standards such as BS 6143 give no guidance as to how this might be achieved, and to follow its advice would cost far more than most companies would be prepared to invest. A further criticism of the Standard is the fact that it is written entirely in mechanical engineering language, and it would prove difficult for those in other industries to interpret its meaning.

Of course, some quality cost data can and should be retrieved. This would include those costs regarded as the important few, such as 'inventory', 'yield', 'energy consumption', 'absenteeism', 'credit period', and so forth. For each of these key criteria, it is advisable to estimate 'What would be the minimum cost of each of these, assuming no deficiencies?'. Then deviations from these norms can be monitored.

Average deviations of this type are referred to by Dr Juran as the 'chronic' problems. The day-to-day fluctuations from the average are 'sporadic' and involve managers in fire-fighting activities. These are the variances which historically might have been judged 'quality-related' in some cases, and of course these problems must be tackled and solved.

However, the real improvements come from tackling and solving the chronic problems, because these determine the overall performance of the organisation. Total Quality companies embark on intensive progressive attempts to identify the causes of these problems, find remedies, apply the remedies, and then hold the gains. It is the intensive application of problem-solving skills to these problems by all levels of organisation which gives the Japanese their extraordinary lead over Western competitors, and is the subject of much of the rest of this book.

The more usual and effective means by which quality-related cost data is retrieved by companies who are successfully implementing Total Quality programmes is the brainstorming method. This participative technique can be used by a variety of different types of groups within an organisation, but at the top level, management can use it to identify the most important problems confronting the enterprise. Using brainstorming effectively, such groups have identified many hundreds of problems which can be resolved successfully using the improvement techniques which are described later in Chapters 19 and 20. The second step is to apply the Pareto principle in order to sort these problems and identify the important few.

Further analysis will usually indicate that the biggest and most costly problems can only be resolved at the highest level in the organisation (Figure 3.6). This may come as an unwelcome surprise for many senior people since it becomes evident that the improvement process of Total Quality is one activity they cannot delegate. In fact it is one case where delegation equals abdication.

Even a 50 per cent reduction of some of these problems may save more than solving a very large number of the smaller problems. Companies which have used this approach to failure cost identification have usually found that failure costs alone account for some 75 per cent of the total cost of poor quality.

Having identified failure costs in this way, it then becomes possible to determine how much monitoring, inspection, and testing is carried out for no other reason that the existence of these failures.

It is important to follow this sequence: failure identification first, followed by the identification of 'appraisal costs'. This is because the latter come in two categories:

1. Appraisal costs which will be there anyway, irrespective of failures.
2. Appraisal costs which are directly failure-dependent. In other words, if the failures ceased to exist there would be no feed for the appraisal.

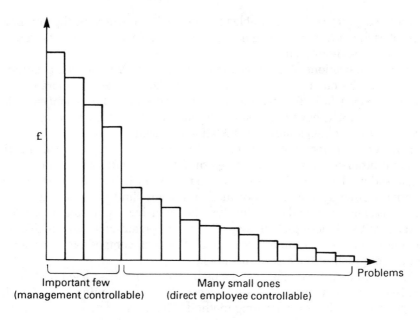

Fig. 3.6

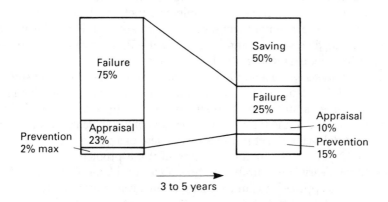

Fig. 3.7

There is little point in including Category 1 in the statistics, since they are part of the process.

The third element of quality-related cost is represented by 'prevention costs'. This includes all the money spent on attempting to eliminate the failures. Again, as with appraisal cost, it is necessary first to identify failures, then to ask, 'How much do we spend attempting to reduce these failures?'. This is because, with many prevention costs, it is difficult to judge whether they are just part of sound business practice, or are directly failure-related.

Figure 3.7 indicates the typical ratios to be expected following such an exercise.

It can be seen that by selective attack on failure cost items, quality-related costs can be progressively reduced. Western companies which have seriously approached Total Quality in the past decade have found that quality-related costs can be reduced by some 50 per cent in 3 – 5 years through this approach. The cost of this improvement is the increase in prevention cost activities.

Using an investment appraisal approach, Total Quality can therefore be justified not merely on the belief that it will help increase market share; there are tangible, measurable, cold hard facts to justify its introduction.

For example, consider the following fictitious company:

Turnover	£100m
Capital employed	£50m
Cost of poor quality	£20m
Profit	£10m

In the normal way, assuming that the organisation is running close to capacity, in order to double annual profit it would have to double the capital employed to £100m. If the statistics for quality improvement discussed above are anywhere near correct, then reducing the cost of poor quality by 50 per cent would also mean an increase of profit of £10m, since the saving in quality cost would go directly to profit. The cost of achieving this at 15 per cent of the cost of poor quality would be £3m. Even at 20 per cent this would still only be £4m, against the alternative of £50m through a more traditional approach.

In the words of John Young, the Chief Executive Officer of Hewlett Packard, when they performed such an exercise around 1980, 'Quality improvement is good business to be in'. Since that time Hewlett Packard have made vigorous progress in the field of quality improvement and are probably one of the West's most progressive companies from the point of view of internal improvement.

In summary, there are two prime reasons why an organisation should embark on the intensive development of Total Quality:

1. As a means of aggressive market penetration.
2. To achieve relentless progressive quality improvement and cost reduction.

The four elements of Total Quality

Despite the obvious advantages of the new approach as evidenced by Japanese competitive success, the West in general still clings to some of the old ideas.

Instead of Quality becoming everybody's job, as in Japan, it has been and still is seen by many as a kind of police force activity parallel to production rather than being inherently part of it. Throughout the 1970s and 1980s the advocates of this approach have stubbornly resisted any deviation from their belief that Quality Systems are the centre of the universe. Even now, when all the evidence points to the fallacy of this approach, and it has become self-evident that Total Quality along the lines of the Japanese experience is the only way to compete, they still argue that Quality Systems are the focal point of what they refer to as Total Quality 'Management'.

Of course systems and procedures are important; of course there must be traceability, calibration, and so forth, but it does not matter how much focus one puts on systems, systems do not hold the pencil of the designer, nor turn the handles on the machines. Quality control does not answer the phone every time a customer calls, nor does it deliver the product or service to the customer. If the people involved do not really care, if they just do their jobs according to instructions, then it does not matter how much system you have, you will never remain in business in the face of international competition. Real quality is all about winning the hearts and minds of all of the people, and there has never been a quality control or quality assurance department capable of doing that.

When the systems-focused approach has failed to produce the results, the advocates of this approach, instead of considering that they may be wrong, have insisted that what is required is more of the same medicine with a larger spoon. Consequently, organisations which have suffered from this treatment have become more and more bureaucratic and people have become alienated from Quality, seeing it only as a negative self-flagellation process rather than the stimulating, exciting concept that it really is.

In reality, systems are only one of four fundamental elements of Quality, which are:

1. Systems
2. Processes
3. Management
4. People

1. Systems

The principles of Quality Systems can readily be found in such documents as British Standard 5750; ISO 9000; Allied Quality Assurance Publications (AQAPs); Federal Drug Association of America Publications; and many variants created by some specific organisations, for example Ford QI.

Third Party Certification

This concept has been gaining popularity in the UK and Europe in recent years as a development of the Ministry of Defence 'Contractor Assessment' Scheme which started in June 1972 in the UK.

Under these schemes, an organisation is assessed by an external audit team and judged on its systems and procedures, usually against the requirement of such standards as BS 5750, etc.

The one merit of such schemes is that at least the assessed organisations, when they meet with the requirements, have a base level of organisation. *This is all that can be claimed as a result of such assessments.* They do not and cannot imply that the said company will produce high quality products. All that can be hoped for in that respect is that some of the worst disasters can be avoided. For example, it is unlikely that the Zeebrugge disaster would have occurred if the ferry company had operated to the spirit of BS 5750, because there would have been a procedure to ensure that the ship could not have left the harbour with the bow door open, or without the Captain knowing, which was apparently the case.

There is nothing which a third party audit can do under the terms of these standards which will put an organisation into a position of competitive advantage, which unfortunately is the mistaken belief of many organisations who have enthusiastically introduced Quality Systems into their organisations.

One company making gas appliances was recently awarded unqualified approval to BS 5750 and yet, on the admission of the plant manager, 40 per cent of the product was rejected on first submission to the customer, and 60 per cent reworked before it ever left the factory gates. The systems and procedures were apparently faultless; the processes were inadequate to say the least. Unfortunately, BS 5750 and its variants are not designed to evaluate processes. Even if this were changed, it is doubtful whether many of the auditors could be trained to conduct the process capability studies which would be necessary.

2. Processes

No matter how good the systems and procedures are, if the processes are not capable then quality cannot be achieved. Another fundamental difference between Japan and the West is the focus on process improvement and process control.

In Japan they have a saying, 'Look after the process and the product looks after itself!'. Unfortunately in the West we lack the means to look after the processes, even if we had the desire. The reason is that to do so would require the harnessing of all the resources of all the people, on a scale never dreamed of even today in Western organisations.

In Japan, following the original introduction of Quality Circles in 1962, millions of workers have been educated, trained, and developed over the years to a level unheard of in the West. Quality Circles of these workers are capable of solving work-related problems of the same level of sophistication as those solved by systems analysts and production engineers in Western organisations. In the West, many companies have, over the past decade, introduced Quality Circles, but none has been developed to anything like the standards reached in Japan.

Consequently, the only problem-solvers are the managers and engineers. The sheer volume of process-related problems in even the simplest of organisations goes well beyond the capacity of such personnel, who in any case will be so involved in fighting day-to-day sporadic fires that in no way can they engage in consistent project-by-project process improvement on the scale of that being achieved in Japan.

The message is clear: unless Western companies can unlock a similar resource, the gap between East and West will continue to grow.

In the next decade we must see a massive change in the levels of involvement in process improvement, otherwise failure is inevitable. Even today the car giants such as Jaguar, Porsche, Rover, Benz, etc., are facing almost lethal competition from Japan, not necessarily in product performance, but in marginal cost. The return on investment of most Western car giants is pitiful compared with the Japanese, and these costs are hidden in the processes.

3. Management

It is accepted that managers are also people! – but 'management' has a critical role to play in Total Quality. In fact this group can be regarded as the linchpin or power house in a successful programme.

It is important to remember that managers as such do not make anything. Managers get results through people. Since managers can opt for several different styles of management, it follows that these must be studied very carefully if the performance of people is to be consistent with the exacting demands of Total Quality.

Basically, the two extremes of management style are:

- authoritarian
- participative

Of the two, the authoritarian style is the easier. Given a careful balance of threats, penalties, and rewards, the approach makes few demands on the busy manager, and when span of control is wide, and the manager under pressure, he may feel that this is the only option available, even if he would prefer to manage in a more participative way.

Participative management, on the other hand, at first sight would appear the opposite. If goals are to be achieved through loyalty, job satisfaction, and group activities, it is necessary to know the people on a more intimate level. This is demanding on the busy manager, and many would believe that the main resource of time is not available. Fortunately, experience with Quality Circles indicates that this could be a false impression, provided that the concept is introduced carefully, and is properly understood. Unfortunately in the West most companies appear to be either unwilling or incapable of doing this research first. The concept of Quality Circles is regarded to be of such great importance that much of this book is devoted to the subject.

Another aspect of the management role in Total Quality involves team-work. In Chapter 2 there was some discussion of the cross-functional problems related to the internal customer-supplier concept, and management 'professionalism'. This form of management involvement is the very essence of Total Quality and is very different from the systems approach controlled by the quality assurance department.

The remedies to the problems identified by the managers using the Pareto principle referred to earlier will involve measures to:

- improve systems and procedures,
- improve processes,
- improve management organisation, or
- improve workers' methods.

The fact that it is the managers themselves who are finding the remedies is very different from those managers having remedies imposed upon them by quality assurance and others. The very fact that they have participated in identifying the theories of causes, testing the theories, and finding remedies, will motivate them to a degree far beyond that achieved through more traditional methods.

4. People

Of course, people do not decide how they are to be managed. In many ways one could say that they are the victims. It has been said, 'Show me a company with poor industrial relations and I will show you bad management'. How-

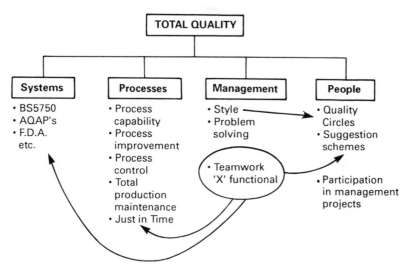

Fig. 3.8 The four elements of Total Quality

ever, one cannot expect a labour force which has become accustomed to one particular style of management for many years to simply accept another, just because management perceives the need. Where relationships have been poor in the past, there will be many suspicions and defensive practices which will stand in the way of progress.

Many of them will not disappear overnight, and it is important for management to ensure that people are fully kept in the picture as to management intentions regarding Total Quality, and to encourage participation. Later in the book considerable time will be spent on these issues, which must be carefully weighed before involvement is considered.

CHAPTER 4

THE JOURNEY TOWARDS TOTAL QUALITY

A divergence of approach

Throughout the 1970s and 1980s Western manufacturing companies have progressively lost ground to their Japanese competitors mainly through a fundamental difference in approach to Quality.

In Japan, from the 1950s onwards they have consistently developed a people-based approach such that Quality has literally become everybody's job.

In the West on the other hand, and in the UK in particular, the so-called Quality 'profession' has opted for a Taylor-style systems-based approach.

It will be useful to look in detail at how and why 'Taylorism', as it came to be known in Japan, was adopted in many countries, including Japan, and how the latter country subsequently rejected it in favour of their people-oriented approach.

The history of 'Taylorism'

It seems a little unfair to Frederick Taylor to associate an entire system of management with his name, particularly as he was only one part of its development, but he did have considerable influence during its formative years. The system began to evolve in the United States during the latter part of the last century. Like most developments, there was no one single factor, but a conspiracy of several elements, which eventually crystallised into a single form. These included:

- The work of Eli Whitney – he had discovered the advantages of inter-changeability of parts, and found this could be achieved by the develop-ment of automatic and semi-automatic machine tools for the manufacture of small arms.
- The arrival in the United States of vast numbers of immigrants, mostly from Western Europe, who went into the American factories with the object of earning a lot of money quickly and then going out West pioneering. These people were, generally speaking, unskilled, and many of them were also illiterate.

In order to make use of this unskilled labour it was necessary to take the skill

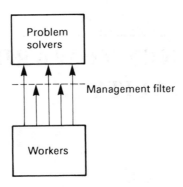

Fig. 4.1

out of the work, and this of course was compatible with the newly developing machine tools inspired by Eli Whitney and his contemporaries.

F.W. Taylor believed that management should accept the responsibility for planning and organising work, and that the task of planning should be separated from the tasks of execution. His main objective was to treat work and management in a 'scientific' manner and to replace the rather inexact and subjective procedures which had hitherto predominated.

In his system therefore, tasks are deskilled by being broken down into their smallest elements, and all problem-solving is carried out by management-level specialists (Figure 4.1), who are often referred to as troubleshooters, or problem solvers.

This system also requires jobs to be defined in such a way that each task becomes a fairly clearly stated sequence of operations or work elements to be performed by the individual. The sequence may be longer in some jobs than others but the elements are still a sequence.

The system developed, and permeated the whole of society throughout the world and has become the accepted form of management in both industry and commerce. It is just as true for telephone operators, clerical staff, nurses, and airline pilots, as it is for production workers in manufacturing organis-ations. Once the people have learned the job routines, they simply repeat their tasks on a continuous basis. No one asks them anything or involves them in anything provided they perform their operations according to the prescribed schedule. If they experience problems, they are usually required to address them to their manager, supervisor, or in some cases, employee representatives.

Unfortunately, problems which are high on their list of priorities are frequently low on their manager's or supervisor's list, with the consequence that rarely is any action taken. This leads the individual to believe that management is not interested in his or her ideas. 'I am just a number on a clock card' or 'cog in the wheel'; 'Why should I worry? I will just do my job according to instructions, and pick up my salary cheque at the end of the week', are all familiar remarks made at the workplace. In other words, the system encourages the individual to switch off mentally and to perform the task mechanically.

If the work is particularly boring, or dehumanised, as in many parts of the automotive and other industries, it is not unknown for workers deliberately to sabotage their work to create a distraction in order tor retain their sanity.

How can we have created such a dehumanised work routine? The answer is that, when it was first introduced, 'Taylorism', combined with the work of Frank and Lilian Gilbreath and others such as Charles Bedeaux, served a purpose, which was to revolutionise the concept of work in the United States. It can be seen that this development was not of cultural origin but was a pragmatic solution to the problems confronting that country at that time. Eventually, through Taylorism, the United States became the most economically powerful nation in the world.

Later on, mainly after the Second World War, Taylorism swept the world, sweeping aside the craft-based systems which had dominated in Western Europe. An understanding of the key social differences between these two systems is fundamental to understanding the new model of Total Quality which is the subject of this book.

The four steps

In any form of work, there are four distinct elements which will exist either formally or informally.

Step 1: Planning
Tasks to be performed, and the prescribed sequence of elements, checks, etc., are determined, in relation to the overall objectives of the task in question.

Step 2: Doing
The tasks determined by the planning phase are carried out.

Step 3: Check or audit
Formal or informal checks are carried out to ensure that the tasks performed in the doing phase have been carried out in the manner required in the planning phase.

Step 4: Action
Following a review of the check or audit stage, action may be necessary to improve the plan in order to achieve the stated objectives.

This is just as true for the housewife cooking the Sunday lunch as it is in complex industrial or commercial operations.

This sequence of operations will be repeated continuously throughout the life of the product or service and the continually improved effectiveness of each phase will ultimately determine the success of that organisation. The main difference between craftsmanship and Taylorism is determined by where the responsibility for each of these phases lies.

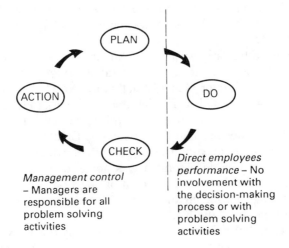

Fig. 4.2 The Taylor regime

Management 'manage' and people 'do'

Under Taylorism, workers are not asked anything, are not involved in anything, they are simply required to do their work according to instructions.

The Taylor concept requires that management be responsible for the planning, checking, and acting and that these phases be separated from the 'doing' phase (Figure 4.2).

Neither Britain nor Western Europe had any need for the Taylor concept at the time it was developed because they had craft-based labour forces and therefore saw little need to deskill work through the introduction of automatic machinery. Neither was the value of high output production of cheap goods identified as a major need.

However, during the years that followed, the Taylor concept was refined and developed. In his book, *My Life and Work*, published in 1922, Henry Ford publicised the development of flow line production. This development led to even greater demands for sophisticated management specialists such as production engineers, quality engineers, work-study engineers, production control, quality control, and the inspection of work by others, and this development effectively completed the destruction of the craftsmanship approach and became referred to as 'scientific management'.

Scientific management

This is merely the ultimate development of the Taylor system, in which the specialists, together with functional line management, totally control the work process.

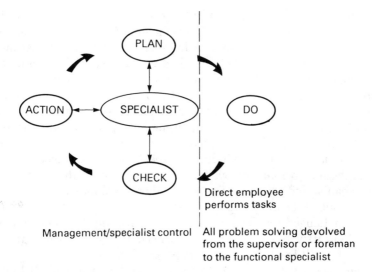

Fig. 4.3 Scientific management

Once formed, the 'scientific management' process (Figure 4.3) becomes self-perpetuating. Management becomes dependent upon the specialist, and the specialist uses this dependence to increase his own influence. There is no pressure from within the model which will enable the mould to be broken.

This concept of management made its biggest impact on the world at large during the Second World War when the Americans used the system to build their massive armament machine. It then became the principal means by which they were able to flood world markets with cheap, mass-produced products when they reverted back to the manufacture of domestic products in the 1940s and 1950s.

This impressed Britain and other European countries, and very soon the world was copying this method of management. American management consultants could earn extremely large fees in any country in the world. It was generally assumed that the process represented the nearest thing possible to an ideal model of management and this assumption has never, until now, been challenged in the West.

The pioneers of Taylorism, namely the specialists, and in particular the work-study specialists, then began to introduce the concept elsewhere, not only into office operations in manufacturing companies but into every form of work activity irrespective of type of industry.

Persistence of Taylorism

Taylorism is proving remarkably resistant to change. This is because the specialists control the system. Only those developments which are in the specialists' own best interests are allowed to emerge and management in the West has consequently become totally specialist-dependent. Because the staff of the management colleges tend to be such specialists, and as they decide what management should learn, it would appear that they therefore filter out anything they find undesirable, or threatening to themselves. In this way the system has become almost totally self-perpetuating. Where their professional interest conflicts with the interest of the organisation, the personal interest will obviously take precedence. It can be seen that this leads to a situation where the individual specialist tends to place his loyalty to his profession before his loyalty to the organisation that employs him. This mechanism effectively stifles any further development and it is likely that this is one of the most important reasons why the concept has remained virtually unchanged for the past thirty years. During that time, almost the whole of industry has become so influenced by this approach that most workpeople at all levels have no perception of any alternative.

As mentioned in Chapter 1, another reason for the persistence of Taylorism in the West, despite its now clear disadvantages, is the fact that the managers who are currently in control owe their own personal career progression to their ability to succeed in this environment. Instinctively, many will be reluctant to experiment with a revolutionary alternative if they are uncertain as to whether they will be equally secure under the new conditions.

This is not to say that people have not identified the problems which this approach brings. All the problems of Taylorism associated with treating individuals as mere extensions of their machine or desk have been identified, but the solutions offered by the specialists have usually been cosmetic. No Western organisation has, until recently, changed effectively the basic tenets of the systems of organisation itself. Even those which have now identified this need and are making progress have a long way to go before they can claim to be on a par with Japan. Until the changes infiltrate society itself, it may not even be possible.

A good example of this lies in the work of such behavioural scientists as Herzberg, Maslow, and McGregor. Each of these famous management scientists made a substantial contribution to an understanding of the problems relating to personnel needs at work, but they were singularly unable to suggest a vehicle for the satisfaction of such needs because they did not realise that the cause of the problems lay in the principles of the organisational structures themselves.

Why Taylorism was broken in Japan

During the critical stages of Japanese reconstruction after the Second World War, labour alienation was the last luxury the Japanese could afford, and the rapid deterioration in labour relations that they experienced in the late 1940s and early 1950s came as a shock. This lead to considerable analysis of the root causes, and they concluded that the most important factor was the introduction of Taylorism.

They were thus the first nation to become aware of the need to break the mould and avoid the problems becoming entrenched. This was because they had experienced the disadvantages of the Taylor system before they had experienced its benefits. For example, if Japan in the early 1950s is compared with Western Europe and the United States at the time, a vivid contrast can be observed.

The West was going through an unprecedented boom, where most enterprises could sell everything they could make. Economies were booming and most people were relatively well off: better off, in fact, than at any time in history. It was at that time that Harold Macmillan, the British Prime Minister, coined the slogan, 'You never had it so good'.

In Japan, on the other hand, things were different. The economy was weak, the export performance of the Japanese was poor, and their GNP was about a third of that of the UK, although admittedly it had recovered to its pre-War levels. They were known as junk merchants to the world, and were noted as cheap imitators of Western products.

Whereas the West believed its success was due to Taylorism, the Japanese identified the Taylor concept with their failures, and associated it notably with low motivation, low job interest, absenteeism, and so forth.

Of course, the West was also confronted with these same problems, but at that time, with the economy in top gear, the disadvantages were easily outweighed by the benefits. Low job satisfaction seemed to be unimportant if the dehumanising aspects of the work method and its social problems were

Fig. 4.4 The success and failure of Taylorism

more than offset by high wages and by the workers' access to consumer durables which would otherwise be out of their reach.

Even the quality problems seemed not to matter. Why should a manufacturer worry about quality when he had a full order book and could sell everything he could make? There was even a perverse argument, widely publicised on management training courses, that suggested that there was a commercial advantage to be gained by deliberately producing poor quality or short-life products. It was argued that this would cause the customer to make frequent replacements, thus increasing the level of demand and the volume of production, while decreasing unit costs. This gave rise to the notion of a 'throw-away society'.

Unfortunately, this approach only works if all competitors do the same. As soon as the market begins to shrink, or a major competitor deliberately changes the rules, the process collapses, with possibly disastrous results for those who fail to respond.

This is probably one of the most important reasons for Japan's recent success in hitherto safe markets.

Not only were the Japanese able to change the rules, they actually challenged the fundamental basis upon which industrial society is based. They attacked Taylorism and introduced aggressive, market-led, customer-first policies. This is something the rest of the world has not yet done, but must do, and quickly, if it has any hope of survival.

Craftsmanship system

For many years it appeared that the Craftsmanship system was the only alternative to Taylorism. The Craftsmanship approach is almost the opposite of Taylorism, since by definition a craftsman is responsible for his own quality.

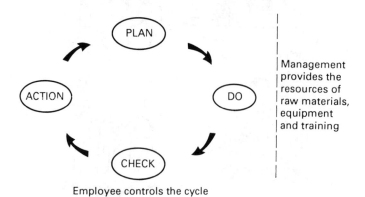

Fig. 4.5 The operation of the Craftsmanship system

Table 4.1 Advantages and disadvantages of Craftsmanship

Advantages	*Disadvantages*
Self-control	High cost of labour
Pride in work	Low output per individual
Self-confidence/self-assurance	Low interchangeability of items
Loyalty to the work	'Unique' product
High level of skill	Scheduling difficulties
Sense of responsibility	Monitoring problems leading to poor control
Motivated and involved	Low wages
Good quality workmanship	Low skills management
Self improving	Reactive to problems of organisation, rather than pro-active
High level of job interest	
'Unique' product	

Table 4.2 Advantages and disadvantages of Taylorism

Advantages	*Disadvantages*
High productivity at low cot	Control by others
Interchangeability of items	Low worker morale caused by frustration, boredom, low self-confidence
Low skill workers	Poor quality, absenteeism, lack of job pride, alienation, tough unions, 'them and us' attitudes
Lower wage costs/unit	Poor company image reflected by workers who interface with customer
Accurate forecasting	Little opportunity for self-development
Predictable results	Supervisory problems due to lack of development and poor selection
Sophisticated, highly trained problem solvers	Loyalty of specialist to specialism rather than to the employer
High wages and salaries	Culture change is difficult
Very economically powerful when not hampered by the disadvantages	'Blame' culture
	Macho-style, egotistical management
	'Grab what you can' mentality at all levels
	Lack of respect for the worker
	Multi layer organisations

The most fundamental difference between the Craftsmanship approach and Taylorism lies in the question of who has control of the process. All work processes contain the same basic ingredients of PLAN–DO–CHECK–ACT, but with Craftsmanship, all these phases are controlled either directly by the employee or by the supervisor and the craftsman together.

In the most simple form of the Craftsmanship system, management only provides the means and facilities by which craftsmen perform the entire operation. Again, the PDCA cycle can be used to describe this system, as with Taylorism, but notice (Figure 4.3) that with Taylorism PDC are in the hands of management, whereas with Craftsmanship the entire PDCA cycle is in the hands of the worker, or craftsman (Figure 4.5).

This system does produce high-quality products, but it has the disadvantage of high cost, low wages, low output, and inadequate forecasting or scheduling possibilities. Inevitably, both this, and the Taylor system have their advantages and disadvantages (see Tables 4.1 and 4.2) but it appeared for many years that whilst Taylorism had its problems, these were greatly outweighed by its obvious advantages over the pure Craftsmanship system.

The alternative–the Ishikawa approach

Professor Kaoru Ishikawa deserves to go down in history as having developed a new system of management that combines all the beneficial ingredients of both systems, but avoids all their disadvantages. In effect he created a method of management that is not in conflict with many of the benefits of Taylorism, but includes all the elements which give it its power, and at the same time includes the most desirable aspects of the Craftsmanship approach. There is nothing cultural in such a concept, because everything contained in its approach already exists at least in part and has done for centuries in virtually every developed country in the world.

Taylorism has never been challenged in the Western world because it has been assumed that Taylorism and Craftsmanship are mutually exclusive and therefore incompatible. Ishikawa's recommendations essentially achieve

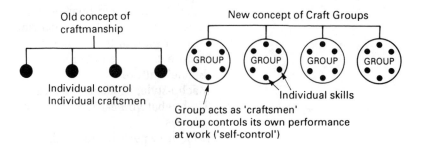

Fig. 4.6 Old and new concepts of Craftsmanship

a revolution in management by bringing the craftsmanship element back to groups of people rather than individuals. This is the essence of the Total Quality system.

Towards Total Quality

So, how do we make the change to Professor Ishikawa's system, and set out on the journey towards Total Quality?

When considering the implementation of Total Quality, we all have to start from where we are. This sounds obvious, but it means that there can be no 'paint by numbers' guide to implementation and for different companies the route will be different. Many consultancies attempt to be prescriptive about the stages and elements of implementation. In reality, this is impossible if success is to be achieved. The issues in any two companies even in the same industry and the same town will be different due to differences in history, share of the market, economics, and a host of other reasons. To be successful, the Total Quality consultant must work from the premiss of helping a company to run its own programme rather than doing it for them. The advice offered here is therefore aimed not at consultants or educationalists, but at the company which is intending to introduce Total Quality as the key business strategic approach to growth.

The first question must be 'Where do we want to be?'. No consultant can answer this question on behalf of his client. To reach an answer, it is helpful to think in terms of some time horizon, say five to ten years. If we were to pick up the *Financial Times* in five to ten years' time, with our company featured on the centre spread, what would we like it to say? Stories of 'phenomenal growth'?, 'World leadership'?, 'Standard bearer'?

Different executives will have different ideas as to where they would like the business to be. Ideally, these should be identified, and the technique of brainstorming is again helpful here. Following the brainstorming session, all of the ideas should be fused into one composite and succinct statement, usually referred to as a 'Mission Statement'. Such statements are normally written in general terms, and it then becomes necessary to identify 'success criteria'. This is important because if success cannot be measured it will be impossible to know whether or not it has been achieved.

A typical example of such a statement has been created by DHA for its own purposes (see Figure 4.8), since the consultancy follows a policy of practising what it preaches to others. Only in this way can new ideas and

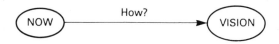

Fig. 4.7

DAVID HUTCHINS ASSOCIATES

CORPORATE STATEMENT

Mission

David Hutchins Associates International Limited and its subsidiaries exist to constantly develop and provide a service to organisations and to society leading to the achievement of never ending performance improvement.

This is accomplished by harnessing the creativity, skill and knowledge of all individuals.

The key concepts fundamental to ultimate success are founded on:

- Self respect and mutual respect between seniors, peers and subordinates.

- Recognition and celebration of successes.

- Pride and loyalty of working for and with a quality organisation and in a quality society.

David Hutchins   27th July 1989
Chairman   Date

concepts be satisfactorily tested. DHA believe this to be one of the distinct advantages which it has over educational establishments. DHA also has to live in the same commercial world as its clients. (This is of course changing in the case of educational establishments, but not without trauma!)

Policy deployment

The company mission statement does not usually contain any time horizon. It is a statement of intent and beliefs, created by the directors of the enterprise. Its aims are achieved in incremental steps over a several-year period. The goals and targets for each successive year must be identified, together with appropriate success criteria. Some of these goals and targets may be achieved simply by good management, others will only be achieved through break-through or projects.

Once these goals and criteria have been agreed, they must be shared with the next layer of management. This layer will then identify the specific requirements on them individually in order that collectively the summation of all of their targets equals the overall business targets and goals for that year. At this stage the model looks like Figure 4.9.

Once agreed at this level, the individual divisional or departmental heads share the plan for their department with their subordinates, who then create targets and goals for their own function. This process is continued all the way down to each individual employee. The completed model of this form of deployment looks like Figure 4.10.

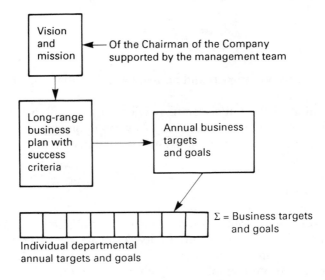

Fig. 4.9

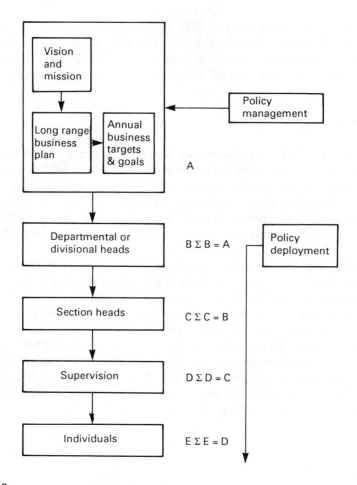

Fig. 4.10

At each level, both projects and normal daily activities will be required to achieve the targets.

The creation of the initial company-wide targets and goals is generally referred to as 'policy management' or policy development, and the devolvement down through the organisation as 'policy deployment'.

Policy control

At each level down a feedback loop is created. This is referred to as 'policy control'. At the lower levels, this feedback occurs on an hourly or daily basis. In many Japanese companies it is continuous. For example, at Daikin Industries, manufacturers of Air Conditioning equipment, an LED-type display board, similar to that shown in Figure 4.11 is positioned above

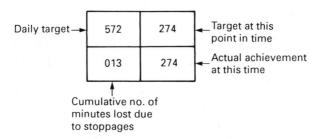

Fig. 4.11 Example of LED-type display board

each assembly line. Variants on this approach can be found in most major Japanese plants.

At each higher level, feedback becomes progressively weekly, monthly, half yearly, and at the highest level, the entire organisation is subjected to an annual audit by the Company Chairman.

Such audits are thorough and extensive. The object is to examine the achievements at all levels against the original plan or policy development the use of problem-solving skills, the activities of problem-solving groups such as project teams, Quality Circles, and also the suggestion scheme (see later, Chapter 7).

It can be seen therefore that the three elements together–policy management or development, policy deployment, and policy control–represent the structure through which the strategic requirements of Total Quality can be achieved. It is the most effective means by which an organisation is able to harness the resources of all of its people to work towards making that company the best in its business. Such organisations can if required change direction at astonishing speed to outflank their competitors who are less effectively organised.

For example, on a recent study mission to Japan a DHA group visited Yamazaki Mazak, one of Japan's leading machine tool and machining centre manufacturers. It was a large plant, very modern, and extremely well organised. Only nine months earlier a similar group had visited the plant led by the same two DHA consultants. In the time between the two visits, not only had the plant been totally reorganised, it had also been extended by some 30 per cent, and yet there was no evidence that this had taken place other than from the photographs taken on the two occasions. We were told that the entire operation, including gangways being repainted, and robot sensors relocated for the materials handling machines, had taken place over only a few weeks with little lost production. This is all the more remarkable when one considers that the plant is fully automated, and whilst it is only manned for two shifts, it runs for three. On the third shift it is totally un-manned and operates in darkness! For a plant of this complexity and scale to be able to change so dramatically and in such short time is an incredible achievement.

Chairman's audit

The annual audit of the whole operation, conducted by the Company Chairman, is known as the 'Chairman's Audit'. From his point of view, it is through this structure of organisation that his policies and goals are achieved. Consequently, he will regard this audit as of the highest importance. It will be carried out by him personally, and he will have a detailed knowledge of all characteristics to be identified in a well run operation. In Japanese organisations, the Chairman's audit is one of the most important activities in the annual calender.

All of the feedback from the daily, weekly, monthly, and half-yearly returns, together with the results of the annual audit and changing market situations, provide the basis upon which the next year's annual plans, goals, and targets are formulated. Again, in Japanese organisations, the formulation of the next year's plan is one of the most important activities of the top management team. It can take these executives anything from one to six month's full-time involvement.

How many Western executives would spend anything more than a few days a year on what they might refer to as a 'back to the woods' exercise? Some companies do set annual goals and targets, and these may also be cascaded down so that individuals have some idea what is expected of them, but they are not usually specific, and few are capable of measurement on a daily basis. Also, even where this does exist, there is no evidence that the improvements required are broken down into specific improvement projects, and tackled on a regular project-by-project basis, using structured problem-solving techniques, as described later in this chapter.

Flagchart

In Komatsu, the policy development, deployment, and control process is supported by what is referred to as the 'flagship' approach. In Japan, it is conventional for fishing boats to advertise their catch by hoisting flags to indicate its size. Komatsu have adopted this as a theme for the means by which they give exposure to quality improvements.

At each level of deployment, charts are prepared to show the goals for the year, as in Figure 4.12. For each parameter a separate chart is prepared. These are made out by everybody at every level, and are posted in the work areas. As the weeks and months go by, the actual performance is plotted against targets. In order to achieve targets, individuals and groups may choose improvement projects in order to break through to new levels of performance. This is the essence of that company's approach, but it is essentially similar to most others.

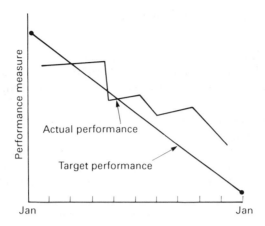

Fig. 4.12

Fig. 4.13

Recognition, celebration and reward

The final element of the Total Quality structure is the organisation to celebrate successes, to provide recognition and reward, and to encourage greater efforts in the future.

Total Quality is a very human concept. It is based on several human principles:

1. That recognition of achievement is very important to people.
2. That people like, and feel a need, to share their experiences.
3. That group achievements have the effect of group bonding and creating a sense of belonging.
4. That success breeds success—people are encouraged by achievement and feel a need to equal or surpass their best.
5. That people want to be listened to and to feel important.
6. That no-one wants to feel like an extension of their machine or desk. Everyone wants to have an opportunity for continuous self-development and self-respect.
7. That if you treat people like responsible human beings they are likely to behave like them.

These principles are absolutely fundamental to the achievement of Total Quality and are almost the opposite of Taylorism and 'scientific management'.

When the celebration and reward elements are included, the completed model appears as in Figure 4.14.

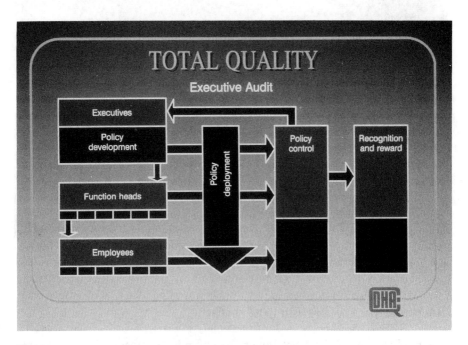

Fig. 4.14

CHAPTER 5

ORGANISING FOR IMPROVEMENT

Theoretically, there need be no organisational support for a totally participative programme once everyone is properly educated and trained in their roles, and the process is working on an organisation-wide basis.

In practice, whilst this may be an ideal goal to strive towards, it is unlikely that a successful programme exists anywhere in the world which does not have some form of supportive infrastructure.

Some quite significant differences appear between the structures which currently operate in Japan and those which seem to be effective in the West. However, this is hardly surprising since a difference of some twenty to thirty years' development separates the two, and it is conceivable that ultimately Western organisations may find that structures which exist in Japan today will be suitable for them in the future. Students of these differences will straight away find variances in terminology. In the West, the top supportive organisation is usually referred to as the 'Quality Council', or 'Company Quality Group', or some such title. In Japan, activities at this level are invariably referred to as 'TQC Promotion Committee', and 'TQC Secretariat' – TQC being 'Total Quality Control'. A typical structure would be similar to that shown in Figure 5.1.

It can be seen that in Japanese companies, there is a considerable supportive infrastructure just for QC Circle activities. With regard to Total Quality on a company-wide basis, most Japanese companies would produce organisation charts similar to the QC Circle chart in Figure 5.1 for:

- new design and product development;
- education programme for all levels from the top down;
- quality assurance;
- cost management organisation;
- standardisation;
- customer complaint procedures;
- management by policy – policy deployment;
- TQC activities.

This is much more highly structured than would typically be found in most Western organisations, but it is not as bureaucratic as it may seem and these structures have evolved through constant and detailed application of the continuous improvement process. Unlike many Western organisations which produce charts showing the way that things *should* happen, the Japanese

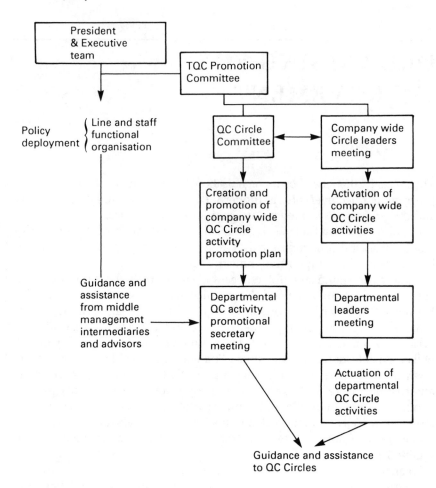

Fig. 5.1

charts describe the way things actually *do* happen. The reason for the difference lies in the fact that the charts are the result of improvement activities which have *involved* the line people themselves (the teamwork referred to in Chapter 4). They participated in the process of identification of symptoms, causes, and remedies. Apart from the fact that people are far more likely to support processes which they themselves helped to construct, there is also the fact that peer pressure from colleagues who also participated will ensure maintenance of the process.

Many British or Western companies may produce similar charts which form part of Quality Manuals, but a significant difference is that in these cases they are generally produced by 'off-line' functions such as 'quality assurance', and there is considerable evidence from opinion surveys that such systems lack credibility in the eyes of line personnel, mainly due to lack of consultation when the systems were created or because the system itself is fundamentally flawed in some way. The result is that many people attempt to short-cut the procedures to such an extent that two systems exist – the one which appears in the manual, and the real one which represents what actually occurs. This second informal system is rarely written down anywhere. In such cases, when the quality assurance department is used to enforce use of such systems, the quality function is seen as a police force process remote from line operations rather than an inherent part of every process as it should be.

There are many instances when even if people do attempt to follow the procedures, they prove to be too cumbersome and bureaucratic to be workable and are therefore not even supported by upper management who are really only interested in results, and are not too concerned with how they are achieved. All this adds up to a fairly depressing picture, but it does represent reality, and goes a long way to explaining why British and other Western companies are not competitive when they are faced with head-on Japanese competition.

The answer is to provide the mechanism for participation at all levels so that these companies too become more efficient, better organised, with everyone collaborating in the application of the right and most appropriate and effective systems and procedures.

Quality Council

The first step towards this goal should be to establish a Quality Council. This is the Western equivalent to the Japanese Total Quality Control Promotion Committee. It comprises mostly of the same people who are supposed to be running the company anyway, namely the executive team of directors.

Many people ask 'Why is it that we need this additional structure if "Total Quality" represents the way we should be running the business anyway?'.

The reason is that the ultimate state of 'Total Quality' requires the change to a very different culture from what is likely to exist in the company at the time the decision is made to embark on this approach. Therefore, we are talking about a fairly massive culture change. This raises many issues and these would flood the agenda of the normal routine business meetings. Of course the business must carry on its day-to-day activities, and it is therefore recommended that a separate meeting and a separate agenda be created for the purpose of Total Quality development. It is also important to maintain a high profile for executives' involvement in Total Quality development, and the use of terms such as 'Quality Council' or 'Company Quality Team', etc., will help to achieve this. The very fact that the members have given themselves this form of identity will help to demonstrate commitment, and to ensure that the key issues are addressed on a regular basis. There is no evidence of success among Western organisations which have not adopted this approach.

Another good reason for the formation of a Quality Council, as opposed to making Total Quality a permanent item on the agenda of other meetings, is the fact that from time to time a crisis issue will occur which overrides all other considerations, including Total Quality, and consequently, there will be a tendency for Total Quality to fall of the bottom of the agenda for that meeting. It is unlikely that this will produce any immediate adverse reaction from the Total Quality process, and it will therefore become easier in the future to sacrifice discussion of Total Quality items when even less important issues arise. A potential decay process would thus be built in to the programme right from the start. Since many executives are always looking for ways to cut down the time they spend on business development, this decay can prove both irresistible and possibly irreversible.

Role of Quality Councils

The Quality Council is created at the highest level, with the organisation Chairman as its Chairman. The mission of the Quality Council is to create the means by which the organisation can change from what it is today, to the organisation of the future, as identified in the organisation's vision or mission statement.

Formation of the Quality Council will usually be the first activity to take place following the decision to implement the process of Total Quality.

The Council's first task must be to agree its own mission, and to identify the roles of its members. Experience indicates that such Councils are considerably more effective when each member has a specific task to perform. These can include responsibility for publicity, monitoring, contact with other orgnisations, sponsorship of projects, etc.

Some attrition of Quality Council membership has frequently resulted from the lack of such direct personal responsibility. Typically, one of the directors is unable to attend a meeting; for example, the marketing director happens to be away on a trip somewhere. Of course, the meeting can go ahead without him without causing serious damage. Having missed one meeting without trauma it then becomes easier to miss subsequent meetings. Eventually he is out of touch with the issues and avoids attendance altogether.

Another director who may not be totally committed observes this and decides to follow suit. Eventually, the group is down to two or three enthusiasts. The process is now hardly the total commitment that it was once claimed to be. This decay is observed by others at lower levels who also drop out, and before long cracks may appear elsewhere.

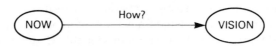

Fig. 5.2 The Quality Council is the means to execute the process

This is by no means an unusual scenario, and many an apparently good programme has failed in this way. It seems that the allocation of specific responsibilities, coupled with the rule that attendance is compulsory, is the best way of reducing the likelihood of this form of failure, and really underlines the personal commitment of the chief executive. Some would say, 'Surely a programme which has already started to produce results cannot fail in this way?'. It is incredible how many times this has happened: Even in cases where the results had been quite beyond the expectations of even the most enthusiastic senior manager, the entire process still slowly but surely sank back into the ground.

How can this happen? There must be many reasons, and much research into these reasons needs to be done. One theory which looks promising relates to the difference between Japanese and Western executives in terms of long-term loyalty to the company. Unfortunately, in the West there is a tendency to put a first loyalty on one's 'profession' and a secondary loyalty to one's company at that time. Career progression and the practice of headhunting take their toll on the loyalties of Western executives. This may be a problem the Japanese also have to face in the future but currently, the 'cradle-to-the-grave' lifetime employment system which emanates all the way to the top is a distinct advantage to Japanese companies.

Once the Council's own mission is agreed and tasks are assigned, the group then becomes concerned with getting the show on the road. It will now be necessary to agree on strategy and timetable.

At the commencement of Total Quality, different organisations will have different strengths and weaknesses, which must be evaluated. In many cases, it may be necessary to hire a consultant to assist in identifying these. Unfortunately, the number of consultants in the West who currently understand Total Quality are fewer than might be estimated from their claims.

Of the many consultants in the so-called 'Quality profession', the majority have their own specialist background which will usually only embrace a small segment of the Total Quality concept. For example, there are literally hundreds who understand BS 5750 – Systems for Quality Assurance – or ISO 9000 – its international version – chapter and verse. Many of these are very competent, know the subject well, and are capable of conducting first class audits to the requirements of these standards. There are others who are impressive when it comes to Statistical Process Control, or even Quality Circles, Metrology, Metrication, and so forth. Unfortunately, the majority of them all think that their specialist topic is the most important aspect.

Therefore advice on when to start, where to start, how to start, and what to do next, will vary considerably depending upon who is contracted. Even more unfortunate, in a lean and hungry world, is the fact that few of them would own up to their biases, if indeed they were aware of them. Most will use the language of Total Quality even if they do not know what the words mean. This criticism applies equally to university professors.

How then can a hapless Quality Council be sure that it is receiving the advice that it needs and wants? There are two alternatives and both should be considered carefully. First of all, there is simply no substitute for seeing for one's self how other organisations have tackled the problem. It is truly remarkable how few senior executives take the trouble to make a serious study of these concepts which are vital to their company's future. This fact never ceases to amaze the Japanese, who would have expected to be flooded with requests to visit their plants. They, on the other hand, although they know that there is little to learn from the West in the way of manufacturing techniques and management science, still visit in their droves to keep abreast of the times. Executives really should take time out, not just to go to Japan but to visit successful companies in their own country, the rest of Europe, and the United States as well. That is the best way to evaluate the state of knowledge of the consultant. Poor consultants get away with murder because they can confidently prey on the likely ignorance of their clients. This simply should not be possible.

The second alternative, which does not exclude the first one, but should rather take place along side it is to check up on the success record of the consultant. Although everyone has to start somewhere, why let a novice consultant learn his craft at your company's expense? The results of Total Quality are too important to fool around with, and to listen to false prophets. Ask to see their credentials and do not simply check up on one client, check several. Do the same for others and make comparisons. The track record of the consultant is what really counts. Whilst bargains are to be had, it is more than likely that fees are in almost direct proportion to value. Many companies have made false economies on this subject. Of course the reverse is also possible, and also highly likely. Again, it reinforces the advice offered above. Ignorance in this field may be one of the most expensive mistakes it is possible to make.

A good consultant will be able to ascertain the status in the organisation of the four basic elements of Total Quality, namely:

- quality systems
- quality processes
- management team work and participation
- employee involvement

In many cases, an organisation is capable of analysing its status with regard to each of these, and it is not necessary to conduct any form of pre-implementation audit.

In the past, many organisations have been dangerously weak in systems and procedures, and when this is identified, and where those weaknesses court potential disasters for the business, it may be necessary to correct this before any further work is done in implementation of participative programmes. For example, with the hazards currently facing the food industry from food poisoning or sabotage, the now severe consequences which can ensue from product liability claims, and the high costs of product recalls, it is obvious that sound basic practices must be introduced before anything else is contemplated. However, whilst this may be necessary, the majority of organisations can usually start the participative programme immediately even if this takes place alongside further work on systems and procedures. Generally speaking, there are merits in waiting until all of these aspects are well established before any further developments are contemplated.

For the purpose of this book, however let us suppose that it has been determined that the participative process should be developed as the next step. In the majority of organisations, this will be a perfectly acceptable approach.

Following the formation of the Quality Council, it will be necessary to organise awareness presentations to the next layer down in the organisation prior to involvement.

For small organisations, the Quality Council may be the only form of infrastructure necessary. As the organisation increases in size, a point is reached where it becomes advantageous to form sub Quality Councils or 'Functional Quality Councils or Teams', whose purpose is to ensure that a sense of ownership is felt right down through the organisation, and that 'Total Quality' is not something that people are simply subjected to, but have an opportunity to participate in. Additionally, it is unlikely that the top team or Quality Council will have such an intimate knowledge of the day-to-day groups on a departmental level that it could effectively identify with any degree of certainty the most important 'local' problems in those areas.

The role of the Quality Council therefore is to develop the overall process of Total Quality. The role of Functional Quality Teams will be to develop the process very parochially in each of the respective functions and departments.

Much of the activity in the Total Quality process is concerned with problem solving and achieving improvements. The Quality Council will be concerned with the identification of major problems, usually of a cross-functional nature. It will also be concerned with the identification of problems which only it (the Quality Council) can solve.

The lower level Functional Quality Teams will be concerned with the identification of problems in those areas which do not impact or require the involvement of other functions. This type of organisation works very well, is not bureaucratic, and is extremely action-oriented.

Having established this basic infrastructure, the next logical step will be to resource the process. There are three key elements to this:

- awareness
- education
- training

These three elements are essentially a top-down, layer-by-layer process. A leading Japanese instructor says, 'In Japan, it is our opinion that the stairs should be swept starting from the top'.

In the early stage, Total Quality programmes are mainly focused on project-by-project problem-solving involving executives and senior personnel. The problems tackled are mostly multi-functional, requiring teams of 5–8 members. The initial education and training should be given to those persons who are predicted to be the most likely candidates for team leadership. Using the

Pareto principle (referred to in Chapter 3), it will be seen that the majority of high-level projects are likely to produce the biggest gains; it would make sense to identify leaders for those projects first, and these are likely to be executives and senior managers.

Team leader training is vitally important, and will be the key to successful projects. Two of the prime reasons why organisations are inundated with continually recurring problems are:

1. they lack the machinery to solve such problems;
2. whilst many people may be trained in scientific investigation, few are trained in a disciplined approach to solving organisational problems.

The techniques for problem-solving are explained in later chapters. Training in these techniques can be effectively carried out on a four-day residential basis for 15–20 people per course.

Prior to the selection of such personnel, it is necessary to conduct awareness sessions for everyone at team leader level and also at the level of team member. The method of awareness training can vary widely from company to company, and it doesn't seem to matter a great deal whether these sessions, which can last anything from two hours to a whole day, are small low-key affairs, or high-powered demonstrations of commitment: whatever suits the culture of the business is the answer.

In parallel with team leader training and awareness, the Quality Council will need to think about initial project selection, general publicity, the rate at which the concept is to be cascaded down through the organisation, and how this will be resourced.

Project selection

Selection of the initial projects is fairly critical and must be completed before the team leaders have been trained. This will enable them to form their teams and begin to work immediately after they have the appropriate skills. There will always be a temptation to select the projects which will potentially produce the biggest gains. This is to be avoided in the early stages. Instead, for the first projects, it is better to select problems that fit the following criteria:

- easy to solve
- reasonable financial return to make it worthwhile
- likely to ensure use of the problem-solving skills
- duration of project, with teams meeting weekly for about 2–3 hours, approximately three months

If all of these criteria can be met, then the first teams will:

- gain confidence in the process and their own ability
- convince others that it works
- demonstrate commitment and enthusiasm to subordinates

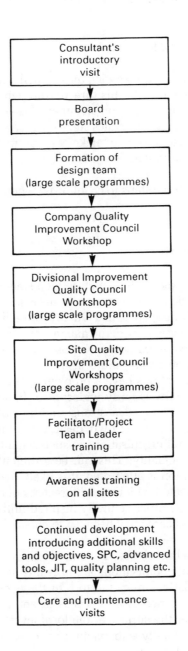

Fig. 5.3

When the team members have tackled one or two projects on this basis they will progress to more substantial projects later. Rome was not built in a day!

Monitoring the process

Once the initial projects are under way, the Council will need to begin monitoring the process. They can do this directly through personal contact, but they can also appoint a senior person on either a full- or part-time basis to do this on their behalf. In most companies such a person is usually referred to as a 'facilitator'. To facilitate means to 'make easy' or 'make possible'. The role and selection of facilitators will be explained in Chapter 11.

Figure 5.3 outlines the basic steps to be followed when implementing a Total Quality programme.

The multi-site organisation

So far we have only looked at the structure for a single location business. In very large single location businesses, it is necessary to develop the sub-structure of functional or departmental Quality Councils or teams as has been explained above, in order to ensure the maximum sense of ownership and to allow the process to be as parochial as possible. This principle is carried through to multi-location organisations also.

Many Western organisations have a problem in this respect. The concept of allowing local autonomy is fairly widespread. In such cases, the central board has frequently developed a strong tradition of allowing local sub-organisations to determine their own destiny within fairly broad limits. Consequently, the central organisations of such satellite operations are very loath to 'impose' Total Quality. This can be a difficult problem to resolve because if such imposition is attempted, it is likely that massive resentment and hostility will be created which could threaten not only the Total Quality programme, but also any other centrally inspired initiatives. Where this reaction is predicted, great care must be taken to obtain the support of the local management.

Even in cases where businesses are centrally organised, the same may be true. It is rare that local organisations are in reality so subservient that they blindly accept all initiatives from the top. In the eyes of the local people, central organisation will generally appear remote, and many counter-strategies are likely to exist under the surface at the local level.

If the object of Total Quality is to maximise and focus all of the energies in the organisation, then clearly these issues must be confronted. The message is fairly clear. Local people must be, and must be seen to be, involved in the process of development at all stages, from awareness onwards. From the point of view of the central organisation, the aim should be to provide a basic um-

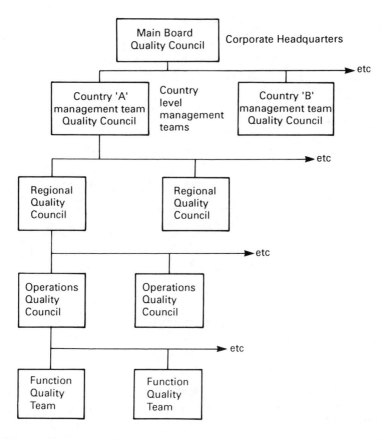

Fig. 5.4

brella of support, and to establish local guidelines whilst at the same time allowing the maximum opportunity for creativity and self-development in the various operations.

The structure shown in Figure 5.4 indicates the most effective means by which this is carried out in multi-site organisations, and this structure applies both to relatively small multi-site operations with only regional operations, and to large, multi-national companies. In the figure, the full model is shown. For smaller organisations, the non-appropriate layers may be ignored.

This model allows for overall development to take place at the appropriate level whilst ensuring that decisions relevant to specific definable groups can be made at the level where the issues are best understood. There are now several organisations operating this structure successfully in the United States and in Europe.

'Bottom-up' implementation in multi-site organisations

Generally speaking, whilst it is theoretically possible for Total Quality pro-

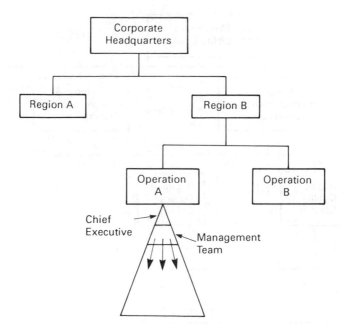

Fig. 5.5

grammes to be started in individual local operations, as shown in Operation A, Figure 5.5, and then to gravitate upwards through the organisation, the track-record of such initiatives is not good, for various reasons.

Typically, the programme is started as a result of enthusiasm on the part of the operational chief executive. The concept is sold to his management team and a vigorous programme is developed. Many such programmes look very impressive in the short term. In theory, success at this level could be transmitted upwards and horizontally through the organisation. In practice there is little evidence of this. Horizontal development in other operations is frequently prevented by rivalry. If success of such a programme does prove irresistible to other operation, then rather than attempt to copy they will seek alternative initiatives with the object of either upstaging their internal rival, or simply to appear different. The net result is that far from a co-ordinated, organisation-wide process which harnesses the powers and energies of all the elements, a patchwork quilt emerges which only serves to continue the age-old rivalries and conflicts of the past.

In other cases, failure results from the continued reorganisations which take place in many Western organisations. Typically, the chief executive will hold his position for some three years, after which he will move elsewhere and be replaced from some other part of the organisation. With no central support and co-ordination of the Total Quality process, it is likely that the selection criteria for his replacement will fail to include any assessment of his attitude towards or ability to support the process of Total Quality. The new executive will wish to make his own mark on the organisation, and will be reluctant to continue initiatives which only serve to project the abilities of his predecessor. He is unlikely to withdraw support immediately, since this would probably reflect on him. Therefore, he will simply allow the process to die by gradually removing the success criteria. This is by far the most common cause of a programme's failure in large organisations.

There can be no doubt that the only way for the full potential of Total Quality to be realised is for a top-down initiative involving the corporate directors of the business. When executives are replaced at any level the new encumbent must be selected on his ability to support Total Quality, and be left in no doubt that one of the key performance measures of his success will be the support he gives to the Total Quality process.

Project teams

Improvement activities ultimately involve all employess at all levels. These activities fall broadly into seven categories:

- mandatory cross-functional teams
- mandatory within-function teams
- normal daily staff activities based on goals and targets
- voluntary cross-functional teams
- voluntary within-function teams (ad hoc)
- individual voluntary suggestion activities
- voluntary within-function teams (continous) – usually referred to as Quality Circles or in Japan Quality Control Circles.

Mandatory cross-functional teams

These can be formed at any time and at every level in the organisation. Experience indicates that the formation of such teams, initially at the highest level in the organisation, is the most desirable strategy with which to commence the Total Quality process. The reasons for this are as follows:

1. they demonstrate genuine commitment down through the organisation;
2. on the Pareto principle, most of the big money-saving or saleability projects will be at this level;
3. these projects will usually result in organisational changes which will have a permanent beneficial effect on the organisation.

Mandatory within-function teams

The development of these groups will usually follow the establishment of functional quality teams which have identified 'within-function' problems.

Sometimes, the analysis carried out to discover the causes of such problems leads into other functional areas. In such cases co-operation will be required between the respective functions, either by forming a joint team, or by the second function providing an individual to work with the first. This latter course is likely when the team simply requires some specialist input from the other functions.

Sometimes it may be necessary for the functional quality team to propose upwards to the next level of Quality Council that such collaboration is necessary. This is particularly likely when the related functions are on different locations.

Normal daily staff activities

The effectiveness of improvements during normal operations is dependent upon the effectiveness of the policy deployment process. The clearer the understanding of departmental and individual goals and targets, the more efficient will be the staff activities. This is applicable at all levels. Frequently, staff will identify opportunities for improvement which are outside their authority or experience. In this case, the means should be created whereby such individuals can formally propose their suggestions to the appropriate level of Quality Council or to their supervisor/manager/senior.

In Japan, realisation of the importance of identifying very clear and specific objectives for all levels motivates the directors of the organisation to spend as much as six full months in each year doing nothing other than the quality deployment process, and creating that year's policy goals and targets.

Again the maxim: in the dynamic organisation, 'Managers do not make decisions, they make sure that good decisions are being made'.

Voluntary cross-functional teams and voluntary within-function teams (ad hoc)

These may take place on an 'ad hoc' basis when the Total Quality process is becoming well established. Sometimes they happen as a result of problems thrown up by mandatory improvement activities. These are a very positive sign both that there is widespread acceptance of the improvement process and also that cross-functional relationships are being developed. This development should be actively encouraged and used as success criteria when evaluating the health and viability of the Total Quality process.

Individual voluntary suggestion activities

The widespread failure of Western suggestion schemes should not discourage a return to this concept, but only after the other improvement activities have become well established. Prior to that time, the chances are that regardless of the presence or absence of financial incentives the response will be similar to past experiences.

Voluntary within-function teams (Quality Circles)

In the early stages of implementation of Total Quality, it may be premature to introduce the concept of Quality Circles. Many of the failures or unconvincing successes in Western companies have been due to introducing Quality Circles before the right supportive environment has been created. Ultimately, the real power of Total Quality will be achieved only when the entire payroll is involved. The early chapters of this book are focused specifically on this concept, and it is recommended that the advice given is considered very carefully before Quality Circles are introduced or re-introduced. This is one case where it may be better not to have tried than to have tried and failed. The value of this total power in an organistion is so great, that it is a tragedy when companies are forced either to wait several years before launching a second attempt, or alternatively change the name and many features just to make it look different from last time.

CHAPTER 6

THE EVOLUTION OF TOTAL QUALITY

We have seen that, although the term Total Quality Control originated in the West, the concept known today as Total Quality has its roots firmly in Japan and not in the USA. It is true that the United States introduced the concept of Quality Control into Japan, and this book explains how Quality Control is an integral part of Total Quality, which also embraces Quality Circles. But the Americans also introduced Taylorism to Japan, and as we have seen, it was the failure of this concept in Japan that led eventually to Quality Circles and ultimately to Total Quality.

The first recorded post-War application of Western-style statistical Quality Control in Japan appeared in the telecommunication industries as part of the plan to restore the entire Japanese telephone and telegraph communication system. Although there is evidence that statistical techniques were being used even before the Second World War. During 1946, the Japanese Union of Scientists and Engineers (JUSE) was formed, and began to further the application of Quality Control throughout Japanese industry. This early work was based on American Standards Organisation publications Z1–1, Z1–2, and Z1–3, W.A. Shewhart's *The Control of Quality of Manufactured Product* (Van Nostrand, 1931), E.S. Pearson's pre-War articles, and publications which were the only materials available at that time.

The first major Quality Control training programme for the restoration of Japanese industry on a nation-wide scale was introduced in 1949 by the Chairman of JUSE, Ichiro Ishikawa (the father of Professor Kaoru Ishikawa). At the same time, the Japanese Management Association and the Japanese Standards Organisation independently commenced Quality Control training programmes.

Dr Edwards Deming

In 1950, the Japanese Government, in collaboration with GHQ, American Occupation Forces, invited the American statistical expert W. Edwards Deming to lecture on statistical method in Japan. This was followed by an invitation from JUSE to give a further eight days of Quality Control seminars.

Dr Deming did not, as many Westerners think, introduce the Japanese to statistical quality control. These concepts and their importance were well known to the Japanese long before he ever went there. However, the Japanese were struggling with the problem of conveying the mathematical concepts to their people (a problem which still exists today in the West). Dr Deming's contribution was to help them cut through the academic theory, to present the ideas in simple ways which could be meaningful right down to production worker levels. Unfortunately for the West, the Japanese listened to him and the West did not.

Furthermore, Dr Deming did not introduce the Japanese to the 14 points for which he is currently so well known. There is no Japanese material which indicates any connection with these ideas, and particularly not the idea of avoiding goals and targets. In fact it could be said that much of the material on which the 14 points are based was derived from observations of Japanese post-War Quality development, rather than the other way round. Policy deployment is totally dependent upon goals and targets.

Dr Deming's teachings about the power of statistical approaches, decision-making based upon facts, and the need for simplification, had a profound impact on the Japanese love to give recognition, and so they created the Deming Award to encourage companies, divisions within companies, small

Fig. 6.1 The Deming Award Medal

companies, and individuals, to learn and use the techniques he advocated for the improvement of their enterprises.

This prize has the same status as the Queen's Award to Industry has in Britain, but it differs in the sense that it is awarded for Quality achievements, whereas the Queen's Award is based upon export performance and technical achievement.

When the Deming Award was instituted it was estimated that to rely upon the existing education process as the means by which the Deming ideas could be introduced could take as long as 35 years. Clearly, industry could not wait that long. Consequently by 1955, the Japanese had begun a massive series of 'self-improvement' programmes on radio and throughout the media. By this time, they had extracted all they usefully could from the statistical techniques, and they needed to take Quality up to the level of upper management.

Dr Joseph Juran

In 1954, Joseph M. Juran was invited to lecture in Japan where he led seminars for both top executives and middle managers. During these seminars he emphasised the concept of 'Management of Quality', which formed the basis of the present Japanese concept Total Quality (TQ).

Dr Juran suggested that the application of the statistical method, whilst vitally important, was nevertheless only one aspect of the real issue and that the ultimate responsibility for quality achievement could only come from the top of the organisation.

He had already developed what he refers to as the 'breakthrough' process, by which all improvements are made. Put simply, he suggested to the Japanese that:

- All real improvements are made on a project-by-project basis.
- The most important projects are most likely to be management-controllable.
- Management usually spends much of its time dealing with the sporadic fire-fighting issues, but it is the chronic underlying problems which must be tackled if an organisation is to remain competitive. These include such issues as 'yield', 'credit period', 'down time', 'utilisation'; etc.

He also suggested a universal sequence of events by which all problems can be solved. First of all it is necessary to define the undesirable 'symptoms'; then the cause must be discovered; and ultimately a 'remedy' is sought. Thus there is the journey from symptom to cause and then a remedial journey from cause to remedy. This seemingly basic idea is in fact quite profound, and the means of making the two journeys involves use of the problem-solving techniques which will be described later in this book.

It does Dr Juran a grave injustice to describe the contribution he made to the Japanese business world in the space of a few lines in this book. Those familiar with his work will be aware that he is both a prolific author and an even more prolific originator of quality-related concepts. Even in his late eighties, Dr Juran is proving to be a formidable asset to the development of world thinking on quality, and it is highly recommended that anyone concerned with the implementation of Total Quality make a serious study of the contribution made by this great man.

The supervisor

Although many of the original theories which led to the development of Total Quality were developed in the United States, few Western organisations have as yet managed to apply it successfully. This is because Total Quality is a people-based philosophy which cannot operate in Taylor-based organisations. Fortunately for the Japanese, however, they had already begun to remove the road-blocks of Taylorism, and the development of the supervisor was an important step forward.

Although significant improvements in performance had been achieved in Japan in 1960, management was still faced with serious industrial relations problems. The Japanese believed the problems were due mainly to having adopted the 'Taylor' system of management from the USA. They concluded that this system was alien to their culture, but initially were concerned mainly with its effect on supervision. They realised the importance of the role of the supervisor and began to concentrate the bulk of the new training effort on foremen and supervisory grades.

In Japan unlike elsewhere in the world this training was not conducted in colleges but organised and executed on companies' premises. The training was intended to build up the confidence of group leaders and to teach the basic quality improvement and control techniques. It was realised that an opportunity to make presentations of achievements in problem solving was a valuable form of recognition for those achievements and at the same time, a good way of transferring ideas to others. Consequently, the trained foremen were given the opportunity of making presentations of their achievements at public seminars, to which other foremen were invited. At that time, no other country had developed such an approach to training. By 1960, not only had this concept spread throughout Japan, but there were already large conventions devoted especially to foremen.

Quality Month

Awareness of the importance of Quality Control to the economic success of Japan had reached such proportions by 1960 that the concept of 'Quality Month' was introduced, and November 1960 was designated as the first of these. Nowadays any visitor to Japan in November will become aware of the large number of Quality conventions and Quality-related functions that take place both nationally and within companies. During the first Quality Month,

Fig. 6.2 The Q Symbol

the Q-mark and Q-flags were both formally adopted as the symbol of Quality-related activities (see Figure 6.2).

Professor Kaoru Ishikawa

Together with Drs Deming and Juran, Professor Ishikawa will go down in history for having made an equal and significant contribution to the development of Total Quality. He suggested that the industrial relations problems prevalent in Japan at the beginning of the 1960s could only be resolved by increasing the job satisfaction of employees. It was then that he proposed the idea of reintroducing the craftsmanship concept, as discussed in Chapter 4.

Regrettably Professor Ishikawa died in April 1989 after a short illness, and whilst he has made many constristions to the development of the concept he will be best remembered for having been responsible for the creation of the Quality Circle concept.

Quality Circles

In April 1962 the magazine *Gemba to QC* recommended the formation of Quality Circles (known as Quality Control Circles in Japan). At the same time, the editorial committee began organising and propagating the idea, and the concept of Quality Circles proper was born.

Definition of Quality Circles

A Quality Circle is defined as a 'small group of work people who, under the leadership of their own foreman or supervisor, are trained to identify, analyse, and solve quality-related problems on a voluntary basis and present their solutions to their managers'. Whilst Quality Circles theoretically are groups of workers who do similar work, they can be made up from any group who share the same work area and interrelate with each other, provided that they can identify common problems.

In May 1962, the first Quality Circle was registered with the QC head-quarters of JUSE. This Circle was formed at the Nippon Telephone and Tele-graph Corporation. By the end of the year over 35 companies were reported to have commenced QC activities.

Besides recognising the importance of training supervisors, the Japanese quickly realised that presentations to management were an essential part of Quality Control Circle activities, and this idea was incorporated into the concept. They also realised the value of making presentations to a wider audience, and Circles were given the opportunity of making their presentations at public functions. The effect of this was not only to boost the confidence and self-assurance of the Circles still further, but it also became a significant means of introducing them into other organisations.

Once established, the growth of the concept was phenomenal. In November 1962 the first annual Quality Control Conference for foremen was held and because of the rapid growth of Quality Control Circles, extended sessions were introduced at subsequent conferences to discuss this topic. In May 1963 the first Quality Control Circle Conference was held in Senai, Northern Japan.

In 1964 the first regional chapters were established in Kanto, Tokai, Houriku and Juki districts. Later, the entire country was divided into 14 chapters under nationwide organisation, and each chapter was to hold its own conventions and other activities for members.

The rate of growth continued to increase and by June 1967 there were 10,000 Circles registered with JUSE and many more in existence but not officially recorded. By 1969 the total number of Circles registered had risen to an incredible 20,000. In that year the 100th QC Circle Conference was held in Tokyo, and one year later the figure reached 30,000 registrations. By this time the Circle concept had become truly nationwide and formed an integral part of Total Quality. By 1978 there were an estimated 1 million Circles, involving 10 million Japanese workers.

Responsibility for the spread of the awareness of the the existence of Quality Circles to non-Chinese character countries is largely attributable to Dr Juran. It was he who recommended that the European Organisation for Quality Control (EOQC) should hold a special session on the subject at its conference in Stockholm, Sweden, in June 1966. After the conference, Juran wrote several articles referring to it, and it was included in his now famous seminars and textbooks.

Juran declared in the late 1960s: 'The Quality Circle movement is a tremendous one which no other country seems able to imitate. Through the development of this movement, Japan will be swept to world leadership in quality.'

Development in Brazil and the United States

Whilst many companies in many countries had attempted to imitate Quality

Circles in the 1960s and early 1970s, none had proved entirely successful. This led to several adaptations of the concept. All these variants failed because they were really only cosmetic adaptations or additions to the entrenched Taylor system of management, and to date, there is no foreseeable competitor.

The first real breakthrough in Quality Circles came almost simultaneously in Brazil and the United States. Oleg Greshner of Johnson & Johnson in Brazil managed to develop a successful programme based entirely on the Japanese approach, with company-wide Quality Control as its basis. This programme is well described in the book *The Japanese Approach to Product Quality*, edited jointly by Naoto Sasaki and David Hutchins. After Greshner's success, Quality Circles began to spread throughout Brazilian industry and by 1979 it was claimed that 30,000 Quality Circles were active in that country.

In the United States the first recorded success occurred at the Lockheed space missile factory in California. Interest at Lockheed was initiated by a visit to the factory by a Japanese team of Circle leaders in 1972. This was followed by a visit to Japan by a team from Lockheed in order to discover more about the concept. From this experience, Lockheed adapted Japanese materials to create the first training materials of their kind written in English. These were largely developed by Jefferson F. Beardsley, the Quality Circle Training Co-ordinator, with assistance from his colleague Donald L. Dewar, Quality Circle Co-ordinator under the authority of Wayne S. Rieker, the Manufacturing Manager.

The first Circles in Lockheed were formed in October 1974 and proved to be incredibly successful, not only in their projects, but in their effect on morale. In less than three years Lockheed claimed that these first Circles had produced a net saving of over $3 million, and a benefit to cost ratio of an estimated 8:1.

Following this initial programme Beardsley, Dewar, and Rieker left the company to establish consultancies. Those three practitioners then, independently of each other, began to develop the Circles movement in the United States. The first companies to follow Lockheed include Northrop, Rockwell International, Honeywell, Hughes Aircraft, and Westinghouse Corporation. Towards the end of the decade the success of these companies and the three consultants had reached international proportions.

An international society, the International Association of Quality Circles, had been formed and the number of companies that had commenced Quality Circle programmes was increasing exponentially. By the summer of 1982 it was claimed that there were over 5,000 organisations with Quality Circles in the USA, including national banks, and airline, the US Airforce, naval dockyards, hospitals, and a wide range of manufacturing organisations.

However, the widespread interest in the concept in the USA and the ensuing publicity attracted other consultants into the field. This unfortunately has led to an alarming dilution of the philosophy, and fears are now being expressed by some of the pioneers that the entire field is being undermined by this development.

In an article on Quality Circles which appeared in the August 1982 edition of *International Management*, Kaoru Ishikawa expressed doubts about the long-term survival of Quality Circles in the West because of the lack of understanding of the importance of Total Quality. This view cannot be expressed too strongly. The Quality Circle conventions, inter-company visits, training seminars, the national activities including 'Quality Month', and the general awareness of the importance of Quality Control, are all essential foundations for ultimate success and so far these ideas have yet to take root in Western countries.

Variability – a source of cost

Another purely Japanese discovery was the fact that variability is a major cause of high cost. Of course, this appears obvious, but until that time, and even today in Western organisations, variability was regarded as acceptable provided that it was contained within specified limits.

For example, it is well known that no two things in the universe are exactly alike, and therefore, in the case of products or services, the acceptable degree of variability is contained in a specification.

For dimensions on manufactured products, a target dimension is given for each parameter of the product, e.g. hole sizes, distance between dimensions, shaft sizes, etc.

The popular Western belief is that, provided the manufacturer or process operator keeps the dimension between difined limits, then the component is OK and quality-related costs are zero.

This concept was successfully challenged in Japan in the mid 1960s by an engineer, Dr Jonji Taguchi. He discovered that quality costs follow a quadratic function which increases as variability increases from the target dimension, irrespective of the process parameters. The rate of increase will be determined by the consequential costs of such variation.

This discovery led to an increased awareness of the value of statistical control techniques, such as the 'Shewhart chart' as a means of identifying the causes of inherent process variability, and their elimination. Data provided by the use of these techniques is hopelessly beyond the resources of technical staff, managers and engineers, but in Japan, with the development of Quality Circles, the means had been provided. Quality Circles, trained to use control charts as diagnostic tools, began an intensive study of process capabilities on an unprecedented scale. In the course of one single decade, the effect of this dramatic expansion of quality-related skills had enabled Japan to virtually eliminate inventory (the 'Just in Time' concept) and to achieve levels of quality which were beyond belief to their Western competitors. More recently, the Japanese have extended the focus of these activities to include what is referred to as Total Productive Maintenance (TPM), which is resulting in process es being available for operation for over 94 per cent of the time.

To the Japanese, this total involvement at all levels is their perception of Total Quality Control, referred to in this book as Total Quality, and it is only the achievement of a similar intensity of skill and drive which will enable Western competitors to survive.

CHAPTER 7

IMPROVEMENT TEAM REWARDS – DIVIDING THE SPOILS

Improvement team rewards

Surprisingly, this topic is rarely ever a major issue, at least in the case of those who are to become involved in the improvement process. None of the companies which have successfully introduced Total Quality has any record of direct financial reward to management improvement teams, staff improvement teams, or Quality Circles. Having said that, there is however considerable evidence of other forms of reward, or recognition of achievements.

As a general rule, an organisation should state as policy right from the outset that it does not intend to pay one penny (or anything else) as a direct ratio of the financial value of an improvement suggestion. However, there appears to be nothing wrong with making some *nominal* payment for successful projects, provided that it is not directly related to *savings* made resulting from projects. Such nominal payments may be awarded simply as recognition of acceptance. They should preferably be used for internal social improvements rather than cash handouts to individuals.

In Japan, most companies make some sort of payment on this basis. Generally, the payments are quite nominal. No one would get rich from them, and they are usually regarded as beer money to celebrate success, or to brighten up the work area.

The principle behind the idea of non-payment is quite clear. One of the key aims of Total Quality is to create an organisation in which everyone becomes involved in working to make 'their' company a better place to be, to share equally in its success, to feel part of the total community, to develop a sense of pride and loyalty, and to feel that their company is better for them being there. This cannot be achieved by making one person or group the envy of others. Everyone should have an equal opportunity both to make improvements and to share in the overall successes.

Financial rewards determined as ratios of saving made fail on three counts:

1. Not everyone will simultaneously be able to participate in improvement activities.
2. The sheer value and volume of materials in one area will be more than the total budgets for some other areas.
3. Not all improvement projects can be expressed in financial terms. For example, projects to improve saleability or service may produce in-

creased turnover in the future but at the time of presenting the project, this will be speculative.

Few if any companies in the West have considered the payment of rewards to *mandatory* project teams. This is because most managers, and many staff people and specialists, accept that making improvements is part of their job, and that project work just happens to be a more effective way of doing that.

Nevertheless, any company which ignores the importance of some form of recognition does so at its peril. It is a natural human reaction to want and to expect recognition. It does not have to be directly financial, but there is no question that people all have a need to justify their existence, and to be seen to be contributing to the success of their community. Therefore, the means by which anyone at any level can be given recognition for their achievements must be carefully considered. In most cases, a feature in a company newsletter will be more than adequate, but many creative alternatives exist. These include:

- opportunities to present at conferences
- industrial visits overseas
- award ceremonies
- opportunities to present to the main Board etc.

However, before turning to these specific activities it should be noted that, as a general principle, whilst no one should be paid directly for quality improvement, there should be a direct link between overall rewards and the financial performance of the company.

Award/reward in Japan

In Japan, awards are frequently effected by giving all employees annual bonuses, usually in two six-monthly increments. These are a form of profit-sharing, and are measured in the form of days', weeks', or months' pay. In the more successful companies such as Toyota, Nissan, Matsushita, etc., these bonuses amount to as much as six months' full pay bonus per year. A typical worker will obtain a total of around £23,000 per year take-home pay at the time of writing this edition: hardly the 'bowl of rice' which is still the impression of many people in the West!

Commitment through lifetime employment

Whilst on the topic of pay and reward in Japan, there are also many Western misconceptions regarding the concept of lifetime employment. It is widely believed that this is endemic in Japanese culture, is responsible for much of the structural differences, and is significantly different from the West. This is wrong on two counts:

1. Whilst lifetime employment is natural in Japan, it is not taken for granted. The main benefit to Japanes companies is that it provides them with stable, long-term, committed managers and stable, long-term, committed policies. In the past, the West has also been able to enjoy these advantages. The incentives for employees, to stay with a company consisted of:

   - pay based on years of service and contribution to the company's success
   - merit awards
   - attractive pension schemes and other forms of welfare

2. Lifetime employment is far more prevalent in the West than many think. For example, banking, legal, commercial, and the medical professions all have a high degree of permanent long-term employment. Also, there are many manufacturing and primary industries where the level of lifetime employment is very close to the Japanese situation.

If a Japanese employee at any level chooses to leave his company for a competitor he is likely to take a substantial drop in pay. The reason for this is that the new employer will fear the effects of resentment by the existing staff if the newcomer is rewarded for the achievements they made in the past, and to which he did not contribute. For this reason, anyone who changes jobs is regarded with great suspicion. Whilst there is evidence that this structure is breaking down a little, nevertheless the Japanese are very aware of the advantages that this method affords them over their Western competitors, and it is unlikely that they will allow the concept to decay to Western levels.

Rewards for Quality Circle activities

Current experience in the UK, the USA, and Western Europe suggests that in the early stages a Quality Circle programme should produce a yield somewhere in the order of 1 to 3 or 4 cost to benefit ratio. On the cost side, this would include all of the costs relating to start up, consultancy, facilitator salary, and other items identified in Chapter 5. This cost : benefit ratio should improve through the second and third years due to the amortisation of start-up costs, together with the continued benefits accruing from some of the early Circle projects.

It must be stressed that these benefits are only suggested as a reference point. In practice, it is impossible to even guess at the true benefits. In one company, a Quality Circle saved nearly half a million pounds by its first project, which was quite simple and took very little time. This achievement would have paid for the entire programme many times over. However, in another company, it may be several months before any great tangible benefit is realised, although it is unlikely that a negative situation will exist for very long. If it does, it is more likely either that the consultancy fees are excessive or that there is some other fundamental flaw in the development.

Many may feel that such attention to cost : benefit ratios is alien to the philosophy of Quality Circles as part of Total Quality, and that a management whose heart is in the right place should want to introduce them regardless of these considerations. At individual Circle level this is true, but taken over all, we must refer back to the original motive for commencing Circles in the first place, and in particular to policy deployment.

Quality Circle represent an opportunity to develop a more successful organisation by improved utilisation of the resources of its people, and this is of benefit both to the individuals and to the organisation as a whole.

Measures of success of course depend to a large extent upon the objectives of the organisation, but cost is always an important consideration. There would be no value in developing the most friendly, happy organisation in the world, if it became insolvent in the process.

Therefore, it is unavoidable that the Quality Circle programme, just like any other consideration, must be regarded as an investment, and investments need to show a return. Fortunately, with the Quality Circles element of Total Quality, the returns are usually so impressive that the cost of a programme is rarely, if ever, a problem.

In addition to the tangible cost benefits, there will be further gains which in many cases will far outweigh the value of the cost-cutting projects. For example, there may be:

- lower labour turnover
- fewer grievances
- higher morale
- general improvements to productivity
- general improvements to quality

and many problems which will simply have 'disappeared' because people are taking more care. In fact, these are the true benefits to management of Quality Circles, and the cost : benefit gains from individual projects should be regarded as a bonus.

Rewards for Quality Circles and other voluntary improvement activities

As already discussed, one of the suggested inviolable rules of Quality Circles is that members should never, under any circumstances, be paid directly in cash as a ratio of any Circle achievement. In fact, one would go so far as to say that the moment a decision was made to violate this rule, the true spirit of Quality Circles as such would cease to exist in that organisation. Eventually, the entire programme would be threatened.

There are many reasons for this, but the principal one is that direct reward is alien to the entire philosophy of Total Quality, including the Quality Circles aspect. The object of Circles, as has been emphasised all along, is to create an organisation where all are made to feel that their organisation is better for their being there, and that their contribution is recognised. The aim is to develop a sense of corporate loyalty by treating one group of people no differently from another, with no one being paid directly for solving problems.

If an organisation did attempt to make direct payments to Circle members, it could run up against the following problems:

1. A policy would be required to determine who should be eligible for payment. This could create enormous difficulties. If payment were made only to Circle members, they would immediately be alienated from others, such as non-Circle members and specialists who might have helped in their work, and such help would be unlikely to be forthcoming in the future.
2. As with project teams, a Circle in one area might be able to save more in one project, just by the sheer value and volume of work flowing through the section, than the entire budget for some other department.
3. Remembering that the primary aim of Quality Circles is to create a better work environment, and that many of their projects will not normally produce tangible results, assessment could be difficult. Also, it will tend to make Circles concentrate on problems that look as if they will produce a good return, and so the concept of Quality Circles will be reduced to a money-swapping trade-off process. The idea of 'self-control', described later, would be lost, and Taylorism would flourish.
4. The levels of direct incentive would have to be negotiated, with the consequence that the Quality Circles concept would be forced into the industrial relations arena and would almost certainly become a negotiating counter for some other non-related objective. Again, the co-operative spirit of the concept would be lost.

As with the project teams and all other forms of improvement activity, rewards for Circles can be given in several ways:

- recognition;
- attendance at conventions, seminars, and workshops;
- exchange visits to other organisations operating Circles;
- allowing Circles to decide how some of the savings may be spent

Let us now consider each in turn.

Recognition

Many people grossly underestimate the importance of recognition of achievement as a form of reward. In fact, people get very considerable satisfaction from being listened to, and the Circle presentation to management is the highlight in the whole process for most Circle members.

Many companies operating Quality Circles who are aware of this frequently give their Circles the opportunity to repeat their presentations to others. These presentations may include:

- other Quality Circles;
- public or semi-public functions;
- the steering committee;
- in-house Circle conventions;
- presentations at national Circle conventions, such as those organised by National Societies of Quality Circles.

Additionally, special projects may be recorded in news-sheets, articles on noticeboards, or in magazines such as *Quality Review*.

The Japanese system of reward and recognition is described in some detail at the end of this chapter.

Attendance at conventions, seminars, and workshops

An extremely powerful form of gratitude for Circle achievements and re-cognition of the value of their work can be shown by allowing Circles to attend public and semi-public functions. Not only will the Circles find this enjoyable and rewarding in itself, it is also consistent with the idea of self-control (see later). The Circles will almost certainly pick up new ideas from the presentations of other Circles, and from the ensuing discussions. More-over, it means that Circles are being treated like managers who, of course, also benefit from learning at seminars.

Exchange visits to other organisations operating Circles

This is another of the key forms of reward for Circles in Japan, and is already becoming well established in Europe. Many British companies have an almost formalised relationship with each other for this purpose.

Allowing Circles to decide how some of savings may be spent

This is the essence of self-control. Nothing could be more impressive as a means of showing trust in a group of workpeople than to allow them to decide for themselves how some of the gains may be utilised. Those managers who might be sceptical of such a revolutionary approach are probably not yet ready to accept the philosophy of Quality Circles. The idea of allowing Circles this degree of responsibility is new to most companies in the West, even those with established Circle programmes. In Japan, however, such practices are almost universal, although the method of application varies widely, and some differences in approach may be evident in all programmes.

Basically each project is evaluated in much the same way as reward-based suggestion scheme programmes (see later in this chapter). A proportion of the financial benefits of the project are then allocated back to the Circle. The Circle can then either decide how this money is to be spent immediately, or, as happens in many cases, it can let the savings accumulate until a more substantial sum has accrued from several projects.

The Circle will then brainstorm the possible ways in which the money can be spent, and these will probably include:

- better tools and equipment;
- ideas for improving the work environment, including even such items as pot plants, carpets, etc.,
- better facilities for Circle meetings;
- presentation aids such as flip charts, overhead projectors, etc.;
- visits away from the factory;
- books and training materials.

At the first Quality Circle convention organised by DHA, which was the first of its kind in the UK before the creation of the National Society of Quality Circles, the delegates, who comprised nearly 90 Quality Circle members and facilitators from a range of British companies, voted unanimously that they did not want direct financial rewards, but liked the idea of controlling some of the savings. When asked how they would use the resources, the majority thought better facilities, aids, and equipment for Circle activities would be a high priority. This is still true today.

In Japan, Quality Circles frequently use this income for such purposes as parties to introduce new members, as well as to entertain others outside the Circle who may have given assistance.

In one UK company, a Quality Circle given the opportunity to decide how some of its savings might be used, requested that two table tennis tables be purchased for the works canteen. This was immediately accepted by management. The value of such suggestions is that others in the organisation also benefit, and Quality Circle activities are shown in a favourable light.

Of course, it must be emphasised that in many cases the Quality Circle should present its recommendations before spending the money, but this is a matter for the organisation and is unlikely to affect the Circle programme one way or the other.

Quality Circles and reward-based suggestions schemes

It would seem from the foregoing that Quality Circles are in conflict with reward-based suggestion schemes. Fortunately, this is not so. Suggestion schemes and Quality Circles are fundamentally different, and can live alongside one another quite happily – as is the case in a very large number of companies.

Let us compare the two concepts. In the West a suggestion scheme is usually operated by placing letter-boxes in convenient locations around the premises. They are often accompanied by publicity materials which encourage people to submit ideas for improvements for which rewards will be given. These rewards are usually calculated on the estimated value of the idea, although some reward is often given even for ideas not accepted. Apart from the time taken by a committee every so often to evaluate the ideas, a suggestion scheme does not cost very much to run. Unlike Quality Circles, people are not specially trained to think up suggestions, nor are they given time to do so.

Quality Circles, on the other hand, receive special training in the problem-solving techniques, and meet for one hour per week in company time. In other words, Quality Circle meetings are an hour of work. It may be a different kind of work, but it is still work. Additionally, the management of the company is making a considerable on-going investment in the programme.

Another important consideration is that Circles only work on one project at a time. If any of the members have ideas about any other topic, there should be nothing to prevent their placing such ideas in the suggestion box (if that is how the suggestion scheme is run) in the same way as any other employee. Alternatively, of course, the Japanese approach could be used, whereby suggestions are formally passed upwards to the supervisor, and so on. Neither should there be anything officially preventing a Circle member from putting forward in suggestion schemes ideas relating to the project, if he or she so wishes; however, experience has shown that this never happens. At any time, Circle members have the choice of either submitting their ideas relating to the project they are working on as their contribution to the Circle, or putting them forward for their own gratification. Experience again shows that members' loyalty to their group prevents their seeking personal reward. Basically, it is a matter of trust. If management is prepared to trust its people, it is unlikely that such trust will be violated.

Integration of Circles with suggestion schemes

Whilst Quality Circles and suggestion schemes are different, that is not to say that they cannot work together. If the idea of Circles having some control of their gains is accepted, then it becomes possible to allow the Circles, if they wish, to place their ideas in the suggestion box with the proviso that any award given will not be taken as a direct cash benefit but may be spent by the Circle in whatever way the members choose.

Japanese/Western suggestion schemes – a comparison

Because of the close link is most managers' minds between suggestions and reward, it will be appropriate to discuss the topic of suggestion schemes in

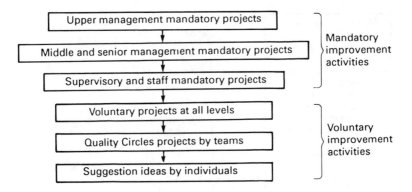

Fig. 7.1

some detail in this chapter. The methods by which suggestion schemes operate in the West do not vary to any great extent from one company to another. In fact the main variation is in the manner or amount by which the suggester is compensated for his or her ideas.

Generally, a suggestion commitee is formed to manage the programme. This usually comprises managers and individuals from key departments, and sometimes also representatives of the Trade Unions. Responsibilities include:

- publicity;
- management of the system – the collection boxes, forms for suggestions, etc.,
- evaluation of suggestions and acceptance criteria;
- appropriation of awards based upon estimates of cost : benefit;
- follow-up to ensure that accepted suggestions are implemented (sometimes!).

In Japan the process is quite different. There is no suggestion commitee as such. Typically, the overall evaluation of the suggestion process (not the evaluation of the suggestions themselves) is carried out by the Japanese equivalent of the Quality Council (the Total Quality Promotion Committee). The suggestion process is seen merely as an extension of the project-by-project process (Figure 7.1). In other words, they see the suggestion concept as a form of catch-all. Anything which hasn't been dealt with by one of the more formalised types of group is picked up by individual suggestions.

Due to the total devolution of problem-solving skills and improvement activities, Japanese workers are highly sensitised to the need for improvement. Consequently, they are more likely to make improvement suggestions than their Western counterparts, and in fact, the achievement of suggestion activities in Japan is phenomenal by Western standards. For example in Toyota, annually, there are some 2,600,000 improvement suggestions, of which over 96 per cent are implemented. From a labour force of 40,000

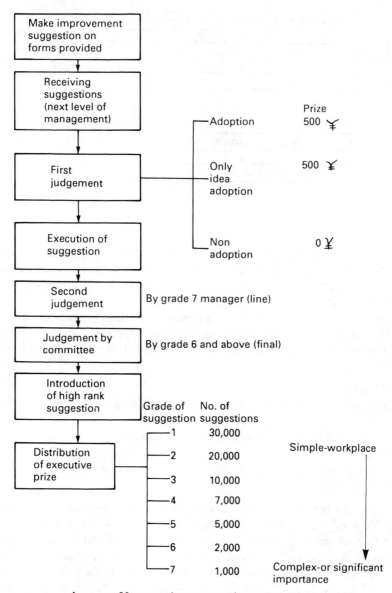

Average: 20 suggestions per employee per year.

Fig. 7.2

people, this represents 65 suggestions per employee per year. There are many companies where 40 per month are being achieved.

Evaluation of suggestions is not made by the Total Quality Council, nor by the Voluntary Improvement Steering Committee, but through normal daily line management activities.

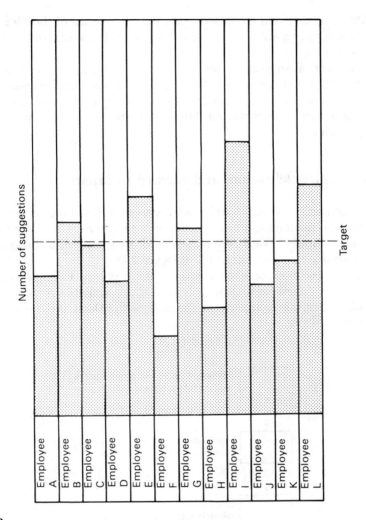

Fig. 7.3

At the bottom level, an individual worker will make his suggestion to his own direct supervisor. The supervisor has the choice of

(a) accepting the proposal;
(b) rejecting it; or
(c) passing it upwards to a higher level.

If accepted at the lower level, the worker will receive a nominal award of, say, 50p. If it goes higher, the same three possibilities apply, and the award will be increased level by level. If it goes all the way up to Company President, the award will typically be somewhere in the order of 50,000 Yen – approximately £200. Typically, about 3 or 4 suggestions per year will reach this level in most companies. The key point is that the award is not based on *return* from the idea; it is entirely based upon the *importance* of the idea. If the suggestion is not accepted, regardless of the level it reaches, the individual receives nothing.

The number of suggestions per employee is monitored in their sections, and the totals are posted on a notice board where they can be clearly seen. Normally, the administration of this is carried out by the Quality Circles, and this again represents a significant difference between Japanese and Western Quality Circles.

Recognition, celebration, and reward in Japan

The recognition, celebration, and reward system in Japan begins with small informal presentations and awards at operator/supervisor level, up through to annual company award ceremonies, and then beyond, to regional and then national award conventions (see Figure 7.4).

Awards can be given both to individuals and to groups, through suggestion scheme achievements and Quality Control Circle activities respectively, or to division, plant, or company in the case of the Deming Award and All Japan Quality Prize.

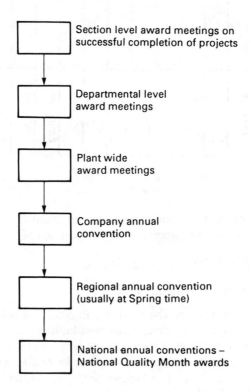

Section level award meetings on successful completion of projects

Departmental level award meetings

Plant wide award meetings

Company annual convention

Regional annual convention (usually at Spring time)

National annual conventions – National Quality Month awards

Fig. 7.4

Most companies operating Total Quality hold regular conventions for the purpose of providing a platform for successful individuals and groups to 'show off' their achievements, and to simultaneously encourage others to greater efforts. This is one of the ways in which Quality improvement achievements are shared across an organisation, and is the most powerful form of reward.

As mentioned earlier, any cash award are usually nominal, and are often used to brighten up a work area rather than being pocketed by the individuals. Of greater importance are the certificates, trophies, and badges which accompany these token rewards. In many cases, there are no direct financial incentives.

Quality Circle Conventions

National Quality Circle Conventions were established by JUSE, under the presidency of Professor Ishikawa. In Spring every year, each of the 14 regions into which JUSE divided the country will hold Quality Circle Conventions for member companies in its area. Each Circle will make a presentation, and they are judged on the quality of this presentation, their use of the problem-solving skills, their use of data analysis techniques, and the credibility of their conclusions.

The Conventions for Quality Control Circles were organised for two basic reasons:

1. To provide a vehicle for recognition.
2. To enable others to share the achievements and learn from each other.

Today, the organisation of Conventions in companies, regions, and nationally, is the main means by which the concept of Quality Control Circles is sustained.

The following examples have been taken from various Japanese Quality Control Circles Conventions. At these Conventions all over Japan the procedure and layout (Figure 7.5) are the same. The presentation is usually made by one or two members of the Circle at a lectern on the right-hand side of the stage. Other members of the Circle, usually working in pairs, operate overhead projectors. The presentations are generally well rehearsed, and slides are changed on cue. Frequently the members who change the slides participate in the narration, and the presentations, which are very slick, usually take around 20 minutes. Following this, questions are taken from the audience, and these are usually either technical or relate to the use and interpretation of data gathering and analysis techniques. These questions are often quite searching and will expose weaknesses in the argument if such exist.

Participants at regional conventions range from several hundred to well over 1,000 at the more highly populated locations. There will then be multiple streams, with simultaneous presentations being made. At the National Convention which takes place in Tokyo in the first week in November and

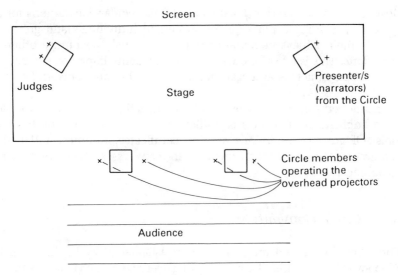

Fig. 7.5

lasts for two days, there will usually be a capacity audience, limited only by the seating of the venue, of around 2,000 people.

The following examples, which have been taken from various Japanese Quality Control Circles Conventions, show the standards achieved by such groups.

Presentation 1: Improving the quality of beauty treatment

This presentation was made at the National Quality Circle Convention held in Tokyo in 1980. The Quality Control Circle comprised of six members. In their presentation they described how they had first of all collected data on problems by designing a questionnaire to give their customers. They used the technique of Pareto analysis to separate the most important problems from the remainder. For this technique each of the identified problems are ranked on some agreed scale. These scales can be either subjective or measurable. Examples of subjective possibilities include:

- aggravation to customer
- nuisance
- discomfort
- customer satisfaction, etc.

These will require some form of ranking, and many techniques exist to enable this.

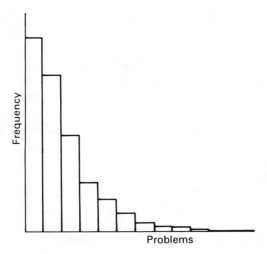

Fig. 7.6

Examples of measurable parameters include:

- cost
- frequency
- time to solve
- cost to solve.

Whatever other criteria a group may use to select problems, Circles are always encouraged to identify 'cost' whenever possible.

In the case of the Circle in this example, frequency of occurrence of the problems was the key parameter.

The Pareto diagram is a form of column graph where each column represents a specific problem. The height of the columns is determined by the measure being used, in this case 'frequency of occurrence'. The columns are always arranged in descending order with the highest on the left and the shortest on the right, with the exception of a 'miscellaneous column' which always appears on the right and may sometimes be longer than the last one or two columns. A completed Pareto diagram is shown in Figure 7.6.

The Circle presented this data to the audience and then proceeded to explain how they had dealt with the most important problems. They also explained that over the course of a year, not only had they dealt successfully with most of the problems, but they had at the same time increased the number of clients coming to their salon by over 100 per cent.

Presentation 2: Leaky bottles

This presentation was made by a Circle of six workers from Kosi Cosmetics in Tokyo, who worked the machines which screwed the tops on the bottles of cosmetics. The Circle explained that they were concerned that reports came back of leakages from the bottle tops. They decided to investigate this and to find a remedy.

This was one of the first presentations of Japanese Quality Control Circles ever seen by the author, and the content was stunning. Members of the group used overhead projector slides to show how they had used designed experiments to study the possible effects of variations in hydraulic pressure, viscosity, temperature, torque to close the tops, shape of top, shape of bottle, type of content, washers, no washers, etc. They used histograms, regression analysis, and other statistical tools to study the data.

It was amazing to realise that this group represented a typical group of Japanese workers. The interpreter explained that the team members had a typical education, that they were aged between 17 and 23, and were no different from average Japanese workers. They would have learned most of the techniques demonstrated during a standard Japanese education!

Presentation 3: Plant tour guides

This presentation was made by a team of six plant tour guides from Komatsu. It was their job to take groups of foreign visitors around the plant.

As with the team from the Beauty Salon, they explained how they had collected data from their 'customers' through the use of questionnaires. The data showed that the principal problem faced by the customers was that they frequently could not understand what was being explained. The Circle looked into this further and discovered that the problem was greatest amongst visitors whose own native language was other than English. Whilst the tour guides spoke fairly good English, it was, nevertheless, not perfect. Although the visitors who elected to choose the English-speaking tour guides could all speak English, it was evident that the greatest difficulties occurred when such visitors had English only as a secondary language. The Circle analysed the data again, and identified, using Pareto analysis, the principal first languages of these visitors. They then approached the Marketing Department to identify the most important aspects of the tour that should be clearly explained, bearing in mind that many of the visitors could be potential customers. The group then obtained support from the company to have audio cassette tapes produced which contained these aspects in each of the key foreign languages. In the presentation, the group went on to explain how they had resolved further secondary problems.

Summary

Articles have appeared in management magazines expressing disbelief that workers, particularly in Western countries, will produce ideas if they are not to be directly rewarded. The evidence now available from a very large number of organisations totally refutes this view. The carrot and stick theories and the approach of Taylorised management have, largely through the activities of Quality Circles, been totally disproven and rejected.

Given the right environment, people do want to work, do want to improve both themselves and their organisation, and provided they are given a fair day's pay for a fair day's work, gain considerable satisfaction from recognition of their talents and creativity. This is the main reward of Quality Circles, and the evidence of five years' development in the UK shows that the question 'What's in it for me?' is never asked by active Quality Circles.

CHAPTER 8

DEFINITIONS OF QUALITY

A successful Quality Circle programme is part, and only part, of the new philosophy of management called Total Quality, and represents an essential ingredient if the full potential of the concept is to be realised. This philosophy regretfully even today, is, still outside the experience of the vast majority of people in industry and commerce anywhere in the world except Japan. The details of the philosophy expounded in earlier chapters should be studied carefully and properly understood before Quality Circle-type groups are even attempted; it is essential that top plant management has both the desire and will to enable it to develop its full potential.

If the principles outlined here are properly understood and heeded when a Total Quality programme develops through to Quality Circles, then within a few years the whole culture of that organisation will have been changed fundamentally and irrevocably. If these principles are allowed to continue to grow and develop throughout society, then we shall soon have created a totally new industrial culture which will alter the relationships between everyone in society, both inside and outside the working environment.

At first sight, Quality Circles may appear to be a simple idea, but nothing which has this potential could possibly be that simple. In this chapter we shall look at the reason for calling the groups 'Quality Circles', rather than some of the alternatives that may be suggested.

Why 'Quality' Circles?

Basically, a commercial organisation exists to make a profit for its backers and to provide employment for those involved. It aims to achieve this through competitiveness and success in the marketplace. To achieve this it must optimise the twin factors of selling price and demand. Selling price is determined by the utility of the product or service in relation to alternative choices available to the consumer. The attractiveness of the service itself is determined by the combined ability, talent, and attitudes of the employees. These factors influence the production cost and hence the pricing flexibility and therefore profit margin of each unit of sale.

It is the 'people' aspect of quality which provides the sparkle to those organisations who know how people should be treated, and it is through people that the breakthroughs and advances can be made. However mechanised we become, people will still be the dominant factor, even in the highly automated factories of Japan they are under no illusions as to the importance of this fact.

It was suggested in an earlier chapter that systems and processes do not motivate people and it is the management of people which has presented many of the problems of Western organisations. If people do not really care, if they just do their jobs according to instructions, then no amount of system is going to make any difference.

Unfortunately it is this side of quality, the motivational and involvement side, which has proved to be the most difficult for most managements to comprehend. One of the key reasons for this failure is that very few managements have ever challenged the fundamentals of the system of management they operate.

Most Western developments in job design have only involved cosmetic changes which, because they lack substance, have been difficult to sustain. This includes many manifestations of job enlargement and job enrichment.

As explained in Chapter 4 the reason why Total Quality emerged in Japan as opposed to the West was largely due to the fact that during the early stages of their post-War reconstruction, the Japanese found themselves confronted with precisely the same industrial problems that the rest of the world is still faced with today: labour alienation, worker indifference, strikes, absenteeism, excessive sick leave, and grievances. It was as much a result of the way they addressed themselves to these problems that led them eventually to Quality Circles, as it was their awareness of a much broader perception of the meaning of the word 'quality'.

Many people are frequently puzzled by the use of the word 'quality' in connection with the concept of Quality Circles, claiming that many of the problems tackled by Circles are not 'quality' problems! This is because they do not realise that the word 'quality' has different connotations to different people, and in different situations, and these differences are quite important to a proper understanding of the philosophy.

Most people have too narrow a perspective of the meaning of the word 'quality'. They associate it with defects in products: scratches, cracks, missing parts, and so forth, but quality is much more than that. It was stated in Chapter 3 that quality is everything that an organisation does, in the eyes of its customers, which will encourage them to regard that organisation as one of the best, if not the best, in its particular field of operation. In other words, quality is a measure of the achievement of customer satisfaction.

For example, we do not give customer satisfaction if our staff are unfriendly or unhelpful when dealing with a customer. This would be regarded as 'poor quality service'. Neither do we achieve customer satisfaction if our telephone operator is untrained and does not sound very efficient, or unplugs the call in the middle of a conversation, or is a long time answering. The customer would also be unimpressed if he were invoiced for the wrong amount, or the products were sent to the wrong destination. These items would indicate a 'poor quality organisation'.

Customer satisfaction has several dimensions, for example:

- fitness for use
- reliability – the life aspect of quality
- value for money
- after-sales service and support
- packaging
- customer information and training
- maintainability
- variety
- speed of service
- civility of service at all levels
- image of the company and customer confidence in the organisation

All these factors added together form an image of the organisation in the eyes of the customer. This image may be good or bad. The confidence of the customer will be determined by it, and that will be a major influence on the company's share of the market. The company is just as much affected by the attitudes of employees who are in contact with the customer as it is by its own products or services.

In the Western world there persists a widely held view that the requirements of quality and productivity are in conflict with each other, and that one is achieved at the expense of the other. This is, in fact, a fallacy. Productivity is a measure of the effective use of resources. If people work twice as quickly, they do not increase their productivity, only their production. They only increase their productivity if they can produce more for the same effort. Productivity therefore is a measure of efficiency. In a manufacturing organisation, productivity is reduced by scrapped, reworked, or repaired items, wastage of materials, time loss, machine delays and breakdowns, items not in the right place at the right time, excessive energy consumption, disputes, and low motivation. They are all quality-related in one form or another, and in different ways each can be described as a quality problem – but not in the way that Western people would normally define quality. If one could regard all these as quality items, then rather than seeing a conflict between productivity and quality one would argue that if everything is concentrated on quality, productivity will look after itself. This is why the word 'quality' is used in connection with Total Quality and, hopefully, the concept of Total Quality in the course of time will broaden the general perspective of the meaning of the word 'quality' around the world.

Quality is dynamic

Perhaps another dangerous misconception about quality is the belief that it has some kind of absolute value. People sometimes say, 'What happens when we have solved all our quality problems?'. The question itself indicates a failure to understand what quality really means. In a competitive world, it is impossible for an organisation to solve all its quality problems, because with the solution of each individual problem, the organisation, by improving its performance, has improved its competitiveness in the marketplace, at the expense of its competitor. If the improvement continues, there will come a time when, if the competitor fails to react, he will be forced out of business, and this may happen in some cases. However, not all competitors will ignore this changing balance, and some will develop their own counter-strategy. Ultimately, only those organisations that are capable of this form of continuous improvement, and at a pace at least equal to that of their competitors, will survive.

Quality therefore is not an absolute entity but a relative one. The quality standard of a product or service is judged by the consumer, but is set by the best performer. If there be any ultimate quality goal, it can only be perfection: a perfect product, perfect service, perfect packaging, perfect instructions, perfect organisation, perfect staff, and so on. Of course, perfection is impossible, and consumer demands are ever-changing, but it does mean that it is always possible for one organisation to be better than another (and this includes the ability to change direction if necessary), and for improvements to be continuous and unlimited. Perfection in this context means 'perfect satisfaction' and not necessarily 'perfectly defect-free' or 'perfectly to size'. These forms of perfection, if not required by market forces, only serve to increase cost, which may be a disadvantage to producer and customer alike.

If we are the best, in the eyes of our customer, and can sell our products cheaply, at low cost, then we are successful. If we are second best, then we are in trouble. As soon as we become the best, the pressure is on to remain there. Others will be all too anxious to remove our crown.

As organisations become more competitive, the tensions in the marketplace become more severe. Quality, therefore, is a dynamic process, which enables the good to survive. To be successful, it is necessary to attempt to be better than the competitor across the entire spectrum of the organisation's activities, at all levels, and at all times. It is just as important for a truck driver wearing the company's overalls to be civil to someone obstructing the traffic, because at that moment he represents the organisation, as it is for the marketing director to 'pull off' a good deal!

In the future, as competition globally becomes more and more intense, it will no longer be good enough to rely upon the past reputation of a good product. It will be necessary to galvanise the resources of all our people to work towards making our organisation the best in its particular field. 'Our' people must project an image both at work and in their private lives, of pride in the organisation of which they are a part. This can be achieved if 'our' people think that their organisation is better for their being there, and that they are recognised for their contribution. This recognition comes in the form of being listened to, being given an opportunity to participate. It is impossible to achieve these objectives under the system of management operating in our society at present. To achieve even partial success it is necessary to change fundamentally the system of management operating currently across all

105

sectors of industry. The quality of working life is at least equal in importance to the quality of the product or service. Ultimately, quality is the basis of everything. Again, this qualifies the term 'Total Quality'.

The difference between the Western and Japanese perception of the meaning of the word 'quality' can best be seen by comparing the European definition of quality control with that of the Japanese.

EOQC definition (fifth edition, 1981)

'Quality Control

The operational techniques and activities which sustain a quality of product or service that will satisfy given needs; also the use of such techniques and activities.

'*Note 1*: The aim of Quality Control is to provide quality that is satisfactory (e.g. safe, adequate, dependable, and economical). The overall system involves integrating the quality aspects of several related steps including the proper specification of what is wanted; design of the product or service to meet the requirements; production or installation to meet the full extent of the specification; inspection to determine whether the resulting product or service conforms to the applicable specification; and review of usage to provide for revision of specification. Effective utilisation of these technologies and activities is an essential element in the economic control of quality.

'*Note 2*: When Quality Control is used in the total system sense, as it normally is without a restrictive adjective, it has to do with making quality what it should be. When used in a more restrictive sense for a particular phase or function within the total Quality Control system, the phrase 'Quality Control' is modified by an adjective or used as an adjective to restrict some other operation. For example: process Quality Control; manufacturing Quality Control; design Quality Control, etc. In the same sense,it is often used as an adjective to restrict other operations to that part which belongs within the Quality Control system, as, for example, Quality Control inspection; Quality Control testing, etc.'

Note that this definition makes no reference to the involvement of people or, specifically, the buyer.

Now consider the Japanese equivalent.

Japanese definition (JIS*Z8101)

'Quality Control

A system of means for economical production of commodities or services of the quality that meets the buyers' demands.

---

* Japanese Industrial Standard

'Quality Control is often abbreviated to QC. Also, since modern control employs statistical approaches, it is sometimes specifically referred to as Statistical Quality Control (abbreviated to SQC).

'To effectively execute Quality Control, *participation by and co-operation of all members of the enterprise activities covering market research, research and development, production planning, designing, production preparations, purchasing and subcontracting, manufacturing, inspection, sales and after-sales service, as well as finance, personnel and eduction.* Quality Control thus executed is called Company-Wide Quality Control (abbreviated to CWQC) or Total Quality Control (abbreviated to TQC).

This definition reveals that quality activities should be as follows:

'**1.** Activities targeted at the consumer in realising the product performance, reliability, safety, usage, economy, servicing, and the like that consumers demand.

2. Activities for rationally and economically realising the above objective through utilisation of statistical and other scientific approaches. Rather than insubstantial spiritual arguments, the activities have to enhance and manage the processes for production of satisfactory results through the employment of specific means and techniques.

3. Activities not only implemented by manufacturing divisions such as production and inspection alone, but in which all the individual divisions ranging from surveying, through planning, developing, and production, to sales, co-operate with one another and endeavour as an organisation for resolution of quality assurance problems and other problems that the enterprise faces.

4. *Activities in which everybody participates, including the management staff all the way through operators on the floor, and everybody advances by playing his role properly under the leadership of the owners, rather than something a handful of designated specialists alone push forward.'!*

(Author's italics and exclamation mark.)

It is obvious that the Japanese approach specifically requires the total involvement of all people at all levels for Quality Control to exist. Not only does the European definition not emphasise these same requirements, it is in fact impossible to do so, because it is prevented by the Western system of management (or 'Taylorism'), which must be changed before the concept of Total Quality can be successfully introduced.

Basically, the impression given by the wording of these two definitions is that the Western approach to Quality Control is heavily committed to the establishment of sophisticated systems, plans, and procedures and inspection, whereas the Japanese approach relies far more heavily upon the development, training and involvement of its people. This is carried out in practical terms through the co-ordinated activities of Quality Circles or other similar concepts such as task force and project group activities. Collectively, these are referred to as 'small group activities'.

CHAPTER 9

QUALITY CIRCLES – WHAT THEY ARE

Small group-type activities can be organised in several different ways, and should also include task force operations, value analysis teams, value engineering, project groups, action centred groups, etc. Each plays a different but important part in participative activities but true 'self-control' at the work place can only be achieved through the introduction and development of Quality Circle-type activities.

The Quality Circle is a specific form of small group activity, and serves a distinctly different purpose from other kinds of group, team, or committee activities. The purpose of this chapter is to define precisely what Quality Circles are, and what they represent.

The principle of 'self-control'

Most Western people confuse Quality Circles with problem-solving groups and this in itself accounts for many of the failures of Quality Circle programmes.

The essence of Quality Circles is to bring the craftsmanship, or self-control element back to groups of people rather than individuals. The aim is to provide all the means by which employees can control their own performance, both individually and in group-based activities.

This concept goes far beyond simple problem solving, although problem solving is usually the point where they start. The results currently being achieved in Japanese organisations would never have occurred if the Japanese had seen Circles as merely problem-solving activities.

The size of the group that comprises a Quality Circle is important. Too large a group makes it difficult for everyone to participate. If there are more people in the work area than can be accommodated in one Circle, there is no reason why other circles should not be formed to involve the remaining employees. They are unlikely to conflict with each other. Most Circles have between 6 and 10 people, and the concept works well with groups of this size. Sometimes there are Circles of only 3 to 5 people simply because there are only that number of people in the section. However, it is vitally important to ensure that all employees in the work area, whether group members or not, have an opportunity to participate. The Circle must be seen as 'our section Circle'.

Circle development

Once a Circle has been formed, all being well, it will pass through three distinct phases of development, to the fourth ultimate stage. Whether or not it ever reaches this final stage is entirely dependent upon the objectives and support of management and whether the more philosophical ideas presented in this book have been absorbed and understood.

Phase 1 – problem solving

During this phase, the Circle will have been trained in simple techniques which will enable its members to identify, analyse and solve some of the more pressing problems in their own work area. These problems will include:

- wastage of materials
- housekeeping problems
- delays, hold-ups, etc.
- inadequate job instructions
- quality
- productivity
- energy consumption
- environmental problems
- handling
- safety
- the quality of work life generally

These will usually be the problems that are uppermost in the minds of most employees. At this stage of development it is not essential for team members to be made aware of policy deployment.

Phase 2 – monitoring and problem solving

After a short time, when several of the simpler problems have been resolved and many others have just 'disappeared' as a result of other improvements in the work environment, the Circle will begin to develop a 'monitoring' mentality. By this time the members should have been trained in simple control techniques, and will be encouraged to use these to maintain the improvements already made.

Phase 3 – innovation: self-improvement and problem solving

There is almost a natural progression to the self-improvement phase from Phase 2. As the Circle begins to mature, and most of the techniques taught have been well practised and understood, the confidence of the group will have grown considerably. The members will also have gained wider acceptance by their colleagues in their own and other departments, they will be treated with greater respect, and it is the responsibility of management to encourage this development and to introduce policy deployment. It is about this time that the Circle will progress from 'just solving problems' to the mentality of seeking ways of making improvements. Obviously, this will take longer in some cases than others.

Phase 4 – self-control

It is doubtful that any Circles in Western Europe have reached this stage of development. Whether it is reached at all is as much dependent on managers and others outside the Circle as it is on the Circles. Until more Western managers take the trouble to visit Japan and see for themselves what can be achieved, it is unlikely that any will ever reach this point. The managers have to get there first, and there is little evidence so far of that happening, despite the levels of competition.

If the Circles pass through Phases 1, 2, and 3, they develop maturity and should be seen to be trusted by management. The organisation should have begun to realise much of the early potential available from this style of management, and must seek ways of both furthering the continuous development of the existing Circles, and encouraging new ones. The latter is only a question of continuing the same form of development with new groups, but the continuous development of existing, mature Circles will be breaking fresh ground in most societies, and is relatively recent among even those companies with 20 years of development.

The development of existing Circles involves two factors – internal and external. Internally, it is necessary for the organisation to ensure that such Circles have access to all the information, training aids, and techniques necessary for them to progress when encouraged to do so. They may indulge in self-study. It will be necessary for management consciously to give them help and information such as quality control data, and access to courses both inside the company and externally. They should have access to technical journals relating to their work and attend in-house seminars in order to be kept abreast of the latest developments in their field. In Japan there is a direct link between self-education and promotion opportunities.

Externally, Circles should be given the opportunity of communicating with the professional, educational and specialist institutions, and also of making either direct or indirect contact with suppliers when relevant to their activities. They should be permitted to attend conventions such as the National Society of Quality Circles or other national bodies, where they can meet Circle members from other organisations, and can trade experiences and seminars to help them progress in their work.

Opportunities should be created to encourage Circle members to participate in self-development outside of work, as we did in the 1950s. In Japan, there is a direct link between promotion and workers who voluntarily engage in this type of activity. Hopefully, the technical colleges will not only respond to the demand, but will actively engage in encouraging people to return to vocational part-time studies.

All this may seem a little advanced at the early stages of development, but the best programmes are all planned a long way in advance. It will be appreciated that if this stage is ever reached we will have created a fundamentally different industrial society from that with which we are so familiar today.

Definition of Quality Circles

There is a great variety of types of group operating in the West all using the term Quality Circle. This is regrettable, because when such groups fail, the impression is that the Quality Circles concept itself is invalid. The definition of a Circle is important, and groups which fail to meet the criterion of this definition should not be called Quality Circles.

The definition of Quality Circles was given in Chapter 6, but it is appropriate to restate it again here, before considering the definition in further detail.

'A Quality Circle is a small group of between three and twelve people who do the same or similar work, voluntarily meeting together regularly for about one hour per week in paid time, usually under the leadership of their own supervisor, and who are trained to identify, analyse, and solve some of the problems in their work, presenting solutions to management and, where possible, implementing solutions themselves.'

(This definition was created by David Hutchins in 1980 and is based upon other definitions produced by Professor Kaoru Ishikawa and Jeff Beardsley, an American Quality Circles Consultant. It has been adopted as a standard in the UK by the NSQC and by many organisations in Europe.)

The confusion over the definition of Quality Circles is very relevant to the success or failure of such programmes. Organisations which have failed to realise this are usually disappointed with the programme they have developed when it is compared with programmes developed by those who have followed the classic approach. In fact it is a strongly held view of the author that the persistent failure of many Circle programmes can be directly attributed to an appalling lack of understanding of this fundamental definition.

Taking each aspect of the definition in turn, the basis of each point will now be reviewed.

1. *'A small group of people who do similar work'*
The Circle should comprise a more or less homogeneous group of people, usually from the same work area. They will usually have a similar educational background, speak the same work language, and no one member should be inhibited in any way by the presence of another. Whilst in excep-

111

tional circumstances some variation of this important rule may be necessary, generally speaking where such variations exist, the resulting groups should *not* be described as Quality Circles.

Circles comprising members from different disciplines or with different work experience invariably illustrate that the more fragmented the experience of the members the more difficult it will be for them to select projects which are of interest to all members. Those least directly affected by the potential achievement will show less interest than the other members, and, if some of the work-related jargon is unfamiliar, boredom may be induced, with a resulting loss of morale and possibly the loss of some individuals.

Other problems may arise if some members have higher educational back-grounds than others. In such cases there is a tendency for the more educated members of the Circle to 'take over' the problem, and solve it on behalf of the group. Whilst in most cases this may not be evident to those outside the Circle, the essential 'craftsmanship' principles will have been lost, with the result that the group will still be suffering the effects of Taylor-type disadvantages.

That is not to say that the Circle cannot utilise the services of specialists or others if it so wishes. On the contrary, this is to be vigorously encouraged. For example, the members may invite such people into the Circle for a specific project if they feel it will help produce a more soundly thought-out solution. In such cases, these guests are really acting as consultants to the Circle, and a supportive management should actively encourage this process.

This arrangement fits in well with the concept of 'self-control' which should be the ultimate aim of corporate management in developing Circles in the first place.

2. 'Between three and twelve people'

The size of a Circle should be limited to ensure that the Circle is a team and not a committee. The section members must also see it as 'their section's Circle' and *not* as an élite group in their work area. Although some members of the section may not wish to participate in the weekly meetings, group members should actively encourage them to make suggestions, and solicit their ideas on Circle projects.

If the work area contains more enthusiasts than can be included in one Circle, others may be formed progressively once the earlier groups have be-come established. Those as yet unfamiliar with Quality Circles specifically may fear that such a development can lead to conflict and rivalry between groups, but this is extremely rare. It is far more likely that they will co-operate with each other, even helping to collect data for each others' projects, and occasionally, if need arises, form cross-Circle subgroups for the solution of specific problems. Such developments are a sign of maturity in Circle activities and are to be encouraged wherever possible.

In cases where there are only one, two, or three people in the work area, it may not be possible to form them into a Circle, but usually, they will have considerable interaction with other more heavily populated sections. Not only will there be plenty of opportunity for them to become involved in the projects of Circles in these areas, but it may frequently happen that the Circle will repay the help that they give by working on some projects of their own choice. Again this is a sign of maturity and cannot be expected in the early stages of development.

3. 'Voluntarily meeting together'

The meaning of the word 'voluntarily' is hard to define, but basically, in the context of Quality Circles, it means that no one *has* to join a Circle. People are free to join and free to leave. If someone joins a Circle and subsequently chooses to leave it, there should be no pressure, inquests, or recriminations. Obviously, if someone does drop out it should be regarded as a danger signal that all might not be well in the group, and the leaver should be discreetly asked the reason for leaving. If there is a problem, and it can be overcome, then that individual may, if he chooses to do so, return to the group if the opportunity arises.

The fact that people join a Circle because they want to, rather than because they have to, means that they are prepared to work. (You can lead a horse to water, but you cannot make it drink.)

The reality of this was very quickly learned by the Japanese when they first introduced Circles in 1962. Those companies which recognised the value of voluntariness soon developed strikingly more effective programmes than those in which membership was compulsory.

Whilst the number of volunteers may be quite small in the early stages, when people may possibly be suspicious of management motives, the number should begin to increase dramatically as soon as the achievements of the earlier Circles become known and confidence is gained.

If a pilot scheme of, say, five Circles is successful, then in a matter of days, weeks, or months, depending upon the circumstances, people should be saying, 'Why can't we have a Circle in our section?' or, 'Why are all the Circle on the day shift? Why can't we have a Circle on nights?', and so forth.

When managers from other departments realise that the sections which have encouraged Circles are improving their performance, they will soon begin to request equal opportunities.

The fact that membership is voluntary does not mean that the organisation will have to wait until people knock on the door and request a Circle to be formed. Many people, possibly most, in the early stages have been invited to join but are not compelled. They should be free to drop out at any time if they wish, even in the middle of training. In a sense, they are actually only volunteering to attend the next meeting.

4. 'Meeting regularly for about an hour per week'

Whilst considerable variation in the time Circles are allowed to meet exists even in Japan it is generally agreed that when circumstances permit, the regular weekly meeting is preferred to once fortnightly or to irregular times on a weekly basis.

A regular meeting time is habit-forming, and the day of the meeting will soon be associated in the minds of the members as 'Circle Day' and so members are much less likely to forget to attend. This sometimes happens in other cases.

Two diametrically opposite attitudes are frequently held to the idea of Circles meeting for one hour per week. Some people cannot imagine that much can be achieved in such a short time; others are more concerned that they might be losing ten hours per week production from a group of ten people. In the latter case, the facts show otherwise, for two important reasons:

- Circles will usually agree to hold their meetings at a time which causes least interference with work schedules. For example, in process work, they may hold their meetings during a maintenance period, a job change-over, or after completion of the weekly work schedule. When this is impossible, they may agree to hold the meeting at the beginning or end of the shift, or during the lunch break. Of course, in these cases agreement as to payment will have to be reached.
- The activities of Circles are such that a company would be extremely un-likely to detect any loss of production or output from any section as a result of Circle activities. In fact, one of the most striking benefits of Quality Circles is an increase in productivity which will more than com-pensate for the lost time. This is because Circle members are usually ex-tremely conscious of the factors that interrupt their work, and these problems are likely to become early targets for a Quality Circle.

In the case of those concerned about the short length of Circle meetings, it must be realised that Circles do not work in the same way as committees. Normally Circles do not keep minutes, or spend half the meeting time dis-cussing minutes of the last meeting; they just get down to work straight away. The techniques used by the Circles, described in Chapters 19 and 20, are ex-tremely effective when used in this type of small group activity, and both members and others are usually amazed at how much they achieve in only one hour per week.

5. 'In paid time'

We say in 'paid time' rather than 'normal working hours', because there are some cases, such as those described above, when it becomes difficult or impossible to hold the meeting during scheduled work periods.

This may be particularly relevant in shift work operations, when Circles may sometimes span shifts. If the Circle comprises members from each of three or more shifts, it may be possible to hold the meeting during an overlap between two shifts, but the members from other shifts will either miss the meeting, or have to attend outside shift time. The pay arrangements for this will have to be worked out between all concerned, not of course overlooking the views or the arrangements of non-Circle members. Contrary to popular belief, Circle members in Japan are also paid for their time when these situations arise.

6. *'Under the leadership of their own supervisor'*

Some people ask why the supervisor should be the Circle leader. They may say, 'Why can't the leader be selected or elected from the members of the group?'. Whilst there may be circumstances where this arrangement is desirable or necessary, they are very few and far between. Even when this is the best alternative, it is rarely ever better than using the appointed supervisor.

Some managers who are unfamiliar with the working of Quality Circles sometimes fear that they will lose control and that the Quality Circle is a way of by-passing them. Supervisors might certainly fear this if they did not have the opportunity of being Circle leaders. Additionally, they would fear that their workpeople might use the Circle as a means of highlighting the supervisor's shortcomings and therefore regard the Circle as a threat.

This would be a tragedy, because nothing could be further from the truth. Management's motives in setting up Quality Circles are to make better use of the existing structure, not to create alternatives. Circles are concerned with work-related problems and not with grievances, wages, salaries, or conditions of employment. If these items are contentious then the group must take them up through the appropriate channels in the usual way. Circles are not part of the bargaining, negotiating, or grievance machinery, nor do they impinge upon the activities of those who are responsible for these aspects of a company's affairs.

Because the Circle is purely concerned with work-related problems, and because the supervisor is the appointed leader of the group, it follows that direct supervisors should at least have the first option to be the Circle leader.

However, once the group has been formed, the members and others in the work area will quickly realise that it doesn't matter who the leader is because Circle decision-making is a totally democratic process. When the Circle members are in the meeting room together, everyone has one vote, and no one's opinion is any more or less important than anyone else's.

The smart Circle leader will soon learn that it is not easy both to be the leader and to think up ideas at the same time, and so may, after a short time, offer to rotate the leadership of each meeting around the group. Not only will this enable the official Circle leader to contribute his own ideas, but it is also a very effective part of the people-building process, and gives confidence to the members of the group. A leader who develops in this way will usually gain considerable respect from the members as a result.

From the leader's and the organisational point of view, this development may lead to further advantages. If the work area is large, and there are others wishing to form a Circle, the leader may allow the original Circle to become self-propelled while he forms a new Circle in the section. When this Circle has developed, the supervisor may then keep an eye on both groups.

Should there be any reason why the supervisor cannot be, or does not want to be, the Circle leader, then assuming the desire is there amongst the members of the work group, an alternative must be found.

First of all, the supervisor must be given confidence that the Circle, if formed, will not constitute a threat to his authority, and the group should be made very much aware of this. The group must be encouraged to discuss its work with the supervisor and where possible solicit his ideas. When it comes to the management presentation, the supervisor should always be invited to attend.

In situations where the supervisor neither wishes to participate in the Circle, nor is prepared to allow a Circle to be formed in the work area, it is up to the management to make a decision whether one of its appointees should be allowed to continue in a position which obstructs the wishes of both management and workpeople alike, and the action taken in such circumstances is beyond the scope of this book. It is, however, encouraging to note that such situations are extremely rare.

7. 'To identify, analyse and solve problems in their work'

The key point about this part of the definition is the fact that the Circles identify their *own* problems in their *own* work area. That is not to say that other people may not make suggestions. Indeed, the essence of Quality Circles ultimately should be that the Circles really become managers at their own level.

People can only manage if they are fed with information, and the more information which is fed to the Quality Circle from management, management specialists, people in other departments, and so on, the more effective the group will be.

People volunteer for Quality Circles for a variety of reasons and when they arrive for their very first Circle meeting, some of them may have been attracted by the possibility of using the Circle as a means of highlighting the faults of others. For example, they could complain about the quality of the products they receive from the previous departments, and so on. However, when they join the group they realise that this is not at all the purpose of the Circle. They are told that 'whilst we can complain about those other people, we cannot do anything about them'. In almost all cases, there are plenty of problems in their own work area, which can be under their control, and where they can apply their own knowledge and experience to get results.

It is this aspect of Quality Circle activities which gives the members the greatest satisfaction. Because they are not meeting to criticise the work of others, they find that they can make real progress with their projects. When asked what they like most about Quality Circles, one of the most frequent answers comes back: 'We find we can get things done'; 'These problems have been around for years, and now we are making progress'.

The techniques used to identify problems are discussed in Chapters 19 and 20.

8. 'Presenting solutions to management'

This should be the focal point or highlight not only of Circle activities but of all improvement activities around the world. After collecting data, trying out new ideas, and having discussions with all kinds of people, sometimes for weeks, once the members of the Circle have installed their proposal, or are convinced of the value of their improvement, it is necessary to present their ideas to their manager.

The group is usually proud of its achievement and of the teamwork involved. The members will probably have worked very hard, may have spent lunchtimes, evenings or even week-ends working on their ideas if they have been enthusiastic enough, and frequently they are. Consequently, the presentations of their ideas to management are the culmination of all this activity.

It would be unfortunate if they were unable to convince their manager of the benefits of their ideas, simply because they were badly presented or because they were forced to present their ideas in the form of a report which might not be read. Therefore, training newly formed Circles in presentation techniques is extremely important. They may use two or even three meetings to plan and prepare their presentation.

It would be unfortunate too if an unthinking manager, given the enthusiasm and hard work of a Circle, was 'too busy to listen'. It would probably mean the end of the Circle. Therefore, management has an obligation to allow the group to make a formal presentation of its proposal, and to make constructive comments afterwards.

It is important that all members of the Circle participate in the presentation as members of a team. Whilst there is no obligation on management to accept the ideas of a Circle, they must be given serious consideration. If management decides to turn down a proposal, it really owes it to the Circle to give a good explanation for its rejection. Fortunately, Circle projects are usually so carefully thought through that outright rejection by management is quite rare.

9. 'Implementing the solutions themselves'

Because Circles are usually concerned with problems in their own work rather than with those over the fence in the next department, they can often implement the solutions themselves. This is particularly true of housekeeping problems, reduction in waste material, energy saving, and so forth. They also frequently find better ways of doing their own jobs.

For example, workers in the credit control department of a division of a fairly large company formed a Quality Circle. For their first project the members decided to analyse one of their work routines that they found to be particularly tedious. The result was that they reduced the work content by 16 hours per month. In the process of this work they highlighted another problem which, when solved, saved a further 17 hours a month, making a total monthly saving of 33 hours. For their third project, they decided to brainstorm all the possible ways they could make use of the time saved. Someone suggested that they might follow up all invoices with a telephone call. The effect of this idea was to reduce the average credit period by nearly two weeks, thereby making available to that company a considerable sum of money.

CHAPTER 10

ORGANISATIONAL DEVELOPMENT FOR QUALITY CIRCLES – CHANGING THE CULTURE

For Circle-type programmes to be successful it is necessary to prepare a smooth path for their introduction. Failure to do this is almost certain to lead to disappointing results. If Circles are to be a major element in altering the culture of an organisation for the better, then people must be made aware of, and be prepared for such changes. Even in the earliest stages of development, the Quality Circles element of a Total Quality programme will make at least some impact on top management, middle management, supervision, specialists, trade union representatives, and non-Circle members at each location of the organisation where Circles are being established.

Conversely, the attitudes of each of these groups will greatly affect the newly formed Circles whose members will be very sensitive to adverse reactions from their seniors and elected representatives.

Generally speaking it is strongly recommended that the temptation to introduce Quality Circles be resisted until the concept of Total Quality and management-led project teams has been well established, and only then, when it is clear that support from these levels can be assumed. This may require a good deal of prior education in some organisations.

At the time of writing this book, the number of failed Circle programmes in the UK far exceeds the successes, and the failure rate of such programmes may exceed 90 per cent. This is probably true of the whole of the rest of Europe and the USA also. Even in cases where they are successful from an enthusiasm point of view, their achievements are usually far below those of Japanese companies, who in many cases may not have been involved for any longer. There are many companies in Japan who have only introduced Circles recently, although most will have been operating Total Quality amongst managers for many years.

At the same time, the author and his colleagues have trained Circles in over a hundred locations in the UK and have met very few major problems in getting people involved and management supportive. The reasons for this success are twofold:

1. Very careful preparation and involvement of higher levels in the organisation has been made before commencement of this stage of Total Quality.
2. Every key group and level in organisations trained by DHA has been fully briefed on the full implications of Quality Circles prior to their introduction.

Friends from companies trained by DHA frequently say that they have been contacted by various organisations who have attempted to introduce Circles without outside help, and have come unstuck.

In many cases of failure the training has been almost non-existent. 'We showed them a video tape', or 'Our Training Officer gave everyone a talk' are extremely frequent replies to questions about an organisation's preparations. There are also an incredible number of organisations who seem prepared to entrust the introduction of Quality Circles into their companies to self-appointed experts with the weakest of credentials, simply because they are local or inexpensive.

Many of them see Circles as an entity in itself, and have frequently been misled into believing that Quality Circles can by themselves solve the company's problems. It is quite extraordinary that the owners and directors of sometimes quite large companies are prepared to entrust the management of the most profound change they are ever likely to contemplate in their entire careers to an 'expert' who had probably never even heard of Total Quality or its philosophy and who in most cases would be unable to supply a list of satisfied clients, if he were indeed asked.

Even the most expert advice available in the world need not be expensive, and a properly introduced programme will pay for itself over and over again. In fact, some companies go so far as to claim that they could not survive in the face of international competition if they had not introduced Total Quality, and gained the commitment of their workforce with Quality Circle-type activities.

It is better to select a consultancy which is prepared to train the organisation to run its own programme, rather than to use one which wishes to flood the company with consultants, at no mean cost. Transfer of ownership from consultant to client is the critical factor on which competing consultancies should be judged, in addition, of course to their track record.

The current climate of the organisation is a key factor in determining the approach to introduction of Total Quality, and consequently, once the decision has been made to commence a programme, a key consideration is that of culture. Basically there are five different levels of culture (Figure 10.1): the 'culture of the organisation', the 'culture of the industry', the 'national culture', the 'local' or 'regional culture', and the culture of the individual department or section itself, i.e. 'departmental culture'.

Many people believe that culture is cast in tablets of stone, and use this belief as an excuse to avoid attempting change. 'It will never work here', and 'It doesn't suit our culture' are frequently heard comments when Total Quality or Quality Circles are mentioned. To this the response should be 'What will

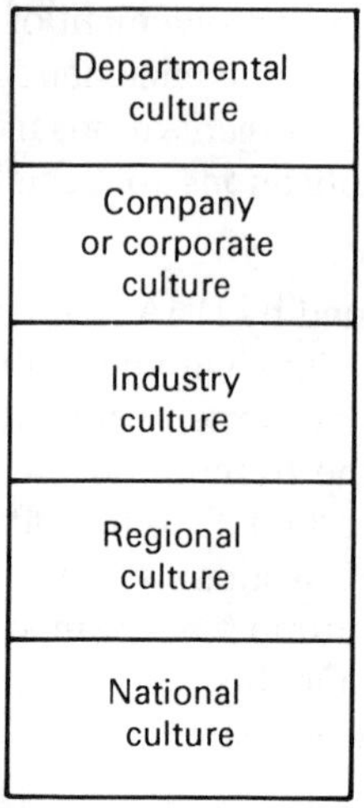

Departmental culture
Company or corporate culture
Industry culture
Regional culture
National culture

Fig. 10.1

happen if we do not?'. The chances are that, without Total Quality, the company will fail. There will be many more companies in trouble, like Ferranti and Jaguar in 1989, before Total Quality has been properly and substantially introduced into industry.

Let us consider national culture first. Of course there are vast cultural differences between Japan and the rest of the world. The Japanese were isolated from the civilised world for over 200 years prior to the Meiji Restoration in 1868; they are one of the few pure mono-culture races left, and their religion, which is a mixture of Buddhism, Confucianism, and Shintoism, also makes them unique. This uniqueness, together with the traditional Japanese culture, is a constant source of fascination to the rest of the world, and stories about the strange customs of the Japanese are constantly distorted to make good entertainment in magazines and on television. All this unfortunately clouds the extremely important question as to whether management concepts which evolved in such a unique culture could possibly have any relevance in another. Unfortunately, it was the belief that this could not be possible that accounted for the long delay in Total Quality being taken seriously around the world, even though its concepts were well known to some people. (The author ran courses on Total Qualityes as far back as 1972: see Figure 10.2).

The reason why Quality Circles do work in non-Japanese companies is not because the concept is cross-cultural. There are many company cultures in which Total Quality and its derivative, Quality Circles, most certainly would not work, but these are not national cultures, they are company created, and they can, and must, be changed. It will not always be easy, but it can be done if the will is there. Survival is a strong motivator, but only if the threat has been properly identified: in the case of McMichael, Sobell, etc. (referred to in Chapter 1), it obviously was not.

SLOUGH COLLEGE OF TECHNOLOGY
DEPARTMENT OF ENGINEERING
QUALITY ASSURANCE

A course of four weekly meetings to consider the concept of a *Total Quality Control* programme. For Managers and Senior Inspectors responsible for the setting and maintenance of quality standards.

Course Details: The course is of four weeks' duration commencing Wednesday, *1st March, 1972*, 3.00 – 5.15 p.m.

Course Fee: £3.00.

Course Lecturer: D. C. Hutchins, C. Eng., M.I.Mech.E., A.M.B.I.M.

Programme:-

1.3.72.   Concept of Total Quality Control
Setting of Design Standards and Specifications.
New design control, in process control, goods inwards control, special process studies.
Despatch and Customer Service.

8.3.72.   Organisation of the Quality Control Department.
Closed loop feedback of management delegation.
Use of relationship charts.
Quality organisation related to size and type of firm.

15.3.72.   Quality Costs
Failure appraisal and prevention.
Minimum overall cost, vendor control and rating, material specifications, calculation of most economic A.Q.L.s for incoming materials.

22.3.72.   Inspection Personnel
Training of Inspectors.
Relation between inspection staff and other personnel.
Role of the supervisor, craftsmanship and indifference theory.

Fig. 10.2

Circles do require certain cultural attitudes to exist in the organisation prior to implementation, after which they will themselves help to create the ultimate cultural values as they become established, and people can see the benefits for themselves.

Not only Quality Circles, but many other aspects of modern Japanese mangement can be introduced unmodified into non-Japanese companies, provided that the company culture is made suitable. Total Quality, and Quality Circles, can only be successfully introduced if the organisation is willing to develop a consensus style of management. The processes of implementation of policy development, policy deployment, and policy control are the most powerful means by which this can be achieved.

Why so many Circle programmes fail

In the West in particular, most organisations have a very individualistic style of management, and operate in a blame culture. In many cases, interdepartmental rivalries are severe and such competition and antagonism between departments or locations is frequently more important in the minds of some managers than the threats from their real competitors in the marketplace. This type of environment is not conducive to Circle activities, and whilst the existence of the Circles themselves will tend to correct this attitude, it is nevertheless necessary for top-level management to make a conscious effort to commence this correction process prior to the introduction of Circles. Implementation of the internal customer—supplier concept, cross-functional project teams, and functional quality teams will go a long way towards avoiding this type of problem.

It is the failure to recognise this necessity that has led to the majority of failed Circle programmes. All too frequently the following scenario takes place: operations manager 'G' has discovered Quality Circles either by attending a seminar, reading an article, or by contact with a colleague in another organisation. The concept appeals to him, and he is faced with three optional strategies:

1. Inform his superior and recommend that the company takes action.
2. Discuss the idea with colleagues at his own level in the hope that they may collectively recommend the concept to top management at a forthcoming management meeting.
3. Regard the concept as a personal opportunity for advancement and, rather than 'give' the idea to others, decide to go it alone and implement the concept in his own department.

Strategy 3 would be extremely unlikely in a Japanese organisation, but may be quite likely in many others, and in fact happens all too frequently.

Let us assume that the operations manager 'G' adopts strategy 3. He will obtain as much information about Circles as possible but will do it in a very low key way in order to avoid alerting others. He is then likely to set up two or three Circles in his section. Before very long one of the Circles will require help or information from another department: let us say Department 'D'. Probably one of the Circle members has a friend in that department, or they meet in the canteen at lunch times. The employee from Department 'D' then begins to co-operate with the Circle, and perhaps carries out one or two tasks to help its members (Figure 10.3).

It will not be long before the manager of Department 'D' discovers what is happening. Given the individualistic or macho style of management mentioned earlier, it is quite likely that manager 'D' does not like manager 'G' and will

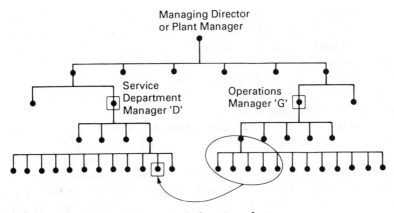

Fig. 10.3 Organisation chart for a single location plant

not want his staff to co-operate in any activities outside the regular scheduled arrangements. Co-operation will be quietly discouraged, with the consequence that the Circle will not get the support that it needs.

This problem will not just occur in one area; it will happen across the entire organisation. The Circle members will quite rightly perceive that they do not have management support and in all probability will disband the Circle. Even if the Circle does not disband, it will probably limp along at such a slow pace that its manager, who was hoping for such big things, will soon come to believe that Circles are not a magic cure after all. He will probably then disband the Circle and subsequently claim, 'We tried it once and it did not work!'. He is unlikely to be keen to make a further attempt. Additionally, he will have another reason for not wanting a further attempt: he will think that the first failure was a reflection on his managerial ability. This could of course be partly true, but really, the failure was due to the culture that existed in the company at the time.

Changing the culture

Far from being static, cultures are in fact in a constant state of change. Whilst cultural change at national or regional level may be a slow process, the rate of change in culture in an organisation can sometimes be quite dramatic. It changes every time a new managing director takes over, particularly if he has a powerful personality. Sir Michael Edwardes made a dramatic impact on British Leyland, as did Ian MacGregor on British Steel. This is not saying that these changes were either good or bad, only that they took place. However, it is unfortunate that such powerful and charismatic leaders are not required to remain in the organisations long enough to see the long-term effects of their actions, as is the case in Japan. This bee-like 'flower to flower' habit which exists in Western organisations puts them at a serious disadvantage to Japan.

Fortunately, the changes necessary to create an environment that will support Quality Circles are readily possible. Of course, they will not happen overnight. Whilst people may change dramatically at a superficial level, some older people will have spent an entire lifetime in their present environment and it will take time for them to become accustomed to a different approach. Scepticism and cynicism resulting from other previous initiatives which have failed will not be helpful, either.

The changes necessary to support a Quality Circle programme must take place both at corporate level and in the way people are managed. It is necessary for corporate management to move towards consensus management: in other words, to develop throughout management a sense of corporate consciousness; to develop a sense of fraternity throughout the organisation so that managers, specialists, and supervisors are mutually supportive rather than antagonistic; to develop a sense of mutual corporate pride, and entrepreneurial drive to promote the success of the whole operation rather than just that of their own departments.

Changing the style of people management

Of equal importance to the problem of interdepartmental rivalry between managers is the problem of management perceiving Circles in their own work area to be a threat to themselves. Some managers may be afraid that the Circles may expose their own weaknesses.

For example, one frequently hears the cynical comment, 'That was a simple problem! You didn't need a Circle to do that! Why didn't you solve the problem yourself?'. Such remarks, if not pre-empted by the preparation of staff at all levels, could be extremely damaging if the manager saw them as criticism of his competence. Even if such attitudes are not stated, given the type of environment they are working in some managers may 'feel' that others are thinking along those lines. This being the case, the manager, who is presumably concerned with his own status in the eyes of others, is unlikely to be over-enthusiastic about a concept that will expose him in this way.

A further potentially equally damaging situation arises after a Circle has completed a successful brainstorming session. Again a question may be prompted: 'How come you have all those problems in your work area? I didn't think you had any problems!' Fortunately, these seemingly intractable problems can be avoided by careful preparation and the prior involvement of the managers in project work concerned with solving the 'management controllable' problems. This will of course be the case if Quality Circles are part of an overall Total Quality strategy.

Management gets results through people!

Prior to the implementation of Quality Circles it is necessary for top management to convince middle management that Circles are not some form of inquisition. Top management must give confidence to both middle management and to direct supervision. They must recognise that of course there are problems in their work area; there are problems in everybody's area, there are problems right across the whole organisation: 'We know that, we accept it, and believe that Quality Circles can help solve them'. If Circles are successful in a given work area, then that work area manager should be congratulated by upper managemention a visible way, because it is obvious that he or she supports the Circles' activities. Support for such activities should be made clear in annual management performance reviews, and be reflected in promotion prospects.

To show them how they affect the performance of their staff, it is necessary to educate managers in the different styles of management and how each of these styles affects the performance of people. Managing people involves three basic factors:

- attitudes
- motivation
- work environment

It is important for managers to realise that they control neither the attitudes of their people nor their motivation. The only factor controlled by management is the environment in which its people work: not noise, smell, and dust, etc., but the environment created by those managers' style.

Management is capable of creating two diametrically opposed managerial styles – authoritarian and participative. Whilst both extremes undoubtedly exist, most managers will be identified as being somewhere between the two. Some may switch from one extreme to the other in different situations. The late Douglas McGregor once summed up these differences when he postulated the theory 'X' and theory 'Y' management concept; the theory 'X' manager is authoritarian and the theory 'Y' manager participative.

The theory 'X' manager will say, 'Work people are lazy, slothful, indolent and inherently work-shy. Therefore I need to use threats, fear, and carrot-and-stick methods to achieve my performance goals'.

The theory 'Y' manager on the other hand will say, 'Work itself is as natural as breathing and sleeping. Man has an innate desire to work, to justify his existence, as part of his social relationship with others in the community, to satisfy his creative desires and to achieve job satisfaction. Therefore, it is necessary for me to make the work of my people rewarding and interesting in such a way that it will give them what they want, which means in turn that they will respond by giving me what I want'.

Quality Circles should be seen by management not just as a problem-solving process, but as a way of creating a theory 'Y' type of environment. If management can accept this principle, then the true nature of Quality Circles is revealed.

Managers must fully understand the importance of the following points:

- The one hour per week is the Circle's hour.
- The Circle's hour is budgeted out on the basis that it allows the members to indulge in those projects that they think are important and not necessarily those which are uppermost in the minds of the manager (the craftsmanship concept).
- Circle meetings should be enjoyable.
- Circles should be given a opportunity to display their creativity, which can be in the form of presentations and access to presentation aids such as view graphs, slides, models, etc.
- Circles should have the opportunity to meet other Circles and exchange ideas.
- Circles should be encouraged to develop a spirit of self-control (the craftsmanship concept – plan, do, check, act).

Management's reward comes from the following:

- Work itself becomes more interesting through greater involvement. Many other problems such as those caused by carelessness, will 'just disappear'.
- An increase in general productivity through higher morale.
- Lower absenteeism because of greater job interest.
- Fewer grievances.
- Greater team spirit.

Quality Circles therefore should really be seen as pure theory 'Y' management.

Top management must convey to middle management that it believes in this approach, and that managers are expected to manage that way because it is the company's policy for them to do so. It is the responsibility of middle management to convey the same attitude to their supervisors, and once this has been achieved, the culture will have been changed totally and irrevocably. However, it is sometimes necessary to use a little theory 'X' to get some theory 'Y'. Remember, in the dynamic organisation managers don't make decisions, they make sure that good decisions are being made.

In one extremely successful company which was trained by DHA, the plant director had a private discussion on the concept prior to a formal presentation to fifty of his senior managers. At the start of the presentation, he said, 'This guy's going to tell you all about participation, and I want you to listen to him, because afterwards we are going to do it!'.

CHAPTER 11

THE FACILITATOR

The appointment of a facilitator will usually be one of the first positive decisions that a company will make, after having decided to implement Total Quality.

Rather than use the term 'facilitator', some companies prefer 'co-ordinator' others 'promoter' or 'organiser' but these terms give a wrong impression of the role. The facilitator does all these things, and in addition he trains, liaises with others, supports, coaches, advises, and consults, and there is no one word which adquately embraces all these activities. To facilitate means to 'make easy' and this is really what the facilitator does. An American once described him as 'the guy with the oil can'!

Given the potential of the Total Quality programme, and the profound effect that it will have on an organisation, it is vitally important to take the selection of facilitators seriously. It is also vitally important to select the right people. In fact experience has shown that the appointment of a facilitator, and the establishment of the Quality Council and voluntary improvement activity steering committees are the three most important and influential factors in determining future success of the programme.

As a rough and ready rule, a facilitator will need to spend about one and a half hours per week on management project teams, and three hours per week per Quality Circle, particularly in the early stages. This means that a single facilitator can handle a maximum of 30 management teams and 15 Quality Circles satisfactorily, given that some of the mature Circles will need less time than the newer ones. In the early stages, however, it might be as well to allow equal time for management teams to ensure that the process is well bedded in, and to allow the facilitators to learn their role.

The facilitator will need to spend some of the available time at the policy-developing Quality Council and steering committee meeting, familiarising himself with his job, discussing project team activities with other managers, and generally 'getting the show on the road', and all of this will also take time.

Part-time facilitators

Sometimes the scale of the programme will not warrant the selection of full-time facilitators, and therefore part-timers will need to be selected. By definition a 'part-time' facilitator is a part-time something else. In those other activities the facilitator will have a boss. That boss will be more concerned with the facilitator's other responsibilities than with the Total Quality programme. There will be many occasions when the pressure of work in such areas will demand the total commitment of the part-time facilitator, and it is extremely likely that these occasions will happen to coincide with a project team or Quality Circle crisis of some kind. Quality Circles particularly often need considerable hand-holding in the early stages, and many will suffer from an initial lack of self-confidence. If the facilitator is frequently absent at this early and critical stage, such confidence as has been developed will quickly be dissipated. This is no time suddenly to realise the problem and then commence a protracted selection procedure for a full-time replacement. It is much better for this to be thought out carefully in advance and for proper decisions to be taken.

Of course, a small company could not justify a full-time facilitator. It probably couldn't afford one even if it were necessary, and it is doubtful whether there would be enough work to fill the time for such an appointment. It is difficult to be specific about the precise size of an organisation that would just be large enough to support a full-time facilitator. This is because there are several factors that need to be considered. However as an approximate guide, the size of the company would normally be somewhere in the region 250–300 employees.

Factors to be considered are:

- number of levels of command
- variety of different skills
- single or multiple location
- degree of participative style within the organisation
- labour relations
- supportive style of management?
- normal day or shift working

If the company is based at a single location and has a short chain of command and a generally supportive management, then a part-time facilitator may be possible, even if the number of employees is slightly higher than 250–300. However, as has already been suggested, it is important not to underestimate the time spent on Quality Circle facilitation in particular, and it would be better to be safe than sorry if doubt exists.

Given that an organisation is unable to justify a full-time facilitator and part-timers are to appointed, the following points should be helpful:

1. First of all estimate carefully the expected time per week to be spent on group activities and make this a clear commitment by senior management. This allocation must be firmly agreed by:

   - the section head for the facilitator's other work
   - the steering committee
   - the facilitator appointed

If group activities prove to require more time than allocated, this additional requirement should be highlighted by the facilitator so that management may make a decision to increase the budgeted time allowance.

2. It is better to have two, or preferably three, part-time facilitators than one. If possible they should be selected from different departments. This will have the advantage that project teams and Quality Circles will be seen as a company-wide programme and not the extension of a single department's influence.

    The main advantage to the teams is the higher probability that at least one of the facilitators will be available when needed. A further advantage can be obtained by carefully choosing other part-time facilitators as the programme grows. Eventually, every manager will become the facilitator of the improvement activities, both voluntary and non-voluntary, in his own area; in other words, facilitating will become just part of normal, everyday management.

3. This is one of the two occasions where the word 'co-ordinator' has some meaning. One facilitator should have higher status than the others, in order to 'co-ordinate' the programme. The term can also be used to describe the senior facilitator in a company with several full-time facilitators.

The selection of a facilitator

As a general rule, it is undesirable to appoint an outside person to the role of facilitator. Whilst advertisements for Quality Circles facilitators do appear in the press, the majority of such advertisements are deliberate head-hunting, often for specific individuals, usually from the same industry and possibly to avoid the use of consultants! However, it is doubtful whether such an individual, new to the company, its culture, and its people, could become sufficiently well accepted by employees at all levels to fulfil the role satisfactorily. Furthermore, the qualities of a facilitator are such that it is very unlikely that an outsider could equal a well selected insider, even when the latter has no previous knowledge of Total Quality concepts. If possible it is much better to make an internal appointment of someone who is liked, trusted, and respected by people at all levels. This usually narrows the field somewhat, but the correct choice really will pay dividends.

Basically, the most important considerations are:

1. enthusiasm (one volunteer is worth 10 pressed men!)
2. influence
3. respect
4. experience in company operations
5. training skills
6. tact
7. full-time availability

1. *Enthusiasm*
The person to be selected must 'want to be' a facilitator, must understand what is required, and see it as a challenge. Although the job is a management appointment the candidate must not be coerced into the job or feel that he or she had moved into a backwater. Such concerns will always be present, and particularly if the company has a reputation for failed initiatives.

2. *Influence*
Good facilitators will be people who have influence on others. This may be a result of their status prior to appointment as facilitators, or their personality. A good facilitator is the kind of person who is not normally brushed aside by an impatient manager, but is likely to be reasoned with in most foreseeable circumstances.

3. *Respect*
A good facilitator is somebody who gets on well with people and is not seen as a political threat. Several good facilitators have been selected from amongst senior managers because they are trusted and respected, are approaching retirement, and have been in the company for many years. They usually see Total Quality as a way of re-establishing some old values which they think have been lost, and accept the challenge of helping to re-establish them in their remaining years of service. Because they will be replaced in their other activities sooner or later, it means that at least they will be able to chaperone their replacement whilst developing the process. One or two companies have even brought senior managers back from early retirement to facilitate the programme.

4. *Experience in company operations*
A good choice of facilitator will be someone who knows the organisation well and is familiar with most departments and their work; who knows where most kinds of information are kept, and who to go to and ask for it.

5. *Training skills*
A considerable proportion of a facilitator's time will be spent in training leaders and in working with them in the training of their teams. Facilitators will also be involved in making presentations to others, and in giving talks to managers and union representatives in other organisations. Occasionally a company may find that the person who is best as a facilitator in all other respects lacks this particular ability. In such cases, many companies have frequently overcome the problem by assigning a training specialist to work closely with the facilitator.

6. *Tact*
Inevitably there will be many occasions when the facilitator will want some information or help for a project team or for Quality Circles at a time when a crisis of some kind is going on. It is important that the facilitator should be

tactful and sensitive to the feelings of those under pressure in such situations. Knowing who to ask and when to ask them is a skill not possessed by everyone, but is essential in a facilitator.

7. *Full-time availability*

This has already been discussed earlier but its importance cannot be over-emphasised. Even if the directly measurable activities appear not to justify fully the time allocation, an enthusiastic facilitator will easily find jobs to do which will more than pay for themselves later. A good facilitator will use every opportunity to write articles for newsletters and noticeboards, communicate with other facilitators, and generally keep up the tempo of the programme. Being visible is vitally important.

In summary a facilitator needs to:

Teach	Support	Consult
Champion	Integrate	Persuade
Lead	Liaise	Use power
Push	Tear apart	
Drive	Listen	

Part-time facilitators in large organisations

Some large organisations have deliberately appointed part-time facilitators even though they are well aware of the time commitment. One large American company developed its programme in this way by introducing facilitator training into its management development programme. It did this initially after it realised that it would eventually have 150 full-time facilitators if it adopted the conventional approach. Now, several years later, every manager is the facilitator of the teams in his own area, and facilitating improvement teams is just part of the way he manages his department.

One or two companies in the UK have begun to develop along the same lines. Experience suggests that whilst this may lead ultimately to a more soundly based programme, there is no doubt that initial progress is slower via this route. Great care must be taken to co-ordinate the programme so that all sections and departments adopt a common policy and do not compete with each other.

It is probably better to start with a full-time facilitator and only develop along the lines outlined under this heading after the initial programme has become well established. This will probably take somewhere in the order of two years.

Facilitator job specification

Because the appointment of facilitators is relatively new, very few organisations will have produced a job specification for the role. The following ideas have now been used, both with and without modification, by a number of client companies of DHA. The specification refers to facilitators in general but in cases where more than one facilitator has been, or is to be, appointed, some points refer principally to the most senior facilitator. The specification is as follows:

(a) Organisation

1. The facilitator will be a member of the Quality Council and the voluntary improvement activities steering committee, and group's main source of information on improvement activities.
2. Preferably the facilitator will report directly to an executive of sufficiently high status, so that he is not exposed to any interdepartmental political defence mechanisms that may exist.
3. Whilst responsible directly to a senior executive, he will be mainly responsible for carrying out the policy decisions of the Total Quality programme which he both advises and serves.

(b) Communications

1. As stated earlier, to facilitate means to make easy and this is probably the best definition of the facilitator's role. Whilst the following tasks will be helpful to ensure the more obvious aspects of this role, it is important that the facilitator should be able to use his own initiative to ensure the success of the company's Total Quality programme within the constraints of that company's corporate goals and objectives.
2. He will keep in regular contact with other facilitators in the company both locally and nationally and, where possible, with facilitators from other organisations.
3. He will be the principal point of on-going contact with the consultants subsequent to the initial training.
4. He will keep abreast of Total Quality and all improvement activity developments nationally, and of the world-wide status wherever possible.

(c) Training

The facilitator will be principally responsible for training new team leaders and working with these leaders in the training of their own groups. During leader training he may call upon additional training skills, both internally or externally, after consultation with the Quality Council or steering committee.

(d) Responsibility

1. His role in team member training is to support and develop the team leader, to build confidence in him, and gradually withdraw from direct involvement with the newly formed group as, in his own judgement, it reaches maturity. Subsequently, he keeps in weekly contact with each team.
2. His long-term relationship with the team is supportive. He is required to ensure the provision of data and help for the team, and arranges for consultative advice for them when requested.
3. In order to make sure that the Total Quality programme develops smoothly, he keeps a close watch on the relationships between team members, and between team members and leaders, non-team members, management, and the trade unions.

(e) Publicity for improvement team activities

1. The level publicity for improvement team activities both individually and collectively is an important factor in the vitality of a Total Quality programme. Visibility for team activities is an important aspect of recognition, and a good facilitator will always be looking for the best ways of achieving this.
2. In-house magazines, news sheets and items in journals all have a place in Total Quality development. The facilitator should encourage these activities as much as possible.
3. Management presentations are perhaps the most important form of recognition, and the facilitator should always be prepared to help and advise the team at this stage in its activities.
4. Mutual visits to other companies may be worth while from time to time. These are normally organised by the facilitator.

(f) Threats to a Total Quality programme

The facilitator should always be on the lookout for signs of trouble. Many problems, if identified early enough, can be dealt with on the spot either by discussion with team members or with members and their managers. More deep-rooted problems, or those involving other departments, are sometimes best tackled after consultation with the Quality Council or the steering committee, and the facilitator should use his judgement as to when this is necessary.

(g) Total Quality programme development

As a Total Quality programme develops, it will occasionally be necessary to repeat some of the early expositions of the concept to managers and union officials – both internal and external - and occasionally in other situations.

It would be worth while for the facilitator to develop visual aids to make such presentations effectively. If a visual aids department exists within the company, the preparation of well-thought-out OHP transparencies or 35 mm slides, professionally produced, will greatly assist in such presentations.

CHAPTER 12

THE ROLE OF TOP MANAGEMENT IN QUALITY CIRCLES

The visible and real support of plant or corporation top management is essential to the success of Quality Circles and all forms of voluntary improvement activity. Circles are only part of Total Quality and there is little evidence to suggest that Circles can even survive, let alone realise, their true potential in the absence of a programme which is fully supported by all levels from the top downwards.

Top management's role in Quality Circles has eight vital aspects:

1. establishment of the overall vision of corporate policy and the creation of the corporate plan, with clear reference to the role of Quality Circles and voluntary improvement activities
2. setting corporate goals and objectives to which people can relate
3. operating policy deployment and policy control
4. management commitment and visible involvement
5. allocation of resources
6. setting up the means for monitoring results
7. auditing the entire Total Quality process at all levels, including voluntary improvement activities
8. visible active support and encouragement

This chapter is intended to give guidance to top management on how this role is fulfilled, if the goals of Total Quality are to be realised.

1. Establishment of corporate policy and corporate plan

Before any organisation can make the final decision to go ahead with the Quality Circles aspect of Total Quality, top management must first of all be certain that it actually intends to proceed, and that it intends to do so continuously, without reservation. This may sound obvious, but it is surprising how many top management teams think that they only have to give the OK for Circles to take place, and then take no further interest. Such programmes always end in failure. Quality Circles are not a form of perpetual motion.

Even in Japan, there is very considerable evidence of direct top management support (perhaps this should have read 'particularly in Japan'!).

Different managers may have a different perspective of what Quality Circles really are, and it is essential that these differences are identified and resolved. These may include differences as to:

- when to start
- where to start
- how many Circles to start with
- what they actually intend to achieve through the programme and why they wish to start

The answers to these questions *must* be part of the overall Total Quality plan, and the decision as to when, where, and how to start Quality Circles must be an integral feature of the process of involving all levels in policy deployment. This can only be a collective decision of the full board of directors.

The most likely reason for starting a Quality Circle programme is to help make the company or organisation better at what it is doing: more successful, and more profitable in accordance with the requirements of the owners, whether the organisation is state-owned or private. It must be believed that Circles will help achieve these objectives and the consensus support of all directors must be received, and be seen to be received, before the process of informing others in the organisation is commenced.

2. Setting corporate goals and objectives

The policy statement is really a statement of intent. It is necessary to be more specific in relation to each function and department, and so goals and objectives for each must be determined. Ideally, as we proceed downwards through the organisation and each level of management these goals and objectives should be more and more detailed. Top management is responsible for estab-

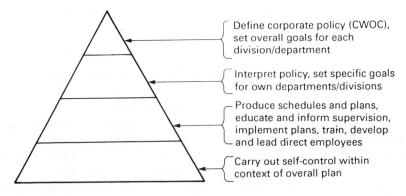

Define corporate policy (CWOC), set overall goals for each division/department

Interpret policy, set specific goals for own departments/divisions

Produce schedules and plans, educate and inform supervision, implement plans, train, develop and lead direct employees

Carry out self-control within context of overall plan

Fig. 12.1 The development of responsibility

lishing the overall policy, but it is the responsibility of senior management to interpret that policy in relation to its own department or division. Each subsequent level downwards should conduct the same operation all the way through to the direct employee, as described in earlier chapters.

When this has been completed, the resulting goals and target proposals should be resubmitted upwards and re-evaluated at each level. Finally, the aggregate of these detailed appraisals will become the corporate goals for the coming year.

The responsibility for achieving these goals and targets should ideally rest within the line management structure rather than being assigned to the specialist support functions. These functions should be developed to fulfil a consultancy relationship with line management which should retain ultimate responsibility (see Figure 12.1).

3. Operating policy deployment and control

We saw in Chapter 4 that once the top management had identified goals and targets with their appropriate success criteria, these needed to be shared with the next layer of management and so devolved through the entire company structure. We also saw that for each level a feedback loop to the level above existed. This loop is referred to as policy control and enables the checking of actual progress against targets and goals set.

4. Management commitment

This is a favourite term amongst management consultants, but its meaning is rarely, if ever, explained. Of course, every programme requires management commitment, and in terms of Quality Circles, it refers to the visible interest in and awareness of the activities of all levels of staff and management relating to Total Quality. Undoubtedly, the most successful programmes are those where the managing director and other directors take an active long-term interest. They attend meetings, raise questions about Circles at management meetings, and ask to sit in at Circle presentations.

In one large company the Chairman told the facilitator, 'If a lack of resources ever impedes the continued development of Quality Circles, you only have to ask'. This was a real shot in the arm for that company's Circles programme, which happens now to be one of the best in the UK.

In another company of international proportions the managing director of the entire operation attended the first Circle presentation in the organisation, at one of its many locations. Afterwards he wrote a personal letter to all the Circle members individually, congratulating them on a job well done, and inviting them to make a video tape of their project. Imagine the effect that this had on the small group who were carrying out printed circuit board assembly work!

Management commitment at the highest level can have a great influence on managers at lower levels, particularly if some of them are reluctant to support the programme. In such cases, the evident enthusiasm of the line manager's report or that of higher management can be very persuasive.

5. Allocation of resources

Resource considerations for Quality Circles can be listed under four headings:

- cost
- manpower
- facilities
- materials and equipment

Cost

Contrary to many people's impression, the introduction of Quality Circle and voluntary improvement programmes should not be expensive, but neither is it free. A good consultant should train a company to build its own programme rather than come in and run it for them. All being well, his total fee is likely to be more than recovered during the first few months of operation, but this cannot of course be guaranteed. This is because Circles do not necessarily start to work immediately on cost-reduction problems. Over the course of a year, many projects will have saved money, and it is usual for the programme to show a benefit: cost ratio of approximately 3 to 1 or better in the first year, and this will improve constantly in subsequent years. (Philips GmbH claimed at the European Organisation for Quality Conference held in Vienna in September 1989 that Quality Circles produce a yield of over 17:1 benefit to cost ratio in that company.)

In addition to deciding the resources to be budgeted for the initiation of a Circle programme, there will also be maintenance and development costs, and a policy decision will be needed to determine how any savings made by the Circles will be used. This latter aspect was covered more fully in Chapter 7. The most important costs to be be considered are:

- consultancy fees
- time lost during training
- facilitator's salary (see Chapter 11)
- steering committee meeting time (see Chapter 17)
- cost of new equipment
- cost of training aids
- cost of Circle meeting time
- budget for Circle projects
- allowance for motivational activities (see Chapter 18)

Manpower

The only additional manpower requirement for the introduction of a Circle programme should be the appointment of the facilitator; the implications of choosing full or part-time facilitators were fully discussed in Chapter 11. In a larger company, further facilitators may be required. As a general rule, one facilitator can adequately support about fifteen Circles once the programme is under way. In some cases the facilitator may be supported by a member of the training department, but this is unlikely to strain existing resources.

(Of course, facilitators will also be required for the mandatory improvement programme.)

Facilities

Meeting rooms for the Circles, free from distractions, are the most important consideration. Initially, this aspect is unlikely to cause problems when there are only three to five Circles, but later on extra facilities may be required.

In the Wedgwood factory in Staffordshire the programme grew so quickly that at the end of the first year there were approximately 70 Circles, which used up all the meeting room facilities. Such was the commitment of management that it built a special Quality Circle centre with a number of new meeting rooms, to enable the continued expansion of the programme.

Quality Circles need some storage facilities such as cabinets, lockers, cupboards, etc., to keep their worksheets and materials. Sometimes, when they are collecting samples of some feature they are studying, they may even need a small room in which to keep their materials, where they are unlikely to be disturbed by others.

Materials and equipment

Circles need very little in the way of equipment and many companies will already have most of the necessary item, which include:

- flip charts – very popular in Circle activities
- carousel slide projector
- tape recorder/player with synchro pulse to connect to projector
- overhead projector

6. Setting up the means for monitoring results

Monitoring a Circle programme at regular intervals gives lower levels of management the clearest possible indication of the importance attached to

Circles by their superiors. A Circle programme can be monitored by the following parameters:

- cost : benefit ratios
- quality improvements
- productivity improvements
- absenteeism
- grievances
- morale – attitude surveys
- sick leave
- accidents/safety
- energy saving
- waste reduction
- inventory control
- schedule improvements
- housekeeping
- timekeeping

and possibly others relating to specific industries.

It must be understood that whilst the overall cost : benefit ratio is an important consideration in assessing whether Quality Circle activities are generally of value to the organisation, individual Circles must not be compared with each other on that basis.

At Circle member level, the most crucial consideration is the level of morale both in the Circle and in the section generally. If an individual Circle appears to be making large financial savings, this should obviously be recognised, but no more than other, less tangible forms of improvement. They should also be attributed to the Circle programme as a whole, since without the existence of the other Circles, these savings would not be achieved. In any case, a circle in one area just by the sheer value of new materials may be able to save more than the entire budgets of some other departments.

The report which monitors the programme will usually be prepared by the facilitator, and endorsed by the steering committee prior to submission to top management. This is likely to be an annual activity, but in some cases may be six-monthly.

7. Auditing

In Japan the annual audit by the company president of every activity within the scope of Total Quality is an essential ingredient in the success of the concept. Not only does it give satisfaction to top management that its policies are being carried out and are working, but it also demonstrates to staff at all levels that top management is not only interested in, but thoroughly understands what is going on. Top management may also instruct the finance department to make an independent audit of cost achievement claims so that all measures of Circle activities are impartially monitored. This will reduce the likelihood of one of the biggest problems in Circle activities – the Circles race!

This is particularly a problem in large multi-site operations. Plant 'A' may justly claim, say, 30 Circles. At Plant 'B', in order to give a god impression, a claim of 40 Circles may be made when in fact it has fewer. This could also apply to claims of savings. One plant makes one claim, which the second plant feels compelled to upstage. Eventually, this rivalry may develop to such an extent that the programme becomes a tissue of lies, and eventually the entire programme is discredited. The independent audit will reduce the likelihood of such problems.

8. Support

Suspending meetings

Occasionally, production pressures and other problems may cause some managers to be sensitive about the time being spent on Circle activities. There may be occasions when there is a desire to suspend such activities. It is on occasions such as this that the support of top management will be crucial. Suspension of meetings should only be advised in the most extreme circumstances. Usually a Circle will volunteer to meet in its own time, if this will help to overcome some crisis in the department. Even in Japan there is much variation from company to company on these issues, based on practical considerations.

Management musical chairs

Direct top management support is also vital in multi-site operations. If management at group level is not aware of Total Quality activities at each location, or does not take an active interest, an otherwise excellent programme can be disastrously affected if the general manager of the location is changed, and the new appointee shows less committment to the concept, – which is frequently the case if the concept of Quality Circles was not part of his selection criteria. In order to make an impression on the balance sheet, he may decide to curtail Circle activities, particularly if he is unaware of any support for the programme at group headquarters. This problem unfortunately occurs all too frequently in many companies which had previously been developing otherwise excellent programmes.

CHAPTER 13

THE ROLE OF MIDDLE MANAGEMENT IN QUALITY CIRCLES

The attitude of middle or line management towards Quality Circles and other forms of voluntary improvement activity is critical. The vitality of individual Circles will frequently be a direct reflection of the relationship between the manager and the Quality Circles in his section or department.

Initially, because a Circle programme is normally only started in a small way with three to five Circles, it is unlikely that every manager will be affected. When managers have been briefed on Quality Circles, a variety of attitudes will become evident. Usually, if the initial briefings are carried out success-fully, there will be a number of managers who are likely to respond by making such comments as, 'I think it's a great idea, pity we didn't think of it twenty years ago', and so on. It is *strongly* recommended that the initial Circles are formed in departments led by such managers. 'Start where the grass is greenest' is a good maxim. Supportive departmental managers are essential to the success of a Circle programme.

Once the early Circles have been established, all being well there should be notable achievements which will not go unnoticed by other managers. Eventually, some of the initially more negative managers will request Circles to be started in their work areas. Of course, there may be some who will never wish to start and this soon becomes obvious. Such hardened attitudes will require decisions to be made as to whether the future of the company can be allowed to remain in the hands of such people!

Middle management support

Enthusiastic middle managers will want to know how they can best help the Circles in their areas. In the early days of Quality Circles in the UK it was thought that the manager should keep well away from the Circle's activities until they requested an opportunity to make a presentation. However, ex-perience has shown this to be wrong. Provided that the manager does not actually 'interfere' in the Circles' activities, or attempt to steer them forcibly in one direction or another, a healthy interest can be of great benefit. Circles like to know that their manager is interested in their work.

The manager must always be aware that the ultimate object of Quality

Circles is to develop a 'self-control' working environment and must always remember the following golden rules (some of which have been mentioned earlier):

- The Circle selects it own problems (the craftsmanship concept again).
- The one hour per week is the 'Circle hour', and the way the hour is used is at members' discretion. Management must not appear too concerned about the total time a Circle spends on a project, although discipline should be strong to ensure that meetings do not last longer than the allotted 1 hour. Of course Circles can, and frequently, do meet outside worktime if they so wish.
- Management's 'pay-off' comes in the other 38 or 39 hours of the week.
- Circle meetings should only be postponed in the most exceptional circumstances, and preferably only after discussion with the higher level of management, or with the steering committee.
- Individual members, including the leader of the Circle, should not be prevented from attending a meeting, except in the most exceptional circumstances. If this is absolutely essential, it may be preferable to rearrange the meeting time in order to give all members an opportunity to attend. This is best done in co-operation with the team members.
- The time of Circle meetings should be mutually agreed between the manager and the Circle and should occur at the least inconvenient time in relation to the work of the department.
- Wherever possible, it is preferable for Circle meetings to take place at the same time and same day of the week. The day then becomes identified as 'Circle Day' and people are more likely to plan other activities to avoid this time. People are also less likely to forget to attend, which sometimes happens in other cases.

There is nothing wrong in the manager 'looking in' occasionally during the Circle meeting. It shows a healthy interest and the Circle will usually be pleased to see him. Sometimes the manager may have some information relating to the subject matter being discussed by the group, and giving this information to the Circle directly is probably one of the strongest indications of support that can be shown.

Sometimes the manager may wish the Circle to look at a problem that affects the department and is of great concern to him. Provided that the reasons for this are explained to the group, and that its members are not pressurised to do so, the Circle will usually be flattered by such a request and will generally respond positively. However, if it happens too frequently the Circle may feel that the manager is attempting to 'take over' the Circle.

Relationships with other Circles

A manager's main concern will most probably be with the Circles in his own department. Sometimes, perhaps frequently, they will need help, advice, or information from specialists or people in other departments. Co-operation between managers in cross-functions will greatly help in this situation, and therefore managers who are keen to promote Circle activities would do well to foster good relationships with their colleagues. Conversely, Circles in other areas may require help and information from that particular manager's department, and his attitude towards such requests will greatly affect the support given by others to his own group's activities.

Voluntary management teams

To be pedantic, voluntary management teams fall outside the definition of Quality Circles, and really should be referred to simply as voluntary improvement activities.

Some companies are beginning to realise that voluntary improvement activities need not extend only to direct employees: such groups can and do work well at both management and supervisory levels. Voluntary teams of specialist trouble-shooters may be referred to as project groups.

There are now also many voluntary improvement teams of supervisors. Voluntary management teams have several advantages:

- By working in the same way as Circles, managers can more fully appreciate the type of relationship which develops amongst the members, and tackle the problems they want to resolve.
- Communications across functions may be improved, and lead to greater co-operation.
- Managers are more likely to develop a 'corporate spirit' rather than a 'departmental spirit' when cross-functional voluntary teams are formed.
- Development of a consensus style of management is encouraged by these activities.
- They are a very effective way of solving management problems identified by the managers, in addition to those determined by the Quality Council as part of the mandatory improvement activities.

Management's role in people development

People are the most important asset of any organisation, even when it is highly automated. However dull and boring a person's job may be, and however alienated people may feel, they have a certain loyalty to their work and to their organisation. When they meet their friends socially outside work they often boast about the company's products or its reputation, and they want to be involved. A good manager should recognise this asset and build on it. Quality Circle activities are an opportunity for them to do so, and the following guidelines are intended to help managers who wish to get the most from their people. The most important considerations for middle management may be put under the four headings:

- responsibility
- recognition
- job rotation
- education and training

Responsibility

The principle of *self-control* really means that people must be offered responsibility, and experience indicates that they will generally accept it. Giving a person responsibility, however small it may be, is recognition of that person's talents and ability. It engenders trust and loyalty, and is fundamental to the re-establishment of the craftsmanship mentality.

Taylorism, discussed earlier, denies people the opportunity to take responsibility. By breaking jobs down into their smallest elements and elevating problem solving to a management specialist, responsibility is removed from individuals and they become mere extensions of their machines or desks. A massive contrast is created between their lives in and out of work. Outside work they have a great deal of responsibility. They may be husbands or wives, they may have families. From their income they have to manage their own economy, pay the rent or mortgage, save up for holidays and Christmas, obtain passports, repay hire-purchase debts, and raise their children. Most people are perfectly capable of doing this. They maintain the same standards as the rest of their community, and are trusted and respected by their friends. They may have hobbies and pastimes, where they have developed considerable skill or acquired considerable knowledge; they may even be regarded as experts. They may be members of some local committee, where their ideas are listened to and acted upon, but the tragedy is that most of them will be required to leave their brains at the gate when they walk into work in the morning and pick them up again when they leave at night. No one asks them anything, no one involves them in anything, and it is no wonder that they switch off mentally. When this happens, their performance becomes purely mechanical. In some cases, as mentioned earlier, the enormous boredom may be so great that they make distractions to break down the monotony. In the extreme, this may even result in the deliberate sabotage of the company's products.

Although this problem is normally identified with manufacture, it does not just relate to production workers doing repetitive tasks, it relates to all forms of work where the individual is confined to a detailed job specification. The indifference often shown by counter clerks in banks, airlines, shops and hotels is indicative of a similar problem in service industries. The sequence may be longer in some jobs than others but it is still, nevertheless, a sequence.

Once the sequence has been repeated several times it can contain little interest, regardless of its length.

The theory 'Y' manager described in Chapter 10 will continually be aware of the dangers of this, and should always be seeking means by which the problems of boredom, fatigue, carelessness due to low job interest, and sullen attitude can be overcome. Many can be significantly reduced through Circle activities provided that the ultimate goal is self-control.

Deliberately feeding Circles with management information such as quality control data sheets, output targets, variance analysis data, and so forth, not only indicates trust and respect from the manager, it also enables the Circle to appreciate management's dilemma, and is far more likely to lead the Circle towards projects concerned with improving the performance of the section.

Recognition

This is one of the most important forms of motivation. A golfer would derive little satisfaction from his first 'hole in one' if there was no one there to witness the event. This is no less true of people at work. People want to be listened to. They like their manager to show an interest in their ideas. It is particularly true of Quality Circles. Good theory 'Y' managers will not only take a keen interest in the projects of their Circles, they will also be prepared to make the time available to attend their Circle presentations. They should see these events as being amongst the most important highlights of the Circle process. The Circles will be proud of their achievements, and will want to tell their story. Their own manager, to them at least, will be the most important person in the audience.

Job rotation

Flexibility at the workplace is a great advantage to management and this may be developed through Quality Circle-type activities. During crises, or when a key individual is absent, it is obviously an advantage to be able to switch people around. Of course, in areas where demarcation problems exist, such flexibility is not always possible, but much can be achieved in many situations, and this problem is in any case far less severe than in the 1970s and early 1980s.

Flexibility is not just an opportunity for management. It should be seen as an advantage for everyone. Whilst undoubtedly there are some people who are content to perform a single operation repeatedly, this is not true of most. People like variety, and a change of activity creates renewed interest. People also like to feel that they have acquired a broader range of skills. They feel more useful. Some organisations recognise this and even award certificates for attainment which are displayed in the work area. Demarcation loses jobs, it does not create them. It is the flexible organisations which are winning the orders, and the demarcation-ridden organisations which are going to the wall.

Job rotation gives opportunities for Quality Circles, particularly where the repetitive nature of work creates problems of carelessness, fatigue, boredom, etc., and at the same time gives greater emphasis to the idea of self-control. For example, in a Japanese factory, a shop full of employees was involved in the assembly of portable radio cassette players. The shop was working on the conveyor-belt principle, with six rows of operatives in lines which ran the length of the floor. The majority of the operatives were involved in the hand insertion of components into printed circuit boards which were the size of an A4 sheet of paper.

During our tour of the work area, some members of the author's study group became concerned that the operatives appeared so intent on their operations that not one of them even appeared to be aware of our presence, and they were working at a very high rate. This was somewhat unnerving to those accustomed to repetitive work in the UK. There, not only would the pace have been slower, but the operators would have taken at least a passing interest in the visitors.

After the tour the study group tackled a senior manager about this observation. At first the manager could not understand why the group should be surprised at this apparent level of job interest. Than he said, 'They did not look up because they were interested in their work'. The group asked how they could possibly be interested in such repetitive tasks, and he replied, 'Ah, well, that is because they belong to Quality Circles. In their Circles' activities they will discuss problems relating to monotony, boredom, fatigue, human unreliability, mistakes, etc., and will seek to reduce them. Although you saw them performing specific operations during the walk around, they would not perform the same task throughout the day. Most probably, an individual would be doing hand insertion of components for approximately one hour, then switch to visual inspection for one hour, then a different assembly operation, then another, making four separate tasks altogether. They would then repeat the same tasks in the second half of the shift. This arrangement of tasks would not be determined by either the manager or supervisor but by the operatives themselves, in order to attain the best results possible. In other words, they were setting their own goals! This is the ultimate in self-control!'.

This form of self-control would of course be impossible if departmental management had not first accepted the responsibility for training the operatives in these diverse skills.

Education and training

It should be the responsibility of each manager to identify the education and training needs of his department in order to ensure that the staff are adequately prepared to perform their tasks in a satisfactory manner and to relate to the goals of the company. This aspect becomes even more important if the principle of self-control is to be realised.

Western organisations focus on task-related training, but ignore education altogether. It is not surprising therefore that people feel remote and isolated form the corporate spirit of the enterprise. Japanese companies concentrate cosiderable resources on education which is designed to capture the hearts and minds of their people.

Department education and training programmes should be designed to:

- Increase task-related skills
- Improve abilities to identify, analyse, and solve problems
- Increase confidence to accept responsibility
- Build teams
- Develop leadership
- Create a sense of corporate identity/loyalty, through sharing of goals, targets, performance, and the performance of key competitors
- Encourage self-improvement and self-development, and an understanding of the PDCA cycle

Some people may not immediately realise the importance of each of the items listed in situations where people are doing highly repetitive, low-skill operations, such as packaging items into cartons, etc. In fact these aspects of education and training are even more important in such situations. The people concerned are probably no less intelligent than others involved in very much more demanding activities, and something needs to be done to occupy their minds. It was the realisation of this fact which was one of the critical factors which inspired the Japanese to develop Quality Circle-type activities in the first place. In the words of Professor Ishikawa, 'Quality begins and ends with education and training'.

Improvement in ability to identify, analyse, and solve problems

A Quality Circle is only as good as the techniques it has been trained to use. The basic techniques which will enable a work group to get started in Circle activities are outlined in Chapters 19 and 20. However, these should be seen as foundation techniques and not as the ultimate development. If Quality Circles are working properly, they should be part of a continuous development process. Additional techniques can be learned in two ways:

1. Formal training through courses arranged by the company.
2. Self-development through reading, evening classes, or correspondence courses.

Formal training needs must be identified by departmental managers, budgeted for, and included as part of the overall company training programme.

Self-development of Circles is an ongoing process, which will happen to some extent regardless of supervisory or managerial input. However, there are several ways in which this can be both accelerated and encouraged.

Managers can make books, periodicals, and technical journals available, and other facilities so that Circles can make contact with Circles in other organisation, for mutual exchanges of ideas. Managers can sanction any or all of the following:

- Correspondence with institutions and learned societies
- Attendance at relevant seminars when the work schedule permits.
- Participation in conventions for Circle leaders and members, such as those organised by the National Society of Quality Circles.
- Mutual visits to other organisations supportive of Circle activities.
- In-company seminars.
- Visits to Japan! Seriously, several companies are already doing this. The Japanese have been sending Circle leaders on overseas visits for over two decades.

All these activities will tend to increase the scope of Circles, heighten their enthusiasm, and encourage others to participate in such activities.

Increase confidence to accept responsibility

The more responsibility can be delegated to others, and provided recognition is given for their achievements, the greater will be their respect and loyalty. Responsibility equates to trust and respect, and it is rare that a normal person would ever violate trust. The more scope a manager affords to his Quality Circles, the greater will be their satisfaction, and their respect for that manager.

Of course the devolution of responsibility must be a gradual process, and measured against the confidence of the individuals concerned. Too much devolution too soon can have the adverse effect if the group lacks confidence. Part of the manager's task in Quality Circles development, then, is always to seek ways of increasing the group's self-confidence. The best way this can be done is by thanking the members and congratulating them on their achievements.

Team building

By their nature, Quality Circles are a team-building process. Where the department includes people who are not members of the Circle, this may present a problem. During the training of Circles, Circle members must be very carefully schooled to regard themselves as 'their section's Circle' and not an élite group in the work area.

This problem is made worse when the manager attempts to use undue influence on the Circle to 'tackle his problems'. The Circle will then more than likely be accused by the non-Circle members of being 'management's favourites'.

However, if the manager fully understands the true nature of Circles, not only is this unlikely to happen, but he can help develop a team spirit throughout the department. If policy deployment is introduced there will be no need for any form of coercion to tackle company problems. The teams will choose them themselves.

The Circle should be encouraged to solicit ideas from non-Circle members, ask for their ideas about possible projects, and involve them in data collection.

Some departmental managers encourage Circles to make their presentations to the rest of the department prior to their presentation to management. On such occasions the non-members may make constructive suggestions on how the presentation may be improved. It may even encourage them to form another Circle, if the existing group has ten or twelve members. There is nothing wrong with having more than one Circle in the same department. They will not conflict with each other. Normally, they will be mutually self-supportive and greatly enhance the co-operative spirit of the section.

Leadership development

During the many years of Taylorised management, the role of the supervisor or management-appointed group leader was in many cases seriously eroded. Quality Circle activities can provide an opportunity not only to re-establish the leader's role, but also to develop leadership and identify future leaders.

A good supervisor acting as Circle leader will quite often rotate the leadership of the group meetings. Not only does this allow the official leaders to think up their own ideas, but it also makes the group more self-reliant. Such a leader may eventually allow the group to run itself whilst a new group is formed elsewhere in the section. The leader will then oversee both groups.

Managers must be keenly aware of the importance of leadership development amongst supervisors and should take every opportunity to encourage their supervisors to take up places in corporate education and training schemes if full self-control is ever to be achieved.

Creation of corporate identity/corporate loyalty

Loyalty to one's family, group, community, or organisation is a natural human characteristic which is latent in most people almost regardless of the way they are treated. Of course, if someone is treated badly or feels unloved, such loyalty is likely to be vigorously suppressed. The importance of loyalty, or the means of achieving it, is often overlooked in organisations, which is surprising because the visible expressions of loyalty by staff are probably the most impressive features of a successful department or organisation.

This is especially important at the point of interface between the supplier and the customer. At company level, the entire status of an organisation in the marketplace can be influenced in many cases more by the visible signs of loyalty of company employees than by the quality of the product or service itself. Loyalty breeds confidence. Loyalty usually equates with pride, and the desire to do a good job.

Of course, one individual manager cannot by himself change the corporate image of the entire operation, but neither can any other on his own. Top management can obtain the loyalty of its senior managers, and the senior managers can obtain the loyalty of their subordinates, and so on down the line. At departmental level, therefore, it is the responsibility of the manager to obtain the loyalty of his own staff within the context of the organisation as a whole.

Managers may consider this aspect to be less important when their section or department does not interface with the user, but this is wrong. Management should instil in the minds of its people the concept of the triple role, described in Chapter 2. One way is to use the perception that the next downstream operations are the customers; we, in turn, are the customers of upstream operations. Those departments that are able to generate this sense of pride and loyalty will find that it becomes infectious in both directions. Not only will the section be more appreciated by the following departments, it will also find that many of the problems it is confronted with among its own suppliers will simply disappear.

Eventually, the organisation will become the sum total of the collective effort of all of its employees. Theory 'Y' management is the only way to achieve that loyalty.

Self-improvement and self-development

Members of staff collectively and individually should be given every encouragement to continue their own development, to read books, attend evening classes, even in non-vocational activities. All these possibilities tend to give confidence, and low self-confidence is one of the biggest problems hampering organisational performance today.

A manager should encourage this form of development and take an interest in his people's attainments.

CHAPTER 14

THE ROLE OF THE SUPERVISOR

A major deficiency of Taylorism emerges when the role of the supervisor under the craft regime is compared with the 'Taylor' approach. Under the craft regime, the supervisor or foreman was usually the leading craftsman in the group. Such was the prestige of the leading hand, supervisor, or foreman in the craftsman age that some people considered themselves fortunate just to live in the same street as the leader.

Under the Taylor system this perception was destroyed. In fact, in the 1950s and 1960s, at the height of the 'work-study' era, many companies sought to eradicate the supervisor altogether by the widespread use of direct payment-by-result schemes. The advocates of these payment methods frequently identified the reduced need for direct supervision as one of the principal advantages of Taylorism. The emergence of the specialist as a problem solver also served to accelerate this process. Whilst there has been some levelling off of this effect in the past few years, there has nevertheless been a tendency in the past two or three decades to concentrate fewer resources on supervisory development. This in turn has reduced the influence and respect of the supervisor and increased dependency on the specialist's technical and other skills.

In ideal organisations, there is a smooth flow of communications from the top to the bottom of the organisation through the line management structure. Corporate policy, objectives, targets, and goals should be established at the top level, but the responsibility for achieving those goals should rest with line management supervision and with workpeople in the various departments and segments of the organisation, as described in earlier chapters.

The specialists should not be a level in that line structure, but separate and parallel to it and acting in a consultancy role (Figure 14.1).

In reality, the specialist must not replace the supervisor, because the specialist has company-wide responsibilities, and has a separate reporting structure; therefore dependency on a specialist will always create a breach in the communication path between management and workpeople. This breach must be eliminated at the same time as Quality Circle activities are introduced.

It can readily be seen that the supervisor must be a key part of the management chain, and is the main link between management and direct employees (Figure 14.3). It is therefore an important feature of self-control by work groups that they focus much of their education and training effort through the supervisory level of management.

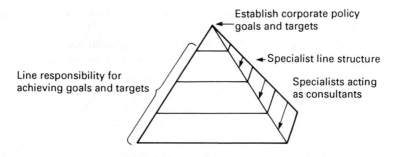

Fig. 14.1

Fig. 14.2

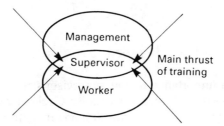

Fig. 14.3

Self-control

In the Total Quality organisation, the training and education of supervisors and Quality Circles is a continuous, life-time process. To reiterate Professor Ishikawa's maxim, 'Quality begins and ends with education'. In the Taylor system managers are responsible for learning new techniques and keeping abreast of the latest ideas. In the Total Quality organisation the managers must give their people the same opportunity.

Self-control is a revolutionary idea for those organisations that have previously regarded task training as a 'one-off', never to be repeated activity. Whilst in some such cases refresher training may be given, this is usually rare. However, it is essential for training to be regarded as a continuous development process if the potential offered by self-control is to be fully realised. Training in more and more advanced techniques should be planned to take place as needs demand.

The process of allowing individuals to make presentations of their achievements in work-related problem-solving training exercises is not only a very effective way of gaining confidence, and improving communication, it is found that by allowing supervisors to present their achievements to each other, a very effective means of cross-fertilisation of ideas is created as part of a continuous self-improving mechanism, and is also part of the recognition process.

Supervisors should not only be encouraged to present their achievements at in-house seminars, they should also be given the opportunity to make their presentations at public functions. These functions may be attended by other supervisors and foreman from across industry who attend both as recognition for their own achievements, and to learn from the achievements of others. In Japan this had become a nationwide movement by 1960 and was supported by a magazine *Gemba to QC* (later renamed *FQC/QC for the Foreman*). This periodical was designed both for foreman and for people in the workshop.

This development has proved to be enormously successful, and that supervisors developed to take managerial responsibility is an impressive advantage. However, it cannot be over-stressd that the problems associated with low morale at the workplace will remain if the opportunity does not also pass down to direct employees.

The supervisor as team leader

Recognition of the importance of the supervisor's role in management in Japan preceded the development of Quality Circles by at least ten years. During that period, the Japanese developed an extremely sophisticated approach to supervisory development which has no equivalent anywhere in the world.

By the time Quality Circles emerged, Japanese supervisors were highly trained, and were better educated and trained managers than many people in non-Japanese societies who are currently two or three levels higher. Consequently, Quality Circles were almost a natural extension of this development. Obviously, it would be unrealistic to expect non-Japanese organisations to spend ten years reproducing this same development before commencing Circle activities. Fortunately that is not necessary.

It has been found that Circles can be formed successfully even in cases where the supervisor or group leader has received no formal management education and training whatsoever prior to the decision to commence Circle activities. This is provided that eduction, training, and development is conducted in parallel with Circle activities. These must never be overlooked. If supervisory development does not take place, it is fairly certain that the Circle programme will suffer, if not fail completely, and some form of supervisory development will always prove to be an extremely worthwhile investment provided that it is done properly.

We shall now look at the role of the supervisor in a post-Taylor environment, the selection of supervisors as Circle leaders, supervisory development and training, and problems relating to Circle leadership.

The supervisor in the post-Taylor environment

It has been explained in previous chapters that Quality Circles are a form of self-control which combines the advantages of Taylorism with the advantages of the Craftsmanship concept, to form a new style of management based on the individual work groups with the supervisor as group leader.

The success or otherwise of Quality Circles is highly dependent upon both the supervisor and the line manager. Both may be required to adopt a different style of management from previously, and their selection and training is a crucial consideration. As Circle leader, the supervisor has two different relationship to consider:

1. The everyday relationship with people in the department which may contain both Circle and non-Circle members.
2. The relationship with the Quality Circle members during Circle meetings.

The critical factors under item 1. that are relevant to a successful Circle programme are:

- Ensuring equal treatment for everyone in the department regardless of their attitudes towards Circle activities and Circle members. Circle members must not be seen as members of an élite group. Some people in a department may be extremely sensitive about this, and the supervisor must ensure that any such accusations, if they arise, are groundless.
- The style of management or supervision that is conducive to the development of a sense of loyalty and co-operation. This requires the adoption of a style of management that can range from consultative at one extreme to participative at the other.

A supervisor who adopted other styles – autocratic or paternalistic, for instance – would be unlikely to create an environment conducive to the spirit of Quality Circles. He would also need to show contrasting styles inside and outside Circle meetings that would be impossible to maintain.

The style of leadership demanded inside the Circle at Circle meetings is critical. It is vital for the Circle leader to remember at all times that when he

155

and the Circle members are in the meeting room together, everybody has one vote, and no one individual opinion is any more or less important than any other. During Circle meetings therefore, it is necessary for the supervisor to adopt a consensus style of leadership.

The main objectives of the Circle leader are twofold:

1. to act as a source of knowledge, and to be an advisor, trainer, and developer of the group;
2. to ensure the participation of all Circle members.

In the early stages of Circle activities the Circle leader, together with the facilitator, will be concerned mainly with the training and development of the group. However, as the weeks go by, and the Circle begins to mature, the training element will gradually reduce. Simultaneously, the Circle leader's confidence will grow, and a healthy relationship with the group will have been developed.

The Circle leader will realise at this stage that it might be worthwhile to allow the leadership of individual meetings to rotate amongst the members. Not only will this continue the people-building aspect, it will also give the members increased confidence in the supervisor and in the open nature of Circle activities. Beyond that, it will enable the supervisor to contribute his own ideas at the meeting - which is not easy when acting as leader and member simultaneously.

After a short time the supervisor may judge that the Circle has become self-sufficient and is no longer totally dependent upon his presence. In a large work area, this may provide an opportunity for him to start more Circles and subsequently appoint deputy leaders. The supervisor may then simply keep an eye on each group and 'sit in' on meetings when necessary. However, in a high proportion of Quality Circles, the supervisor will remain Circle leader permanently.

It may be seen that Quality Circles are by themselves an excellent form of supervisory development. In one company trained by DHA, the plant manager commented: 'The most significant development since we formed the first Circles last year is that our supervisors are now talking like managers. Even if the Circle programme had achieved nothing else, in my opinion, this fact justifies the entire cost.'

In another case a managing director said: 'We have spent a fortune in the past sending our managers away to Management Colleges. They have learned more through Total Quality development then they did on all the courses put together!'

Selection of supervisors as Circle leaders

Because the introduction of Circles is not usually preceded by years of specialised supervisory development, the selection of the initial Circle leaders is critical.

Normally, it would be unwise to consider the creation of more than five or six initial Circles at a given location. There are several reasons for this, the most important being:

1. First impressions are extremely important, and because the organisation is unlikely to have any previous first-hand experience with Circles, it is necessary to be able to give the new Circles all the support they need.
2. A large-scale development is likely to frighten those who are as yet un-committed into a defensive position. People feel less threatened by a pilot programme, which can easily be terminated if necessary.
3. There will be a wide range of management styles, relationships, and atti-tudes within the organisation, some of which may be adverse to the Circle concept. These cannot be changed overnight. Only a small proportion of managers and supervisors have attitudes conducive to Circles in the early stages.

Item 3. demands that before Circles are contemplated the styles, relationships, and attitudes of managers and supervisors throughout the entire location be reviewed.

The answer to the question, 'Where should we start?', is, as stated earlier, 'Where the grass is greenest!'. In other words, start in those departments where the supportive supervisors and leaders already exist.

Again, it is impossible to emphasise too strongly the importance of sup-portive management in the section or department where Circles are to be organised. Having located the most supportive managements, the potential Circle leaders may be selected. This requires much the same approach as was used to find the supportive managers, and the first Circle leaders should be those who already have a good relationship with their people. They should have a natural tendency towards theory 'Y' management, and easily adopt a consultative or participate style with their people. They should also be selec-ted from amongst the more self-assured and confident people.

Whilst they will have been invited to become potential Circle leaders, it must be emphasised that the voluntary nature of Circle activities applies as much at this level as it does at member level. If they do not want to lead a Circle, they should not be forced to.

If they do not want to lead a Circle, and both management and direct employees want to form a Circle, then management is faced with two options:

1. Ask the supervisor if it is acceptable to him for a Circle to be formed with the group electing their own leader.
2. If the answer to 1. is negative, management will be faced with the choice of either abandoning the idea of a Circle in the area initially, or of moving the supervisor to another area.

If option 1. is accepted, it is imperative that the supervisor is kept in touch with the activities of the group, and that he is always given the opportunity to attend Circle presentations. He should never be by-passed.

The above advice will enable most organisations to make a start. Some

157

will find the general attitudes of managers, supervisors, and workpeople more favourable initially than others, but it is highly unlikely that the positive factors will be totally absent, and a pilot scheme will almost always be possible . This pilot scheme should be seen as being rather like a new-born baby. It will need nursing and caring for until it is strong enough to stand on its own feet.

If the first leaders are carefully selected, the first Quality Circles are likely to be successful. Success breeds success, and all being well others will be impressed with the results, and will soon want Quality Circles in their own area. The rate at which this demand will increase cannot be forecast and varies from one company to another. At one extreme, a company may commence five Circles and only progress to seven or eight a year later. At the other extreme, some companies, such as Wedgwood, have created a phenomenal 180 Circles in just over two years.

Paradoxically, whilst the success of the early Circles may greatly influence other supervisors to start Circles, the converse may also happen amongst a minority. Some supervisors, perhaps those who have the least self-confidence, will be reluctant to start Circles because they are worried that they may not equal the achievements of the earlier groups. Such supervisors may need additional education and training designed to increase their self-confidence before they are given the opportunity to lead a Circle.

Supervisory development and training

Whilst some supervisors will display the necessary characteristics to be considered for Circle leadership, they will still require initial training in the basic techniques and group dynamics of Circles before they ask for volunteers amongst their workpeople.

It has been observed that some consultants who claim to be experts in Quality Circles attempt to train the leader and the Circle at the same time. There are several serious defects in this approach:

1. the client is permanently dependent upon the consultant because no one in the company will have acquired the basic training skills;
2. the environment will remain 'Taylorised' because the key aspect of self-control through the development of the leader will not emerge;
3. the leader is suppressed into the group and will not develop leadership skills;
4. the consultant has less credibility with the group than the leader, who shares work-related jargon.

Circle leaders should be trained to train their own Circles as part of their own development. Of course, there are few Circle leaders who would be able to do this entirely unaided, but the initial Circle leader training should be designed to achieve this with the help of the facilitator.

After leader training, which normally takes three or four days, the leader

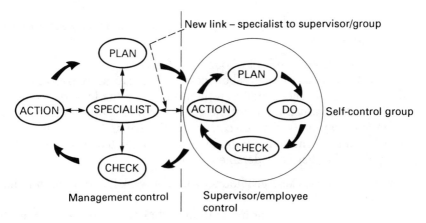

Fig. 14.4

and the facilitator together should train the Circle. The facilitator's role in this training is supportive. At the first meeting of the group, in most cases, the facilitator will probably do most of the work. However, if an informal atmosphere is created, even the most nervous new Circle leader will break in to explain some of the points. As the leader's confidence grows, he or she will take over more and more of the training. The facilitator will gradually recede into the background when it is judged that the leader has effectively assumed control. The rate at which this withdrawal of the facilitator takes place will vary from one Circle to another. In some instances it will happen quite quickly. The leader may already have experience as an instructor, or have been a football or netball coach, and will therefore quickly take over. Others without such experience may require more initial support.

Ideally, supervisory development should precede the development of Circles in the same way that it did in Japan. Although this is not essential, it does not mean that it can be overlooked entirely. Whilst a Circle leader training programme for supervisors will be sufficient to commence Quality Circle activities, it must be regarded as only basic training. Supervisor/leader training should be a continuous development process which may carry on indefinitely within the company's corporate plan. It is this continuous development process in Japan which gives their Circles their enormous power.

The training should be designed to be 'people building', and not simply be concerned with the acquisition of knowledge for its own sake. For example, Etsuro Tani of the Nippon Steel Corporation writes in a paper:

'Indispensible for the promotion to the foreman (*kocho*) rank is to finish the formal special course and the assistant foreman study course, and the foreman cannot be promoted to the general foreman (*sagyocho*) unless he completes the latter special course and the general foreman course. In this way education is inseparably related to promotion.

'Formal courses of importance to supervisory development are summarised in the following:

(a) Introductory Course, full day course … 10 days.
   General introductory lessons about company life are given to all operators newly employed. Inculcated into their minds are the importance of the iron and steel industry, the outline of Nippon Steel Corporation, and the pride and consciousness newcomers shall have as Nippon steel men. This is similar to induction training courses conducted by some Western companies, but has considerable depth.

(b) Foreman's Special Course, 3 hours, twice per week for 40 weeks totalling 240 hours.
   Employees of middle standing with over three years' experience are to be trained in this course on Quality Control with daily standard work operations as the basis for the training. The aim is to give practical and special knowledge essential for jobs assigned to foreman and equivalent in problem solving and leadership.

(c) Assistant Foreman Study Course, full day course of 6 weeks' duration.
   This course is aimed at building up the capabilities of assistant foreman practically to carry out leadership in the capacity of foreman and at teaching the basic techniques to accept leadership in the workshop.

(d) Later Special Course, full day course of 5 months' duration.
   Trainees are foreman and their equivalent who are expected to become general foremen, to teach them the technical knowledge they will require to perform the general foreman's duties.

(e) General Foreman Education Course, full day course of 2 months' duration.
   The trainees are candidates for the general foreman rank, to build up their abilities for management control work and the actions essential for good management.'

In addition to these courses, supervisors and foremen are encouraged to study in correspondence courses, described as self-improvement programmes, and are given the opportunity to attend seminars, give papers, take journals, and operate Quality Circle activities as a part of their normal work activity.

This intensive process of training in management skills does not just apply to Nippon Steel, it is common to the whole of Japanese industry.

If other countries really want to achieve the same level of progress in their industries as is currently happening in Japan, it is necessary for them to develop a similar level of intensity of training. The courses should not be designed by colleges which cannot be responsive to individual needs. but by the companies themselves as part of their own development programme, and based on their own specific requirements identified in the corporate plan. At the begining of each year, the education and training programme for each division or section should be determined from the overall policy and goals of the enterprise. Preferably, this should be worked out by a special committee comprising the heads of each division or section.

The techniques selected to be introduced through the training should be those which will enhance the skills already acquired, so that the individuals may do their work more effectively rather then for purely academic purposes. Basically the objectives should be to:

- create a sense of corporate identity/corporate loyalty and corporate pride
- give a greater awareness of corporate goals
- improve decision-making ability
- improve problem-solving skills
- improve leadership skills
- improve communication and presentation skills
- develop training skills
- increase self-confidence
- improve relationships with the managers and with workpeople.

Problems of Circle leadership

A Quality Circle is comprised of a group of individuals, each with his own personal characteristics. There are many texts which cover the behavioural aspects of small group activities: the threats, fears, and conflicts that emerge: the differences between the behaviour of assertive, altruistic, and analytical types; and the ways of dealing with aggressive or shy characters, etc. It would appear from the complexities which result that the leadership of Quality Circles would present horrendous difficulties to the supervisor who does not have an honours degree in group dynamics..

It therefore comes as a surprise to most people that 'in-depth' training in these skills is rarely given in Circle leader training courses, and is found to be unnecessary. This is due in the main to three important factors:

1. The voluntary nature of Circle activities means that people can drop out if they wish. Although this rarely happens in properly trained Circles, the fact that they are able to do so seems to put pressure on the individuals to come to terms with each others' point of view.
2. The techniques themselves tend to reduce the likelihood of conflict. The basic rules of brainstorming are really good rules for any kind of meeting. For instance, the rule that requires all ideas to be written down, and not evaluated immediately, almost completely eliminates the risk of conflict. When the idea is later challenged by a group member it becomes an attack on the idea and not the originator. In other forms of meeting such as committees the attack is launched immediately the suggestion is made, with the intention of preventing it from reaching the Minute Book. In other words, it becomes an attack on the originator, not the idea.

3. There is a rule that everyone takes turns in offering suggestions and is allowed only one idea per turn. This ensures that even the most shy member of the group has a say equal to that of the most assertive type.

This does not mean to say that the leader will not have problems, only that they are less likely, and that the problems which will be encountered are unlikely to be disastrous, provided that the rules are followed.

The problems that frequently occur are as follows:

- A strong-willed member of the Circle attempts to force the Circle to tackle a problem of his choice – frequently an industrial relations problem.
- The group is made up of people with disparate skills and finds it difficult to choose a problem which all members want to tackle.
- The Circle tackles a problem which proves difficult to solve.
- A non-Circle member is trying to demoralise individual Circle members.
- The departmental manager proves to be less supportive than was expected.
- One or two members are less interested than others in the group and forget to attend meetings, or perhaps hold private conversations at the meeting.
- Fluctuating work demand makes it difficult to fix the timing of Circle meetings.
- The Circle thinks management has been slow in implementing a previous suggestion, and is becoming demoralised.
- The Circle believes that it has run out of problems. Usually, it means it is not brainstorming according to the rules.

All these problems are likely to occur at some time or other. They are rarely more than a nuisance, and most companies overcome them without seeking outside help.

The first two or three on the list are perhaps the worst. The strong-willed member, if not prepared to accept the democratic or consensus approach, could bring about the collapse of the group and sometimes does, if the problem cannot be handled. More often though, the group will either bring such members into line, or it will effectively squeeze the individual out of the group. In the last resort, the leader and the facilitator will have to deal personally with the problem.

The second problem sometimes arises in small offices where it is only possible to form a Circle of staff from different sections. If their skills are too diverse, and it is desirable to attempt to form a Circle, it might be a good idea to suggest different types of project so that everyone can participate. For example, they may choose to design posters for a company Quality campaign or organise functions for the other Quality Circles.

The third problem is frequently avoided by allowing Circles to bring in specialists if they wish. It must always be remembered, however, that it is the Circles' problem and that the specialist is acting as a consultant or adviser because the members requested it. There is always the risk that the specialist will take over the problem and this must be vigorously discouraged. If the specialist happens to discover something important relating to the project he must present it through the Circle and not independently.

Demoralisation by non-Circle members can have many different causes, but is frequently due to fear in one form or another. Steps should be taken to convince everyone that Circles are not threatening, and that the Circle represents the whole department or section. Circles should also seek to avoid appearing as an élite group.

The lack of support of the department manager is a relatively common problem in the early days of a Circle programme. It tends to dissappear as soon as successes become apparent. Managers must be made to realise that it is their section's Circle and that they may be measured by the vitality of the Circle.

The sixth problem, a lack of commitment in some of the Circle members, often occurs when the group is too large and when the leader has not been trained properly. The facilitator should help the leader improve the cohesion of the team.

Problem seven, a fluctuation in work demand, may not be too difficult to live with if the teams are given the opportunity to help determine when the meetings take place to avoid the critical work peaks.

The eighth problem is again very common in new programmes. Circles are often suspicious of management's commitment and expect results instantly. Managers must keep the teams informed of the progress of their suggestions' implementation.

The last problem, finally, can be avoided altogether if adequate training has been given.

CHAPTER 15

QUALITY CIRCLES – THE SPECIALISTS AND NON-CIRCLE MEMBERS

This chapter is about 'everyone else' – all the other people on the payroll who may not necessarily be members of Circles, or in a management capacity, but who may, nevertheless, be involved in one way or another. They can be classified into two groups, the specialists, and non-Circle members.

The specialists can be further subdivided into:

1. the troubleshooting, problem-solving specialists
2. service functions or other functions whose own activities will influence or be influenced by the work of Circles

Both 1. and 2. may of course form Circles among themselves if there are enough people in their section, and if they have the desire and will to do so.

The specialists

1. The troubleshooting specialists

This group will include such specialists as work study personnel, Quality Control, production engineering, O & M, etc. If they are not properly informed about what Quality Circles are, and how Circle development will effect them, they are quite likely to see Quality Circles as a threat. Typically, they will think, 'My job is solving problems, why should you teach others to do my job?'. This observation may be especially pertinent during times of recession. It would be a pity not to dispel such fears before Quality Circles are established because, far from being a threat, Quality Circles, if anything, put more demands on the specialists, not less.

Follow-up visits by DHA to companies they have trained have shown that the specialists rank amongst the greatest enthusiasts of Quality Circles. This is for two main reasons:

- The type of problems usually dealt with by Circles are rarely the same problems that are attractive to the specialist. Consequently there is little conflict of interest.
- The Circle quickly discovers that specialists have access to information and knowledge outside the scope of the Circle, and so they often invite them to join the Circle as consultants, usually for the duration of that project.

Under the Taylor system, specialists are usually regarded by direct employees as 'management'. If the specialists are graduates, or are perceived by the employees to be deficient in direct experience of their particular activities, employees are likely to be hostile and unco-operative. They will also be deeply suspicious of the motives of the specialists whom they will see as management men only interested in cutting costs and reducing the payroll.

It is surprising how quickly these particular clouds are dispelled when Quality Circles are introduced. As soon as people realise that they are being listened to, that management, regards them as sufficiently valuable to give them Quality Circle training time, and that they are recognised as experts in their own jobs, their attitudes change completely. The specialist is then regarded as a potential equal, who happens to possess different skills from their own. Provided that the specialists themselves are prepared to co-operate, a close relation with Quality Circles should quickly develop.

A senior manager in one company with Quality Circles recently commented that one of the most significant changes that had taken place since the commencement of the Circles programme was the relationship between direct employees and the specialists. He said that the specialists were now tending to work in the areas which already had Circles because the people in those sections were more co-operative.

It follows that because the Circles need the specialists to help in their work, the members are more co-operative in helping the specialists in their activities.

2. Service functions

In the context of this discussion, service functions include:

- all other departments or sections
- people from other work areas
- managers
- trade union representatives and committees
- safety committees
- all upstream and downstream operations
- outside organisations including both customers and suppliers
- in-house committees, panels, and groups
- other Quality Circles

It has been stated earlier that Quality Circles must accept the organisation as it is. They must respect all other opinions, and the knowledge, experience, and feelings of others. Circles must work with these groups and reach solutions that are acceptable to those affected or responsible for work which may be related to the Circle project.

Examples

It would be pointless for a Quality Circle concerned with a manufacturing problem to offer management a solution that involved a design change, without first consulting a design specialist. There may be valid reasons, outside the knowledge of the Circle, why such a change would not be advisable. In any case, the Circle would not have solved the problem. It would simply have created another for the manager who, in addition to other responsibilities, would now be required to take up the matter with design. In many cases, he would not be as familiar with the problems as the Circle members are and might easily underestimate the importance of some factors.

If is far better for the Circle themselves to meet the specialists at an earlier stage so that they may together arrive at a solution that is acceptable to everyone. Furthermore, such specialists should be invited to attend and participate in the subsequent management presentation, and give further evidence of the thorough nature of their work. This type of co-operation need not be restricted solely to personnel and departments at one location.

A Quality Circle of welders in one UK company had always experienced difficulty in welding one of the long-standing well-established products manufactured by their company. The members decided to tackle these problems as a Quality Circle project. In the process of their activities they asked management if it would be possible for a specialist to give them some advice. As the company did not employ such a specialist, it sought outside assistance, and a consultant was invited to meet the Circle.

When it became known in the factory that this was happening, the production engineers and one or two designers asked if they could sit in on the discussions, and the Circle agreed to this. During the meeting, the consultant was able not only to give the Circle members valuable advice on improving their technique, but also to suggest that the product be re-designed in such a way that the problem was eliminated entirely. The design department agreed to this, and so an important improvement was made, with considerable savings in defect costs.

Some might say that these improvements could have been made without a Quality Circle, and this is true. But the fact is that they were not, and the problem had existed for many years, mainly because management did not have time to solve all of the problems single-handed. The real benefit of course was not just the direct savings from the project, but other spin-off benefits which accrued from the greater sense of involvement of that group of welders.

In another example, a Quality Circle, faced with problems involving its packing materials, was given the opportunity of visiting the manufacturers to explain its difficulties to the operators engaged in the manufacture of the materials.

The result of the meeting was the elimination of a problem that had plagued the management of the user company for many years. The quality manager had complained on many previous occasions but nothing had been achieved. After the discussions between the two groups of workers, the operatives at the supplier company said: 'We never realised that this caused real difficulties; we thought management was just getting on at us!

Non-Circle members

Almost every organisation will find that most departments will contain one or more employees who are not members of the Circle. This will either be due to a lack of interest, or because the department is too large for everyone to be able to join. In such a case it it hoped that it may be possible at some stage to form another Circle. There is no reason why two or more Circles should not be formed in a section.

However, it must be clearly understood by everyone, particularly the Circle members, that they belong to 'their section's Circle' and they are not an élite group. Failure to recognise this is one of the problems that frequently plagues organisations in the early stages of development. It can lead to considerable alienation between the two groups and cause the break-up of the Circle.

Causes of alienation between Circle and non-Circle members include:

- management pressure
- over-zealous facilitator
- leader showing favouritism
- Circle not involving others
- rival factions in the department

Let us examine each in turn.

Management pressure

Sometimes management does not fully appreciate the importance of the rule that Circles pick their own problems, and that the one hour per week is the 'Circle's hour'.

Interestingly, the Circle is usually less sensitive to this problem than non-Circle members of the department. They will detect quite quickly that management is 'steering or manipulating' the Circle, and will accuse its members of being 'management favourites'. Generally speaking it will annoy one person more than others. This person then attempts to 'pick off' a Circle member whom he thinks is sensitive, and tease that member about Circle activities. The first indication of this to an outsider will be one member of a

Circle dropping out of the group, followed by another. Usually, the defectors will be relucant to give reasons for leaving because that would leave them open to further problems with their colleagues.

If the Circle is genuinely left to choose its own problems and is continually made aware of the importance of involving non-Circle colleagues, the problems it selects will be those that everyone would like to see tackled, and all being well, the Circle members should become popular with their non-Circle colleagues as a result.

Over-zealous facilitator

The pressure on a newly appointed facilitator must never be underestimated. Those selected will usually be well advance in their own career and in all probability will have exercised some considerable courage in accepting the appointment. They will be very sensitive to their interpretation of senior management expectations from the Circle's programme.

The worst situation may occur when they think that top management is looking for a quick payback. This will lead to the same type of problem outlined above under 'Management pressure', only this time it will be the facilitator who is manipulating the Circle. Frequently the facilitator does this quite unconsciously. The most likely time for such interference occurs after the brainstorming session, when the Circle members are attempting to select their problem.

After the problem classification stage, it would be easy for the facilitator, particularly with a new Circle, to 'guide' it towards an 'easy' first problem. Unwittingly he may guide it towards a problem that look as if it has a good payback, or one which has been of major concern to management. As before, the non-Circle members will be sensitive to such manipulation. It is not a bad idea to allow them to participate in problem selection.

Leader showing favouritism

Following the initial introduction of Circles, some non-Circle members may become hypersensitive to the relationship between the supervisor and Circle members. In a few cases, individuals may attempt to evaluate every action of the supervisor to see if favouritism exists. The Circle leader therefore must be extremely careful to avoid the likelihood of such problems and must treat everybody in the department equally, regardless of their attitude towards Circle activities.

Circle not involving others

This is usually a training problem and indicates that the facilitator and Circle leader have not taken enough care to ensure that everyone can participate. Many Circles involve non-members by circulating questionnaires to solicit ideas. Publicising Circle activities by displaying worksheets in the department is an excellent way of encouraging outside interest (provided that there is little risk of graffiti).

In a number of companies, the Circles make their first presentation to the section before their management presentation. Apart from ensuring that non-members are familiar with the Circle's method of working, it enables them to offer suggestions as to how the presentation might be improved and gives them a sense of involvement.

Rival factions in the department

This is problem outside the scope of Circles directly, and does occasionally, but thankfully rarely, occur. The problem usually boils down to there being two conflicting personalities in the section, each with his on her own loyal supporters. If all the supporters of one person are in the Circle, the others may be alienated. If it is possible, the problem may be avoided by attempting to involve members of each group. Occasionally, such a situation has prevented a group from being successfully formed, although this is fortunately very rare.

CHAPTER 16

TRADE UNIONS AND QUALITY CIRCLES

This chapter is intended to assist trade union officials, representatives, and members to formulate their opinions about Quality Circles and their effect on trade union interests. It is expected that the topic will attract much discussion amongst union activists as the concept of Quality Circles continues to develop.

Any change in work relationships constitutes both a potential threat and potential opportunities for trade unions, and it is hoped that this chapter will help those concerned to gain a clear understanding of these important aspects of Quality Circle operations.

It is also intended that this chapter should assists those managers responsible for planning the introduction of Circles in the initial preparation stage. Hopefully the content will enable them to obtain a clear perspective of the matters that are likely to be of greatest interest to trade union representatives, and stimulate the necessary co-operation that is so important to the success of any programme.

Background

At the time of writing this book the British Trade Union movement has not published a policy either in favour of or against Quality Circles, although several leading trade unionists have made varying comments and the British Trade Union Congress published a guidelines document in April 1981, which will be reviewed later in the chapter.

In general, DHA's experience in dealing with trade unions at company level has so far revealed that no one union is either more or less supportive than any other. That is not to say that there have not been problems, or that individuals at all levels have not expressed opinions based upon the knowledge they had at the time. Union attitudes towards Quality Circles at plant level have varied from both extremes, – total hostility to total acceptance and co-operation. However, these differences invariably relate either to the personalities of individuals or to the environment within the company and its industrial relations record, and not usually to the union itself.

In some cases the union representatives on site have been supportive but the local full-time official hostile. On other occasions the reverse has been true. Whenever there has been a hostile local official, it has frequently been due to the fact that he has already had a bad experience of Quality Circles elsewhere in the territory, but in all known cases, this was because the companies concerned had made a bad job of implementing the concept.

Currently, this is the greatest hazard in Quality Circles. There are so many consultants, all offering their own variant of the concept, that it is easy for a misinformed client to introduce a programme that violates the basic rules. In other cases, in order to cut costs, some companies have attempted to introduce Circles without proper advice, with similar unfavourable consequences.

The biggest fear of those properly experienced in helping to establish Quality Circles is that such ill-conceived programmes may bring the entire concept into disrepute and give a wrong impression before sound Quality Circles are properly established. It would be a major tragedy if any trade union were to declare a national policy of hostility to Quality Circles based on feedback from such badly introduced programmes.

In the years since the publication of the first edition of this book in 1985 under the title *Quality Circles Handbook*, this problem has got worse rather then better. In fact, workshop sessions at the British National Society of Quality Circles reveal that there are very few companies which have a common perception of the concept itself, let alone the details. In the opinion of the author this is a serious problem which must be resolved. Analysis indicates that the principal cause relates to ignorance at Chairman and Board of Directors level. It is the old, old chestnut: people in the middle and the bottom know what should be done because they attend the conventions; people at the top do not because they never attend the conventions – and they are the ones who make the policy decisions. If Chairmen and Directors cannot find the time to learn how to direct their businesses correctly, then how is this time spent? One thing is for certain – if they do not learn soon, and apply the lessons swiftly and effectively, they will have all the time in the world, but nothing to manage!

To illustrate the importance of this point, two examples will be given of situations that occurred within the experience of DHA. In the interests of confidentiality it will not be possible to name the organisations concerned.

Example 1

A company trained by DHA had a successful Circle programme which had been in existence for about nine months. Suddenly one day, and without warning, all of the members of the biggest union in the factory received a letter from their full-time district official saying 'on no account should any member have anything to do with Quality Circle activities'. It was later discovered that the same letter had been sent to every member in the district.

The employees who were members of Circles were extremely shocked and upset by this and could not understand why it had happened. They made representations to the branch and found that the problem had originated in another company in the same locality and in the same industry. Apparently, the other company had commenced a Quality Circle programme without assistance. Obviously it did not understand the concept properly, and initiated one Circle in each of its three factories with instructions to look into anomalies in the piece-work system. Apart from the fact that true Quality Circles should be free to choose their own problem, it is a hard-and-fast rule that Circles should not be allowed to tackle problems relating to wages and conditions of work. This is because there are other channels for dealing with such matters. Circles should be concerned with problems related directly to work.

It happened that the shop convener in one of these factories was the wife of the local official, and apparently it took just thirty minutes for her to contact him, with the result that he wrote the above letter.

Fortunately, DHA had been kept informed of these events and were able to contact the company in question. They were offered a presentation on Quality Circles and this was given after normal working hours in the canteen. The following day the district official sent a further letter to the members saying that he had no objection to their being involved in Circle activities provided that they kept within certain guidelines. These guidelines had been spelled out at the presentation the night before.

Example 2

In another company, the author had just finished a half-day presentation to the twenty-two senior shop stewards representing the ten unions with members at the location. As the people were about to leave, the most senior steward, representing the largest union on site, said, 'My full-time official has told me to have nothing whatsoever to do with Quality Circles'. He then promptly left the room together with his colleagues. Things indeed looked black.

The manager who had organised the meeting looked somewhat shocked and thought that the unions were going to resist Circle activities. However, it was suggested that the full-time official be contacted in order to find out why he should take that view. It was felt that perhaps he should be invited to attend a presentation on the topic and that a similar invitation be made to the full-time officials of the other unions.

This offer was accepted, and the officials of all the unions attended a one-day presentation, together with the senior stewards who had been present at the earlier meeting. About half-way through the afternoon, the full-time official who had originally objected to the concept said, 'The reason why I was against Circles was because one of the companies in my area had introduced Quality Circles and in my view management was using it as a way of manipulating people. But on listening to you I can find nothing I disagree with, and if this company is prepared to introduce it along these lines then as far as I am concerned that is OK'.

This example goes back to 1982. The company concerned now has one of the most impressive Quality Circle programmes in the UK, and the unions are fully supportive.

These two examples illustrate the importance of ensuring:

1. That the management of the company thoroughly understands Quality Circles and all the considerations before attempting their implementation.
2. That management operates a policy of total openness with worker representatives and trade unions generally on every aspect of its Quality Circle policy.
3. That the trade unions on site have an opportunity to co-operate in the development of the concept through the steering committee.

A threat to the union?

Circles represent no threat of any kind to any union interest, and there is absolutely no good reason whatsoever why any trade union should object to their introduction.

Circles are concerned with making more effective use of the existing functions as they may be modified from time to time. They are not an alternative to any of the usual negotiation or bargaining channels, specialist functions, safety committees, or any other activity. Neither do they undermine the influence of workers' representatives.

Circles must recognise the existence and interests of all these people and groups. They must never by-pass them in any way. Unions and management must be free to negotiate any arrangements they want to, and these negotiations must not be fettered by Quality Circles. Circles must accept the organisation as it is.

For example, suppose that the members of a Quality Circle decide to tackle a problem relating to their work but the solution they find happens to cut across the interests of the union or a safety committee. There would be no point in their presenting such an idea to management because until they can obtain the acceptance of the third party, they have not solved the problem. All they have done is to create another problem for the manager because he will now have to open up discussions with the third party.

When the members of a Circle request a management presentation, it should be to talk about their achievements, not to present management with more problems. Consequently, in the situation outlined above, the Circle, if it is properly trained, will request a meeting with the third party. If the third party has objections, they will be discussed, and hopefully, a suitable alternative solution will be found. The Circle will then request a management presentation for this new solution, and, all being well, will invite the third party to attend. Apart from the recognition afforded to the third party, in this case the union, it will also convince management of the thorough way in which the problem has been tackled and of the soundness of the solution.

It may be seen from the foregoing discussion that trade unions have a crucial role to play in Quality Circle activities. It is vitally important that all trade unions in an organisation have every opportunity to discuss Quality Circles with the consultant, with each other, and with management *prior* to the implementation of Quality Circles. It must be recognised that the trade unions should be able to satisfy themselves that the motives of the organisation, and the thoroughness of their preparations, have been exhaustively examined before they can be expected to endorse a prospective programme.

Trade unions and Quality Circle steering committees

Trade unions, if they wish, may have an important contribution to make towards the creation of a better working environment based upon the Quality Circle concept.

If Quality Circles really are an opportunity to create a better and more rewarding society for all people then the trade unions should be given the opportunity to participate in their development. They should also receive recognition for that role.

The opportunity for such participation comes at plant level through the steering committee. This is a group of people representing a variety of interests at that plant or location who have volunteered to work together for the success of a Circle programme. The structure and role of the steering committee is fully discussed in Chapter 17 but there is no doubt that Circle programmes which have the active support of the unions on site are considerably more healthy than would otherwise be the case.

TUC guidelines document

The TUC guidelines document on Quality Circles published in April 1981 expressed the concerns of the trade union movement about the growth of Quality Circles, and was the basis of a seminar held at Ashridge Management College where the author and Clive Jenkins of the ASTMS were principal speakers. At the time of writing this 2nd edition, no better document has been produced for discussion.

Under the heading 'The trade union attitude to Quality Circles', eight observations were made. Items 1 to 8 in the TUC text are not included. These were concerned with description of Quality Circles and their background. Items 9 to 16 are now reproduced with comment by the author.

'(9) Trade unions have been urging employers for decades to give workers more control over the jobs they do. QCs are a belated recognition of employees' expertise and knowledge and the need to put them to use. At the same time, trade unionists may be understandably sceptical about the merits of the latest in a succesion of 'vogue' management techniques.'

Comment Not only is this 'scepticism' understood, it is positively welcomed. The reason why so many so-called 'management panaceas' have come and gone over the years is frequently more a result of management misunderstanding of the concept than possible weaknesses in the concept itself.

It is salutary to note that many of the concepts that have been sold as 'the best thing since sliced bread' are very much alive and kicking in Japan, where people appear to have a far more analytical approach to the relative merits of these concepts prior to their introduction.

Hopefully, we have now had our fingers burned sufficiently often to be a little more careful with Circles. Some will have learned their lesson, some unfortunately not.

'(10) *The sophisticated presentation of QCs by management consultants does not disguise the fact that there is little basically new in the idea of QCs. Many companies have already introduced consultative procedures to discuss questions relating to production and quality control which are similar to those connected with Quality Circles. Trade unionists may therefore not wish to dismantle existing arrangements, where they exist, by introducing QCs.'*

Comment On this point it is felt that the outhors of the TUC guidelines document have some misconception of the true nature of QCs. Quality Circles are not productivity discussion groups or a form of consultation process; they are a form of self-control, as explained earlier in the book. Circles do not conflict with the arrangements referred to in Paragraph 10; these should be positively encouraged and hopefully enhanced by the activities of Quality Circles. Neither is there any reason to dismantle any of the consultative machinery which may exist, unless, of course, all interests agree that such arrangements are redundant.

'(11) *Like any other addition or alteration to working methods, QCs must be subject to existing agreed procedures between management and unions.* **Trade unions are likely to oppose QC's structures that are imposed unilaterally by management without reference to those procedures.'**
(The words in bold were underlined in the original document.)

Comment DHA would wholeheartedly accept this comment and so would their clients. As has been stated earlier, Circles must accept every established agreement and procedure. They must operate within all the constraints which management and organised labour agree to accept. Circle members accept this by their volunteering to join. This is another reason why everyone should have the opportunity to know precisely what Circles mean before being asked to join.

'(12) *QCs should not be seen by management as a way of by-pasing or competing with existing trade union machinery at the workplace.* **Trade unionists will be opposed to the introduction of QCs if they challenge in any way existing trade union machinery or practices.'**

Comment Again, this is accepted. That is not to say however that such changes cannot be brought about by discussion if it proves to be in the interests of all concerned. No attempt should ever be made by any party to use Quality Circles as a lever in any such discussions.

'(13) Management cannot expect to 'claim' all the productivity and other saving generated by the work of QCs. These, like other elements of workplace productivity, are a matter for established negotiation procedures. The absence of such negotiation will heighten workers' scepticism of management's motives in introducing QCs.'

Comment This observation raises issues which are far too complex to comment on in a few lines. The whole question of reward or 'what do we, or they, get out of it' is fully discussed in Chapter 7.

'(14) Trade unions will be particularly concerned about the employment implications of QCs on, for example, staff in quality control departments as well as employees in other jobs affected by review of work methods.'

Comment The authors rightly highlight this important point. Fortunately, it is fair to say that so far no one has lost his job as a result of Quality Circles. If he had, it is fairly certain that the news of such an occurrence would very quickly reach Union HQ with inevitable consequences. Workpeople know that, and management knows it. If a Circle project happens to reduce the work content of a particular operation, the Circle and management together, and probably also the union, would come to some agreement on how the time might be spent. In one company it was such a situation which led to the greatest Circle achievement. They had saved 32 hours per month in their department through the elimination of a tedious routine. They decided to use the time saved in such a way that it created over £400,000 savings immediately!

'(15) Despite the tightly limited role ascribed to QCs by management consultants, employers must expect trade unions – and possibly QCs themselves – to emphasise the need for broader workers' involvement in other matters affecting quality and competitiveness, such as research and development, marketing, and investment. In other words, employers cannot expect trade unionists to see QCs as a substitute for other far-reaching forms of involvement of the kind set out in the TUC's views on action at company and plant level by EDCs and SWPs.'

Comment Since the publication of the TUC document Quality Circles have emerged in all the areas mentioned above, including accounts departments, warehousing, cleaning, and many other situations. Circles will work anywhere where people work together and share common problems, and it does not matter what kind of work it is.

Again, Circles will not conflict with the other forms of involvement. It may be, however, that some of these forms may adopt some of the Circle techniques.

'(16) The TUC has been pressing for the establishment of action teams or factory development committees at company and plant levels to discuss issues associated with the work of EDCs and SWPs such as marketing

and investment. If established, such FDCs or Action Teams would clearly devote much time and discussion to aspects of company performance and quality control, the subject areas of QCs. To co-ordinate work on these subjects within the plants or factories, trade unionists would see the establishment of QCs as an extension of the work of FDCs – bodies upon which there be full union representation.'

Comment Perhaps the co-ordination referred to should be bridged by the FDC and the Quality Circle steering committee rather than by the individual Circles themselves. Since, all being well, the union is represented on the steering committee, this should not present any problems. Certainly, the Circle activists in the company should desire such co-operation and hopefully it would be achieved.

Points of special union interest

Trade union representatives and members who are considering their attitude towards Quality Circles, and that of their local organisation, will naturally want some basis upon which to evaluate their company's approach to Quality Circles. To help in this evaluation, the following ten key points should prove to be of interest.

First of all, it is worth referring to the definition of Circles given on page 111. It must be remembered that the word 'Quality' in the context of Quality Circles has a broader meaning than simply 'product quality' and includes the quality of work life and all other factors relating to Total Quality, as described in Chapter 3.

1. The term 'voluntary' means exactly what is says. There should be no pressures on anyone to join a Circle and no recriminations if someone decides to opt out. There are now many recorded instances of Circles being formed as a result of spontaneous demand of people at work.
2. Paid time is usually at the rate at which employees would have been paid had they not attended the Circle meeting, although there are examples now in shift-working departments of Circles that have chosen meeting times outside normal shift hours. In these cases, if trade union organisation exists, it is essential to have their agreement to the meeting arrangements. These will usually have been suggested by the Circle itself. This kind of agreement relates not only to pay, but also to whether the meeting time properly constitutes 'overtime'. Any arrangements made must be compatible with agreements currently in operation.
3. The question of leadership is often raised. Why the supervisor? It is not absolutely essential that the supervisor should be the Circle leader, but he should at least be offered first refusal. Circles are not concerned with by-passing anyone and the official leader of the group should have first choice. Again, there are many departures from this 'ideal' situation, and every case should be treated on its merits.

4. The Circle identifies problems although others may add their ideas to the list. The Circle chooses the problem it wants to tackle withour coercion, or pressure, from any member of management. Management and others may, on rare occasions, invite a Circle to tackle a specific problem, but the final decision rests with the Circle.

  The leader has just one vote like any other member when making the choice of project. In choosing the problem, the Circle should be bound by three simple but effective rules:
   • It must be 'their' problem, not one from another group's work area:
   • It must not involve criticism of identifiable individuals. Circles attack problems, not people.
   • Quality Circles never, repeat *never*, become involved in matters concerning pay and terms and conditions of employment. This is one of the most important rules of any Quality Circle programme.

5. All members of the Circle participate in presentations to management. The presentations are always face-to-face and never in memorandum or report form. Neither are they given by the leader on behalf of the group.

  There will be occasions when management cannot give immediate replies, but if ever a Circle's recommendation is rejected, management should be required to give its reasons for rejection in as clear and comprehensive a form as possible.

6. In making recommendations to management, the Circles will probably be claiming to have solved the problems, but the problems have not been solved if there are still trade union objections to the proposals. The Circle must discuss potentially contentious projects with trade union representatives *before* making their presentation. This will ensure that Quality Circle proposals work within the exsting machinery and do not conflict with long-standing procedures and arrangements.

7. Quality Circles do not undermine the role of the elected trade union representatives or interfere with their right to raise matters with management. The problems selected and tackled by Circles are generally different from issues relating to industrial relations, and other matters of great concern to trade unions. However, if any overlap exists, the Circle must abide by the rule not to become involved in matters best left to the negotiating machinery. (Representatives may even use techniques similar to those of Circles in formulating the case they wish to place before management.)

8. It should be established policy that Quality Circles do not receive any direct financial reward other than the payment for their one hour per week meetings. They do not receive percentages of the savings or fixed sum awards. There are a number of reasons for this, but the most important is that everyone in the organisation should benefit equally. If an organisation is attempting to create a situation where all are made to feel that their organisation is the better for their being there, it cannot do it by treating one group differently from another, and some work areas may have a greater potential for big savings than others.

The wages, salaries, and standard of living of all employees are a matter for consultation and negatiation between organised labour and management, and Quality Circles as such play no part in this process.

9. Many trade union representatives fear that Quality Circle activities may lead to job losses. This is unlikely. Quality Circles consider problems in their own work and are unlikely to cut their own throats. If management seeks the full benefits from successful Quality Circle programes, it would be foolish to take advantage of such situations. Quality Circles are not, however, about job losses, but rather about increased competitiveness, customer satisfaction, problem solving, and improving the working environment. Hopefully, Quality Circles will make a small contribution to creating jobs, not losing them.

10. Finally, there is the function of the steering committee, the membership of which should be drawn from a cross-section of the organisation and include trade union representatives if they wish to join. The committee has a number of functions, which will be discussed in the following chapter. If the union agrees to participate, it will be able to asist in the formulation of the policies and rules relating to Circle activities. The existence of a properly formulated steering committee will enable the individual problems relating to Circle activities to be resolved in a sensible manner. It also gives the union the opportunity to be identified with a concept which hopefully will change the working environment for the better for all people at work.

Conclusions

A Quality Circle programme that recognises the validity of these ten points as far as employee representatives are concerned is unlikely to meet insoluble problems. A programme that ignores them is almost certain to fail.

There will always be issues raised, and problems to solve, but if these rules are followed, Quality Circles can offer substantial benefits to everyone, without arousing fear, concern, or conflict, and lead to better working conditions.

Quality Circles give workpeople an opportunity to control their own work, and the activities should be enjoyable and beneficial to everyone. In the final analysis, it should be remembered that it is all voluntary; if at any time people cease to enjoy what they are doing, they can stop.

Quality Circle programmes must not be seen as a replacement or alternative for any other activity or practice, but only as an additional means of involving much larger numbers of people in making decisions about matters that are important to them. Each person becomes the manager at his or her own level.

The ideas outlined above will not solve all problems for all people, but they will draw together some of the key elements of Quality Circle programmes for consideration by management and trade unions, and they should emphasise that trade unions are important to Circles and vice versa.

CHAPTER 17

THE VOLUNTARY IMPROVEMENT ACTIVITIES STEERING COMMITTEE

In some companies the steering and support of the Quality Circles aspect of Total Quality has been succesfully carried out by the Quality Council. Generally speaking, it is nevertheless better to consider the introduction of a further substructure which is linked to the Quality Council but is specifically concerned with Quality Circles, the suggestion programme, and all other forms of voluntary improvement activity.

Because of the deep-rooted implications of Quality Circles, it would be impossible to commence a successful programme before all people affected have been given an opportunity to decide for themselves whether they want to become involved. To ensure a positive response at all levels, it is necessary to give awareness presentations to top management, middle management, trade union representatives, specialists, and supervisors. Assuming that the general reaction is favourable, and that there are no major objections, it is then possible to draw up an action plan for the development of a Quality Circle programme.

First of all, it will be necessary to determine who will be responsible for this development. Of course, up to this stage responsibility must already have been assumed by someone – usually the chief executive – or some small group, and the Quality Council will have to make the decision to invite an expert to talk to them about this extension of the Total Quality process.

After this presentation, one or two other directors or senior managers may have taken an active interest in becoming directly involved and so a small team may be formed. They will plan the next steps. These steps will normally be the awareness presentations to the other groups mentioned above. In some small companies all of these groups may attend a single session together. In other cases several sessions may be necessary. However, following these sessions, all being well, a number of people from different levels and functions are likely to express a keen interest in the subject and to want to play an active part in the subsequent development. These people, together with those already involved, may form what is usually referred to as a 'steering committee'. Some organisations prefer to use the term 'support group', which does have certain advantages, although the former term is more common.

Membership of the steering committee therefore is, like that of Quality Circles themselves, a voluntary involvement. Not all the volunteers will necessarily have put themselves forward, they may have been invited, but as in the case of Circles no one should be forced to join.

Perhaps the first consideration is why this approach should be preferable to having just one person in charge of the entire programme. For example, some people may think that the facilitator could, or should, take all this responsibility. There are several arguments against this.

First, many of the decisions and plans will frequently be made before Quality Circle facilitators are appointed or the importance of the facilitator's role appreciated.

Second, it is extremely unlikely that there would be any one person who has such intimate knowledge of and familiarity with each department and level of people that he could sucessfully cover all the tasks and work that are to be carried out by the steering committee.

Third, if the steering committee's responsibilities are vested in one person, the Circles aspect of Total Quality would be dependent upon one person and the process could easily become a personality cult. If, as frequently happend in such situations, that person were to leave the company, or suffer some misfortune, the programme might very easily collapse, or at least suffer a major setback. The formation of a good steering committee will prevent all of these risks.

Finally, there are also some very positive reasons for this approach. In an earlier chapter it was stated that most Western organisations have an individualistic style of management compared with Japan, and it is necesary to become more consensus-inclined for a Circle programme to be ultimately successful.

The steering committee can, if properly constructed, very effectively create the necessary consensus-style characteristics essential for the development of a healthy Circle programme.

Who should belong?

If the steering committee is reasonably representative of all interests, it will be 'in touch' or 'wired in' to the feelings of all members of staff. It will also inspine confidence.

For example, shop floor workers in a factory who are worried about some aspect of Quality Circles may find it difficult to talk to a senior manager, or someone from another section or department. However, if there is someone on the steering committee at their own level, or whom they find accessible, then they will have no worries about approaching that person with their observations. Not only is this important from that individual's point of view, it is also valuable to the steering committee itself, because now, they will be more sensitive to the general mood and to people's perspective of the Quality Circle programme.

Union Representation

It is important to give trade unions the opportunity to be represented on the steering committee as an equal member to the others. Union representatives should be approached along the following lines: 'We like the idea of Quality Circles and want to form a steering committee. If you also like it, then we would value your membership of the steering committee in order to help build a successful programme'. Union members therefore should be invited onto steering committees to make positive constributions, not just to 'keep an eye' on things.

Besides ensuring that policies worked out by the steering committee take account of union views and interests, there are also other advantages. If the unions are not given the opportunity of participating in the development of a Circle's programme, they can hardly be expected to be enthusiastic about it.

In many instances, when employees are approached and asked if they would like to join a Circle they will probably seek the advice of a worker representative before accepting the opportunity. If the worker representative has a jaundiced view of Circles, or has not been informed of what is going on, there is every chance that the advice will be negative.

The modern trade union movement had its origins in the middle of the nineteenth century, when the object was to create better terms and conditions of work. Much has been achieved since those early days, but Taylorism has created a plateau. If Quality Circles provide an opportunity for making a further advance, then it is only appropriate that the trade union movement should have an equal opportunity of sharing in that success. If trade unions adopt a positive attitude towards Quality Circles, and their members identify their union with having helped in the achievement of a better society as a result, it must be in the best interests of everyone.

Membership of the steering committee is the best opportunity for such visible support.

Supervision

In some companies the role of the supervisor, group leader, or foreman is more clearly defined than in others. It is just as important that someone from this level should find a place on the steering committee as any other. Some supervisors may be nervous about how Circles will affect their role, and it would be dangerous if the steering committee was not sensitive to these feelings and neglected to have supervisors represented.

Middle management and specialists

This level or group is usually the linchpin of a Circle programme. The attitudes of middle managers both individually and collectively will determine to a large extent the 'flavour' of that company's Quality Circle activities. Middle managers, particularly those who lack confidence, are likely to feel the most exposed by the developing programme. If care is not taken to develop middle managers through involvement in project team activities at the same time as the Circles are being developed, some managers may become afraid of the growing confidence of their people. Also, some managers may become nervous if their people are speaking a language that they themselves do not understand, through the acquisition of skills in using the Circles techniques. Key middle managers therefore – those who are more closely associated with other middle managers – can play a vital role in the steering committee activities.

Top management

A steering committee will be largely ineffectual if it does not contain as a member one of the ultimate decision-makers at plant level, a key member of the Quality Council, and also someone who can sign cheques. Otherwise the steering commitee would lack authority, and all the important decisions would be made by the group seen to be a third party, i.e. top management. It would also mean that the committee would be required to make respresentations to top management or the Quality Council for decisions to be made and, in all probability, top managers might not appreciate the importance of requests made, simply because they would have been less involved.

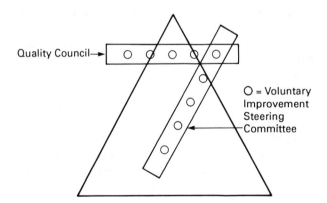

Quality Council→

O = Voluntary Improvement Steering Committee

Fig. 17.1

When Quality Circles form part of Total Quality programmes, and hopefully this will be the case for all readers of this book, the steering committee should be linked directly to the plant or site Quality Council by having at least one senior person common to both groups.

Summary

The steering committee:

- should span all functions and all levels;
- gives confidence to others through accessibility to members;
- gives continuity, and shows commitment;
- must be linked to the Quality Council.

The tasks of the steering committee

Because the steering committee evolves in the manner described at the beginning of this chapter, it must not be assumed that all the items mentioned under this heading will necessarily commence after the final membership has been completed. However, it is advisable to review past decisions of the steering committee when new members join. The aim should always be to have the widest possible consensus. In some companies staff turnover is so rapid that in less than one year most of the members of the steering committee will have changed. It is vitally important that all members of the steering committee are fully acquainted with the philosophy and concepts which were known to the original members. It must never be assumed that this knowledge has been acquired casually.

The basic responsibilities of a steering committee can be listed in 17 separate categories. In individual cases others not listed may become apparent.

1. Integration of Quality Circles into policy deployment
2. Quality Circle programmes policy making
3. Policy review and resolution of social and group dynamic problems; people issues
4. Constraints – limitations to Circle activities
5. Facilitator support
6. Guidance
7. Continuity of support
8. Monitoring the Quality Circle process
9. Presentations/conventions
10. Publicity, internal and external
11. Recognition
12. Reward
13. Assessment
14. Appreciation
15. Liaison
16. Development
17. Linking with Quality Council

1. Integration of Quality Circles into policy deployment

The corporate plan created through policy development for the company must be evaluated to identify the role of Quality Circles in the Total Quality programme. The relationship between Quality Circles and the corporate mission should be clearly defined and published.

2. Quality Circle programmes policy making

Establishing the policy and guidelines for Circle activities will be the most intensive activity of a newly formed committee. Such questions as 'resource allocation' both at plant or branch level and at Circle level; 'constraints' on activities, i.e., 'when Circles hold their meetings', 'where the meetings will take place', etc., are just a few of the items which will require resolution.

David Hutchins Associates recommend to their clients that the steering committee should commence its activities in the same way as the Quality Circles themselves, and conduct brainstorming sessions of all the items which it thinks will be relevant. This will usually produce a list of over 100 items. The steering committee will then discuss each item in turn. When all of the items have been discussed, agreed, and minuted, the result is a Quality Circles policy statement, covering all aspects of the programme. If copies of this agreement are circulated to all steering committee members, each member will be able to give the same answers to any employee and the agreement will become the foundation of that company's programme.

3. Policy review

It is unlikely that any initial policy will be absolutely perfect, and discussion issues are bound to arise. These may stem from the steering committee members themselves or from other employees.

Of course, employees can only influence the programme if the steering committee members are accessible and visible. They must be given the opportunity to know who they are. It is a good idea, therefore, for photographs of the steering committee members to be displayed on notice boards, together with their names, their role in the organisation, and where they are to be found. This will make them more 'accessible' to other employees, who will then air their comments on policy issues more easily. An annual review of all policy elements relating to the Quality Circle programme should be carried out by the steering committee. This review should also obtain inputs from the teams themselves and ideally take place prior to the annual audit of the Total Quality programme by the management team or the Quality Council.

4. Constraints

It has been stated quite strongly in earlier chapters that Circles must never take on as projects issues relating directly to wages, or terms or conditions of employment. There may be special reasons why a particular company might wish to add further constraints, and this should be considered by the steering committee. It is most important that any such constraints are clearly understood by potential Circle members *before* they are invited to join a Circle. People are likely to become quite resentful if they are only informed afterwards.

5. Facilitator support

The facilitator should always be a member of the steering committee, and will usually be the main source of information. In a larger company with several facilitators, it would be unreasonable for all of them to be represented. Usually one of them, who in this case could be termed a co-ordinator, will probably be more senior than the others. The co-ordinator would be their steering committee representative and would report back to the other facilitators at facilitators' meetings.

The steering committee will be the facilitators' main source of support. In companies which have a participative, consensus style of management, this support will not be so important, but in others – particularly those which suffer from strong inter-departmental rivalries – the support of the steering committee may mean the difference between success and failure. This is further evidence of the value of having a broadly based steering committee.

6. Guidance

Occasionally, hopefully not too often, the pattern of work flow might threaten the activities of a Circle. For example, a meeting might be suspended in order to meet a shipping requirement. Individual managers will be uncertain as to when this would be acceptable, and the steering committee will find many instances where it is required to give guidance on such matters. Additionally, the facilitator will also require frequent confirmation on specific points of policy.

7. Continuity

Whilst the majority of companies trained by DHA have very active and involved steering committees, there is nevertheless an awareness, or suspicion, that in a number of companies the steering committee only pays lip service to its responsibilities and leaves everything to the facilitator. Whilst this might appear to be satisfactory in the short term, particularly if the facilitator happens to be a charismatic figure, the committee will suffer ultimately if that facilitator is suddenly lost. A personality cult should never be allowed to develop around the facilitator, and can only be avoided by a visible and active steering committee.

8. Monitoring

The Plan-Do-Check-Act (PDCA) cycle referred to in earlier chapters is no less important in Circle activities than in any other. As the Circle programme develops, each Circle will develop its own innate characteristics, and will be very different from every other Circle.

In the early days of Circles in one company, the facilitator said that at one extreme the Circles were exceeding all expectations, and he felt that if he left them alone entirely he would not have to worry about them. The bulk of the remainder needed some support, but were basically self-sufficient. However, he had one or two Circles that were like cold porridge – if he stopped stirring them, they would set.

If some Circles do appear better than others, there may be lessons to be learned from the more impressive Circles and transferred to others. The same logic applies to Circles in different companies. Monitoring, therefore, can include cross-fertilisation. Steering committee members should be prepared to visit other companies and compare their approaches. In this way, everybody can benefit from everybody else's experience. The National Society of Quality Circles in the UK and others which have been established in other countries provide a forum for this at Circle level. However, the concept of 'Quality Month' with conventions for all levels from Chairman downwards has yet to become established in the West. This is the basis of Total Quality development in Japan under the auspices of JUSE (the Japanese Union of Scientists and Engineers). DHA do publish an occasional journal entitled *Quality Review*, and have organised conventions for all levels for over one decade. As yet there is no Western equivalent to JUSE.

9. Presentations

The management presentation is the culmination of all of the work carried out by the Circle on its project. If the members have been successful, they will be proud of their achievement and will want to show what they have done.

For the majority of projects, these presentations will be made to the members' own manager, and perhaps to others who are directly affected by their recommendations. Sometimes, however, it is a good idea to allow certain projects to be presented to the steering committee, and to the Quality Council, or to an annual in-house convention. This can be desirable for the following reasons:

- The Circle members will be confronted with a number of people they do not normally meet, and the meeting will demonstrate to them the breadth of support that exists in the company.
- Some steering committee members may not be closely and directly involved in Circle activities, and it gives them an opportunity of seeing for themselves what the Circles are achieving and the enthusiasm generated.
- It is worth allowing the early Circle projects to be presented to the steering committee as a whole so that it can see how the programme is developing. DHA have noted that many steering committees have not really 'jelled' until after they have had such an experience.

- It can enable the Quality Council to experience the extent of development.
- Key suppliers and customers can be invited to attend in order to 'sell' the company's approach and to give even more recognition to the teams.

In one company, the steering committee, which was heavily represented by the personnel department and leading trade union activists, was therefore seen by many employees as an extension of the industrial relations negotiating committee. Instead of being constructive, the steering committee members were adopting defensive postures. This resulted in the creation of a Quality Circle policy statement which read like a productivity agreement. Fortunately, however, even in the hostile environment, one of the first Circles managed to reach the presentation stage with their first project and this was presented to the steering committee.

This presentation had a profound effect on both management and union members of the steering committee alike. Several of them admitted astonishment that Quality Circles really did operate in the way that they had been told. This resulted in a dramatic change of attitude amongst steering committee members, who subsequently adopted a totally different approach to Circles, with the result that the steering committee has subsequently been a major influence in the establishment of Circles at other sites.

10. Publicity

This topic can be considered under two headings – internal, and external. Internally, the steering committee will consider the importance of publicity both as a means of giving further stimulation to existing Circles by publicising their achievements, and as a means of encouraging others to participate. Externally, the steering committee may see a value in advertising the company's support for Quality Circles as a means of enhancing the company's reputation in the marketplace.

Internal publicity

The internal forms of publicity may include use of notice boards, newsletters, and a variety of leaflets, pamphlets, etc.

Notice boards may be used to keep employees informed of the activities of Circles in their area. The photographs of Circle members may be posted, and a description of the Circle projects included. In some companies, a separate position on notice boards has been devoted entirely to Circle news, and members are encouraged to contribute material. In Japan these boards are kept up to date by the members themselves.

There are now a great many companies who publish their own internal news sheets, as discussed in an earlier chapter. The production of a news sheet is hard work, but they are generally regarded as worthwhile. They also provide an opportunity to maintain a conscious link between Quality Circles and other improvement activities. Of course, some companies have a regular newspaper anyway, but generally it is not possible to give Circles more than occasional exposure through this medium. Publishing a special newsletter for Circle members gives every Circle a regular opportunity to publicise its own activities and to learn about the achievements of others. This cross-fertilisation is a vital aspect of Circles' development and it was recognition of this important issue that led DHA to produce the first regular Quality Circle journal in Europe entitled *Circle Review*. This has more recently been absorbed into the house journal *Quality Review*, which embraces all facets of Total Quality.

External publicity

External publicity for Circle activities has now emerged in the West as more and more companies become confident of the permanence of their programmes. In Japan, may organisations see this as an extremely valuable way of demonstrating the care they take to produce good products and reliable service. Many sales brochures of Japanese companies feature Quality Circle activities.

11. Recognition

Steering committee members themselves should make every effort possible to take an active interest in Circle activities. This means that in addition to attending the regular steering committee meetings, the members should ask if they can sit in on occasional Circle meetings and presentations. Not only does this give the steering committee members a better insight into the health and vitality of the programme, but also, and most importantly, it demonstrates to the Circles the extent of the committee's interest in their activities.

This personal level of interest is one of the most important forms of recognition for Circles. It must be emphasised of course that steering committee membership does not imply any extra powers than would otherwise be held, and that all such contacts with Circles should be made through the usual channels. This would usually be via the section head, but it would be as well for such impromptu visits to be made also in co-operation with the facilitator.

12. Reward

No topic has evoked so much discussion of Circle achievements as the subject of reward, which was discussed in Chapter 7. All steering committee members should be thoroughly acquainted with the guidelines discussed in that chapter.

Quality Circles can be rewarded for their achievements in many ways, but direct financial rewards should *never* be given. If this rule is ever violated, the Quality Circle programme will have entered the bargaining arena, and Quality Circles of the kind described in this book will cease to exist. In its place, there may remain a money-swapping trade-off structure which will survive until it has been submerged by jealousy, envy, and disagreement.

Part of the attraction of Quality Circles to management is the opportunity they afford to create a sense of identity and corporate loyalty, and for people to feel that their organisation is better for their being there. This cannot be achieved if direct financial rewards are given, but there are many other forms of reward, as discussed in Chapter 7, which contribute positively to this objective and are extremely attractive to Circle members.

13. Assessment

Just as individual Circles vary, so do Circle programmes. Of the many lo-cations initially trained by DHA, whilst all have been successful as far as the Circle programmes are concerned, there are nevertheless extreme differences in the vitality of the programmes. The reasons for these differences are many and complex. Undoubtedly the biggest factor is that in periods of recession some Circle programmes may fail simply because the companies themselves cease to exist. However, apart from such dramatic situations, well-designed Circles programmes have proved to be extremely hardy even during times of redundancy. At Brintons Carpets in Kidderminster, which can proudly claim to have the longest surviving Circles programme in the UK, the entire pro-gramme was almost totally wiped out in the recession of the early 1980s.

The factors which most obviously affect the success of a programme include:

- lack of pre-preparation
- low key steering committee
- wrong choice of facilitator
- entrenchment of Taylorism – a major problem
- Industrial relations tensions (usually relates to Taylorism)
- lack of management support and understanding of the basic concepts
- trade union suspicions
- inadequate leader/member training
- underestimating the importance of all the techniques
- insularity – lack of contact with other organisations
- no linking to policy deployment

These are just a few of the possible causes of dissappointment. The complete list could run to several hundred items.

It is of enormous benefit for a steering committee to establish contact with the steering committees of other companies. This can be achieved by mem-bership of national societies of Quality Circles, or, for those companies which have been trained by DHA, through membership of DHA's International Network of clients.

14. Appreciation

The steering committee should always be alive to the importance of ensuring that all Circles receive adequate recognition for their achievements. Various departmental managers will differ in their personal recognition of this. Consequently, some Circles will feel more appreciated than others. The steering committee should be aware of this and can help overcome any difficulties by giving some Circles more exposure in news sheets, etc. The aim should always be to keep the whole programme at the same healthy level.

15. Liaison

The Circle programme does not exist in isolation from other company activities, some of which may overlap with the work of Circles. In the context of organisational development, it may be necessary for the Quality Circle steering committee to interface with other groups concerned with other concepts such as task force and project group activities in order to produce an integrated programme. Trade unions, for example, may be concerned with the development of FDCs as discussed in the previous chapter.

16. Development

As the programme develops, it will eventually make more and more impact on other activities. The ultimate power of Quality Circles may be realised when Circles become a fully integral part of Total Quality activities – in other words, when everybody can be a member of a Circle or of a management project team. The ultimate aim should be 100 per cent membership, and Quality Circles are simply the way a company manages its people. Before this stage is reached, it will be necessary to establish a formal relationship between functions such as quality control, quality assurance, and Quality Circles. All being well, the people in charge of such functions should have realised the importance of Quality Circles in the achievement of their own objectives and those of Total Quality, and they will be feeding information to the groups. This information will include customer complaints data, articles from Quality journals, and anything else which quality control thinks could enhance Circle activities.

This also applies to other functions such as production engineering, work study, accounts, etc. The steering committee can play an extremely important role in the encouragement of such developments.

17. Linking to Quality Council

With the stong focus of attention which has been given to quality throughout the 1980s it is unlikely that there would be many organisations which have not introduced a quality initiative of one form or another in recent years. It is quite likely that many will already have steering committees for Quality Circles, and are contemplating starting Total Quality programmes, and wish to link the two.

Ideally, the Quality Council should be established first and the Total Quality programme started from the top, with Quality Circles and the suggestion process being the final elements of organisation.

Many people are confused as to the distinction between the Quality Council and the Quality Circles steering committee, or even the need for their initial existence. If such doubts still exist in the mind of the reader it is recommended that Chapters 4 and 5 be revisited and studied carefully. Both are vitally important if a high probability of success is to be achieved.

To summarise the differences:

1. The Quality Council is concerned with
   - The development of Total Quality on a company-wide basis.
   - Establishing the structure for policy development; policy deployment; policy control; and all of the implications of each.
   - Identification of 'management controllable' projects
   - Training of mandatory improvement activities
   - Publicity/recognition/reward, etc.

   This is a horizontal slice of organisation at the highest level.

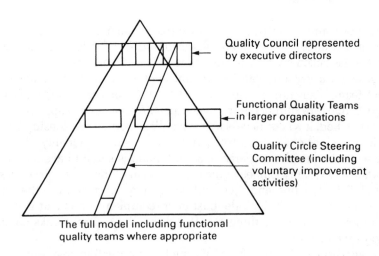

Quality Council represented by executive directors

Functional Quality Teams in larger organisations

Quality Circle Steering Committee (including voluntary improvement activities)

The full model including functional quality teams where appropriate

Fig. 17.2

2. The Quality Circle steering committee is concerned with
   - support and development of the voluntary improvement activities aspects of Total Quality closely linked to the objectives of the Quality Council.

This is a diagonal slice of organisation from the top to the bottom.

Summary

It may be seen from the foregoing that the compositon and constitution of a steering committee is vital to the success of Quality Circles. It may also appear that such activities may be time-consuming. This is not true. The first few meetings may be lengthy and frequent, but once the policy has been established and the Circle programme commenced, the meetings will become shorter and less frequent. In an on-going programme, the meetings would normally last for about two hour's, and occur monthly or bi-monthly.

Those organisations that have already begun Circle programmes but have not yet established steering committees would do well to start such committees immediately. On well-known American company did not do this, and the programme collapsed when the facilitator left. Fortunately, it has since been re-established, and they now have an active steering committee.

CHAPTER 18

VITALISING AND DEVELOPING QUALITY CIRCLE PROGRAMMES

Perhaps one of the more common reasons why Western Quality Circle programmes have produced disappointing results is that many managers think that Quality Circles represent some form of perpetual motion: they perceive that all that is necessary is to light the touch paper and walk away, leaving the Circles to look after themselves.

Far from representing perpetual motion, Quality Circles really to need considerable management attention and management development. The more attention managers devote to Quality Circles, the better will be the results. The development of our people has been neglected for so long that there are years of work ahead before their true potential can be realised. It is likely that the difference in the level of support given by Japanese managers and by their Western counterparts relates to the difference in expectation. Western managers have low levels of expectation, and therefore devote little time to supporting these activities. Unfortunately, this is a vicious circle, because the lack of support leads to lack of results.

Those hard-pressed managers who may despair on reading this can take heart from the evidence which suggests that many of the problems that make their lives difficult in the normal way will be considerably reduced by the increasingly co-operative spirit that will develop in their department when Circles are properly introduced. Consequently, they will be able to devote more time to supportive measures when necessary. Japanese managers are very aware of this, hence the time they devote to the support of Quality Circle activities.

In this chapter, the various ways in which Circles may be supported will be explored. The main theme will be the stimulation and encouragement of Circles during their continuous development. These supportive activities may be separated into two groups – internal and external.

The internal activities are those activities that can be established within the organisation independently of any outside influence. However, a study of Quality Circle activities in Japan shows that tremendous benefits can be gained from giving Quality Circles the opportunity to participate in relevant activities outside their own organisation. These have been developed in Japan to a very sophisticated level through to activities of the Japanese Union of Scientists and Engineers and QC Circle Headquarters. This external support is regarded by the author to be of such critical importance to the survival and development of Quality Circles that the internal and external aspects of support are covered separately in this chapter.

Internal support

It was suggested in an earlier chapter that Quality Circles pass through four phases of development. In this chapter, the supportive measures which may be considered by management, trade unions, and steering committees will be related to each phase.

Phase 1 – The problem-solving phase

At this early stage, which should last for about one year, Quality Circles will be concerned mainly with improving their skills in the use of the basic techniques, and with developing effective presentations. They will sometimes be quite sensitive at this time, and it is important to ensure that their newly won self-confidence is not shattered by thoughtless remarks from overbearing managers or others who expect too much too soon.

The supportive measures should primarily be those aimed to give encouragement and confidence, and may include:

- Features and photographs of the newly formed Circles in house journals. This will show the Circles the importance with which their activities are regarded, and is a very positive form of stimulation.
- Repeat presentations. New Circles may be given the opportunity to repeat their presentations to others. This will enable them to 'polish their act' and will lead to even more impressive presentations in the future.
- Participation in competitions, such as Quality awareness campaigns.
- Exchange visits. Towards the end of this initial phase of development, the Circles may be given the opportunity to make outside visits. This will boost their confidence even further, will show recognition, and lead the group into the second phase.

Phase 2 – Monitoring and problem solving

There is no clear distinction between this phase and phase 1, other than the fact that the Circle will exhibit greater self-assurance. When it seems appropriate (and this will be determined by the level of skill achieved in the use of the basic techniques), the Circle should be introduced to control techniques. The use of simple control charts will enable the Circles to monitor and control the levels of some problems, and skill in this ability will lead the group into phase 3.

Because monitoring and self-control is relatively new to many people outside Japan, there is great value to be obtained from allowing Circles at this stage to witness the presentations of other Circles which have developed this ability. Occasionally, DHA organise conventions of Japanese and Western Circles in London; participants have gained enormous benefit from seeing the current level of achievements of their Japanese counterparts. Attendance at such conventions is to be greatly encouraged. Better still, allow Circle leaders, facilitators and members to visit Japan to see first hand. Many of those who have attended and participated in these conventions have commented on the contrast between the level of development of the Japanese teams and their Western counterparts.

Phase 3 – Innovation: self-improvement and problem solving

The important feature of this phase is that the Circles are becoming innovative. In addition to their problem-solving techniques, which will continue for as long as they remain in existence, the Circles will begin to seek ways of making improvements. In other words, they will no longer be satisfied with maintaining the status quo of their departmental performance. It is at this time that the Circles can be introduced to policy deployment.

The innovative phase can be a very creative and rewarding phase of Quality Circle development, and will demand a greater involvement with others outside the Circle. In particular, the Circles will seek more help and advice from specialists and specialist departments. They will become involved in experimentation, and take an interest in innovative developments relating to their work. In Japan many companies provide facilities for Quality Circles to actually produce the improvements they are working on.

This can and should be a most rewarding time for the supportive manager. The degree of trust and respect between the manager and the Circle will have grown to such an extent that the manager will become increasingly involved in the Circle activities.

Supportive measures that will be particularly useful at this phase, as well as all those measures relevant to the earlier phases, will also include:

- Meeting with quality control and other specialist departments to discuss problems of mutual concern.
- Formal feedback to Quality Circles from quality control, including:
    customer complaint data
    fault analysis
    general quality information
- Formal feedback from accounts and control departments on:
    lost time
    variances
    standards, etc.
- Feeding Circles with relevant technical data relating to new equipment,

sales brochures, and innovative articles from journals relating to their work.

● Giving them further access to textbooks and any other materials that may be of interest.

Phase 4 – Full self-control

This is the ultimate phase in the development of a Quality Circle. The time lapse between start-up and the commencement of this phase will vary considerably depending upon many factors including:

● degree of self-control prior to start-up of Circles programme
● level of education of Circle members
● support of steering committee and facilitator

Even though a few Circles may reach this stage of development quite quickly it is likely to be several years before this phase is reached on a company-wide scale. It may take at least five years and probably as many as ten for some large companies. It will never be reached without the deliberate and planned support of management consciously working towards this state.

To achieve this goal it is essential that the organisation makes the achievement a corporate objective, and works systematically through each of the phases 1, 2, and 3. It is only when the fourth phase is reached on a corporate scale that the full power of the Quality Circle approach will be realised.

Only then, when this full integration of effect has been achieved, can an organisation justly claim to have successfully introduced Total Quality. At this stage, the organisation will have fully integrated the activities of Quality Circles with all other functions in the organisation. Circles in one department will be co-operating with Circles elsewhere, both on and off site. The Circles will also communicate directly with other organisations as part of their activities.

Sadly, there are virtually no organisations in the West which have achieved anything like the potential which this concept affords, even though many of them have been operating Quality Circles for many years. Most have stagnated at phase 1. If more executives and managers had been to Japan on properly organised industrial study tours, and witnessed the state of the art for themselves, the current situation could have been very different. Instead, they spend huge sums of money on courses at Management Colleges, many of which are of dubious real value in terms of achieving international competitive standards. There can be no substitute for the first-hand experience of seeing for one's self.

Additional supportive activities

In addition to the suggestions given earlier, there are many other ways in which an organisation can both stimulate and utilise Quality Circles. Whilst Circles are primarily involved in problem solving, one must never lose sight of the fact that they are also concerned with making work itself more interesting, more rewarding, and more enjoyable. Circle meetings should be fun, and comments such as 'I look forward to Circle meetings' should be frequently heard. If Circle meetings are thought to be boring, there is something fundamentally wrong.

Management and steering committees can do much to ensure that Circles are seen to be an exciting concept. For example, the steering committee might perhaps decide to organise a poster competition where Circles are invited to design posters on some selected theme such as:

- quality awareness
- cost reduction
- energy saving, etc.

Occasionally, one or two Circles may be stuck for a problem. This is most likely in situations where the work is particularly simple and monotonous. Such Circles could be given the opportunity to produce posters, instruction sheets, or other ideas which may be the result of brainstorming by both the steering committee and the Circles themselves.

Quality Month

Another feature of Japanese management is the concept of 'Quality Month': November has been designated 'National Quality Month'. During this month national conventions are held for all levels of employee, but in addition to these, individual companies also organise their own internal activities.

As part of a programme for the development of Total Quality, there is great benefit in such a concept. Each company may designate a particular month in the year as its Quality Month. During this month it may hold special conventions where selected project team and Circle presentations are made, run poster competitions, or allow the Circle to come up with their own ideas on how Quality Month should be organised.

In order to institute a similar supportive approach DHA have suggested to their clients that they collectively designate one month in the year as Quality Month. It is hoped, therefore, that a 'National Quality Month' will develop in non-Japanese countries along much the same lines as in Japan. At the time of writing, this idea had not yet found fertile ground, although there is now a world quality day! The author has also suggested that the Queen's Award be modified to provide the stimulus offered by the Japanese Deming Award. The response of the organisers of this award was that 'We see no need to change our approach at present'. Nero fiddled whilst Rome burned....

External support – Circle network

The external supportive structure to Quality Circle activities is equal in importance to the internal activities of individual organisations if the true potential of Quality Circles is to be fully realised.

Circle programmes run by the more independent companies which deliberately isolate themselves from others are notably less impressive. There is no doubt whatsoever that mutual visits, exchanges of experience, and the general camaraderie that develops from co-operation between different companies is a significant factor which characterises the more successful companies.

From the very outset of DHA's activities in the field of Quality Circles, this interactive spirit has been vigorously encouraged and developed. Commencing initially with facilitator workshops, where trained facilitators were given the opportunity to meet each other at residential workshops, these activities have been extended to embrace the full spectrum of supportive activities into what was originally referred to as Quality Network.

Full membership of the Network was restricted to Quality Circle participants from companies and organisations which have undergone a programme of training conducted by one of DHA's senior consultants. However, with the formation of the National Society of Quality Circles, and the fact that many DHA clients were amongs its founder members, this Network was thought to have served its purpose, and support switched to the national body.

One of the main aims in allowing Circles to attend conventions is to increase their confidence and enthusiasm. This can only be achieved if all participants have been trained in a similar manner. This is particularly important in the case of fledgling Circles which expect to learn from their peers.

National societies of Quality Circles

Awareness of the importance of the Japanese Union of Scientists and Engineers' involvement in the spread of Circles in Japan has led to the development of national supportive movements elsewhere and most countries now have some national form of supportive body. Unfortunately this was in many cases led to conflict with more traditional bodies created originally to promote Quality Control and Quality Assurance. These professional bodies were slow to respond to the concept of Total Quality, with its strong participative element, and consequently, new organisations sprang up to support these activities and in many cases, these are in either open or subversive conflict with the more traditional groups. This conflict must be resolved if any semblance of JUSE-style organisations are to be successfully created.

United States

The International Association of Quality Circles (IAQC) was formed in California in the mid-1970s for the propagation of Quality Circles. Since its inception, the organisation has developed a wide range of training courses, organised conventions, and published a considerable quantity of materials for the advancement of the concept.

Also, in the USA there is an organisation known as the American Society for Quality Control (ASQC). This organisation, whilst taking an interest in Quality Circles, is primarily concerned with Quality Control. Internationally ASQC has links with both JUSE and the European Organisation for Quality Control (EOQC).

Whilst Quality Circles only form a small part of the activities of ASQC and EOQC at present, it is hoped that their importance will increase dramatically when Total Quality begins to emerge from the more well-developed Circle programmes of some larger companies. Unfortunately there appears to be little evidence of this in the late 1980s, and it seems that the preoccupation with certification and standards which has dominated these organisations for over two decades will continue to dominate in the next.

CHAPTER 19

THE BASIC TOOLS FOR QUALITY IMPROVEMENT

All types of group formed within a Total Quality organisation will spend much of their meeting time collecting data, solving problems and preparing presentations.

Sometimes problems can be solved through discussion and consensus but more generally they are solved by using problem-solving techniques. These are techniques to identify problems, to collect and analyse data, examine causes, suggest solutions, evaluate the solutions, and to implement them.

There is also a discipline. All too often people involved in problem solving jump to conclusions and make decisions based on opinions, not facts. Even when facts are used, the results may not match the prediction because the data was inadequate. Even people who have had years of training and experience in problem solving frequently make errors of judgement, and so great care must be taken to ensure that anyone involved in these activities has been made keenly aware of the pitfalls, and the limitations of both the techniques and their own knowledge.

One of the main fears of managers who are as yet unacquainted with Quality Circle type groups in Total Quality is that Circles made up of groups of people who have experienced very little education, and who are performing unskilled and semi-skilled tasks, may not be able to achieve very creditable results. These managers do not realise the power of the simple techniques that are used to solve problems in Quality improvement activities.

These basic techniques, usually seven in all, gravitated downwards into Circles during the formative years of Total Quality in Japan, and form the basis of the problem-solving activities of managers. They are frequently referred to in Japan as the seven basic tools, and have proved to be particularly effective when used in all types of small group activity. It must be emphasised that these are only the basic tools – a 'get-you-started' kit. Later on, as the groups mature, their members will want to use the techniques in more and more sophisticated ways and will add further skills to their list when they are found to be relevant to their work. At management levels, the techniques will be supplemented by a wide variety of additional ones, and even the basic tools can be developed further.

The seven techniques are:

- brainstorming

- data collection
- data analysis
- Pareto analysis
- cause and effect analysis
- histograms
- control techniques

Later on, the groups should be encouraged to learn method study techniques, and a further group referred to in Japan as the 7-M-Tools or Seven Management Tools.

If presentation techniques are included, the list comprises eight basic elements. In this chapter we will review each technique in turn except for the data analysis and histogram techniques, which are discussed in Chapter 20.

Brainstorming

The idea of brainstorming is to use the collective thinking power of a group of people to come up with ideas they would not think of by themselves. It is particularly effective when used in small group activities.

Brainstorming is the basis of much of the work carried out by all levels of problem-solving group teams and is used in one form or another at several stages in a team's project. It is used

1. to help identify problems;
2. to help analyse causes; and
3. to highlight possible solutions.

Some problems, once evaluated, may have only certain obvious solutions, and brainstorming would not be used in those cases, but in others there may be an almost unlimited number of possible alternatives and brainstorming is particularly effective.

Why brainstorming?

Over the years there has been considerable controversy about the value of brainstorming. Some academics have provided evidence to show that individuals can produce equally creative ideas on their own without brainstorming. However, this is usually because the brainstorming sessions they refer to are generally conducted differently from the approach described here.

This approach evolved during the early years of small group improvement activities, and as with the other basic techniques it is very simple. For example, the groups are not usually taught about creative and lateral thinking in the form in which it appears in most brainstorming training programmes.

Not only is brainstorming itself useful in small group activities, but the associated discipline helps create cohesion amongst the members and helps considerably to avoid the conflicts that are so common in other group activities such as committee meetings, public meetings, etc. In fact the manner in which the technique is practised has been found to be so effective that it is generally quite unnecessary to train team leaders and members formally in the handling of group dynamic difficulties because these rarely ever arise.

The method

Teams use brainstorming first of all to identify problems. For this they use large sheets of paper, usually flip charts so that everyone in the group can see what is being written.

The members take turns to submit ideas to highlight the problems they are familiar with in their work. No idea is censured during the brainstorming session and all ideas are written down. No idea should be thought of as stupid or ridiculous, and no discussion is allowed at this stage. In this way, the group will usually highlight a large number of problems. Sometimes as many as 200 to 300 ideas have been recorded in such sessions.

These ideas will be wide-ranging and comprise almost all areas covered by the knowledge of the group's specialists, and others in their section may all contribute their ideas to those of the team members. When the members feel the list is adequate or complete, and is representative of the problems they are confronted with, they will then commence evaluation.

In the case of voluntary teams such as Quality Circles, the goal will be to highlight just one problem out of the many they have identified, which will form the basis of their project.

Figure 19.1 shows the results of such a brainstorming session carried out by a Quality Circle concerned with the subassembly of parts. The Circle took just one hour to produce this list. A list of this length or even longer is quite typical.

One Quality Manager, when looking at such a list, commented, 'Although I recognise every problem on that list, I have never seen them written on one sheet of paper before and I did not realise that there were so many!'. And his comment related to only one of many work areas in the Company!

Because a group should only tackle one problem at a time, it may seem time-wasting to carry out such an exhaustive classification of problems, but this process is really quite important. It is only through this means that the Circle can be sure that the problems identified by each member of the group are given equal consideration.

Once the ideas have been listed they are then evaluated. Basically, they fall into three categories:

1. non group controllabe
2. partially group controllable
3. totally group controllable

Insufficient tools
Parts incompatible
Sub-standard materials
Shortages
Wrong materials issued
Wrong tools
Lack of training
Methods
Presentation of methods
Out of date drawings
Ambiguous work instructions
Bad reporting of defects
Insufficient labour
Incorrect change form issued
Poor quality drawings
Communication with outside
   suppliers
Poor work station layout
Badly worn jigs
Too much waiting time
Acceptable quality standard?
Poor design of tooling
Performance levels unknown
General untidiness of work station
Too much walking about for parts
No system of tooling recall
No first aid in area
Poor lighting
Insufficient assembly aids
Insufficient tooling information

Lack of bench space
Wrong working height of benches
Feedback of fault information
Personality conflicts
Lack of inspection stages
No list of alternative parts
Flexibility of labour
No indication of priorities
Bad tasting coffee
Service operator availability
Standard of supervision
Insufficient cleaning
No job satisfaction
Safety shoes
Morale
Weight of components
Insufficient data
Lack of identification of parts
Poor storage facilities
Too many indents used
Poor deburring of something? parts
No forward visibility of work
Lack of humour
Air conditioning
Unused items in work area
Uncomfortable seats
Job discussion
Lack of management communication
No recreation facilities
Incorrect standard times
Work instructions

Fig. 19.1

Whilst it may not always be possible to separate the second and third categories, it is necessary first of all to remove those which the group believes are totally outside its control. They do this by systematically going down the list one by one, and asking the question, 'Can we do anything about this problem?'. If the answer is 'No', that item is scratched from the list. For example, the team which produced the brainstorming list in Figure 19.1 decided that some of the problems outside their control were:

Insufficient labour
Poor quality drawings
Too much waiting time
Lack of bench space
Wrong working height of benches
Poor coffee

Standard of supervision
Job satisfaction
Safety shoes
Morale
Weight of components, etc.

The members decided that these were matters that they could complain about but not do anything about. Although they had the rest of the week in which they could voice their opinions about these problems, they felt that they were outside the scope of the Circle from a project point of view.

A newly formed Quality Circle would normally take the remaining problems and sort them in order of easiness to solve, starting with the easiest. Sometimes there may be a problem which frustrates the group so much that it decides to tackle it regardless of its complexity, and there would be nothing wrong with that. It would be as well, however, to warn the team not to tackle anything which it feels will be too complex or time-consuming in the early stages, since failure can lead to a loss of confidence at this sensitive stage and the group may even disintegrate under such circumstances. A quick success, however small, is very important to a newly formed team. Not only do the members acquire a sense of achievement, but others outside the group will notice that they are getting things done.

Once the team has completed its brainstorming and perhaps solved one or two simple problems, it will want to pick a problem which will make some impact. Gradually, with encouragement, they will select progressively more challenging problems.

The members of the group are likely to say, 'Let's pick the problem which costs the most', or 'Let's see if we can reduce customer complaints', 'reduce losses', 'reduce handling time', or many other items. In other words, the group has now progressed to selecting a theme. This is consistent with the concept of policy deployment.

The teams are likely then to select projects which help in the achievement of the goals determined by policy development. If they have decided on a theme, such as 'delays', they will have to identify the problems that cause delays. This will take them back to the brainstorming sheets, from which they will identify all the problems that cause delays, and these will then be listed separately. Naturally the members of the group will want to tackle the problem which causes the longest delays. For this it will be necessary to collect data.

Data collection (check sheets)

Whilst data collection itself may be easy there are many pitfalls:

- Where to collect data?
- When to collect?
- How much to collect?
- Who is to collect?
- What data?

and so on.

One only has to look at the results of opinion polls and compare them with

CHECK SHEET OF DAMAGED PARTS								
DESCRIPTION	Mon	Tues	Wed	Thurs	Fri	Total	%	£
PART A	HHT ||| HHT	HHT HHT ||						
PART B	||	||||						
PART C	HHT ||	HHT |||						
PART D	|HH HHT HHT ||||	HHT HHT HHT HHT ||						
PART E	||	|						
PART F	HHT |	|||						
OTHERS	||	HHT						

Name of Group____SOUTH SIDE PROJECT TEAM____

Date _____

Part Nos .... /Description ...Torn Bags.................................

Fig. 19.2

General Election results to know that data collection even when carried out by experts sometimes goes wrong.

Obviously, one cannot spend the time and effort giving team members 'in-depth' training in sophisticated data collection and analysis techniques, and so once again, the message is 'keep it simple'. In doing so, one must make sure that members are made aware of the limitations of the techniques they are using, and if they need to be more certain about the accuracy of their data, they should enlist the services of a trained statistics specialist to work with them.

The data gathering technique most frequently used by teams is the check sheet. Here the items about which the data is to be collected are listed on the left-hand side of the sheet. The time period for data collection is determined and listed in columns across the sheet, as shown in Figure 19.2. The tally check method is normally used as the data is obtained.

Before groups progress to the collection of data, they should be made aware of the ever-present dangers of reaching misleading results. Practical training using aids such as bead boxes, dice, and rods, should be used to acquaint the members thoroughly with the risks of errors due to:

1. bias
2. wrong sample size for accuracy required
3. non-repeatability of results
4. inaccurate measurements

Members should also be made aware of the importance of agreeing standards when subjective measurements are being made for such features as 'feel', 'taste', 'colour', 'shade', 'surface roughness', etc.

There can be no doubt whatsoever that the effectiveness of a group's problem-solving activities will be very dependent upon the quality of the training given in these important aspects of its work. Indeed, the foundations laid in the members' basic understanding of simple data will become the basis of all subsequent development of their skills. This training should never be skimped or bypassed, however compelling the reasons may seem at the time.

Pareto analysis

Having collected the data relating to the problems highlighted, the frequency of each occurrence is shown in the Totals column (see Figure 9.2). If the costs of these events are known, then it would be a simple matter to present the results on a cost base, which obviously has more meaning and makes a greater impact on management. However, whilst this data may be meaningful to the team members, it will mean very little to others outside the group who have not been involved. Lists of numbers are usually extremely unimpressive and if they are to be used to communicate ideas to others, it usually makes more impact if they are presented in more graphic forms. This is where the Pareto form of column graph becomes useful.

Pareto was an American Italian scholar who discovered that about 80 per cent of a nation's wealth was in the hands of about 20 per cent of the population. At about the same time another academic named Lorenz found that this relationship seemed to hold good in a wide variety of situations; for example an analysis of the value of items held in a store is likely to reveal that about 80 per cent of the value is contained in about 20 per cent of the items. The same is frequently true of quality failure costs, such as scrap, rework, customer complaints, etc., machine or equipment breakdown time, delay, telephone usage, etc.

When such relationships exist, column graphs with each column representing a separate feature will usually result in one or two bars being considerably longer than the others, as shown in Figure 19.3.

However, the Pareto diagram is not drawn in this haphazard manner. It is usual to place the longest column on the left-hand side of the diagram, with the bars going in descending order of size towards the right-hand side. The final column, regardless of its length, contains the miscellaneous items which were not itemised individually. The Pareto diagram, therefore, when properly constructed will usually look like the one shown in Figure 19.4.

This diagram indicates far more dramatically than a list of numbers that the biggest problem or the most frequently occurring event is item D.

There are several advantages in using this approach:

1. The team members themselves will be more impressed by the length of the first one or two bars, and this enables them to become goal orientated.

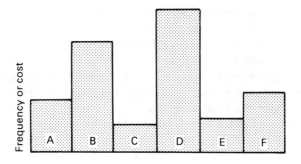

Fig. 19.3

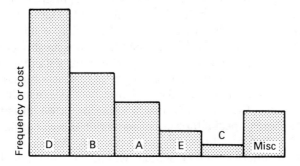

Fig. 19.4

2. It is a useful way of communicating the results of the data collection to non-team members, particularly those who may have asisted in the collection of the data.
3. It makes a big impact in a management presentation, and shows the thoroughness with which the group has carried out its work.
4. Once the data has been illustrated in this way, the team can really see whether it has made improvements as it can compare similar data which may be obtained after implementing its ideas.
5. It is a goal-setting mechanism which tends to concentrate the attention of members and non-members alike on the few important problems, rather than spread it across the many trivial ones.

Cause and effect analysis

Basically there are two principal forms of cause and effect analysis, and both may be used, depending upon the type of problem being tackled. Whilst many variants of both techniques exist, the most popular are the cause classification and the process analysis technique.

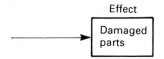

Fig. 19.5

When the principal problem has been selected by Pareto analysis, the next stage will be to classify the most probable causes. To do this the team may construct a cause classification or fishbone diagram. This diagram is also known as the Ishikawa diagram, after its inventor, and is constructed by using the brainstorming process described earlier. However, this time, instead of simply listing the ideas, it is helpful if similar or related ideas can be grouped together. The cause classification diagram enables this to be achieved.

The problem or effect is written in a box on the right-hand side or a large sheet of paper, fixed to the wall or on a flip chart where it can be seen by everyone, as before in brainstorming. An arrow is then drawn pointing towards the box, as shown in Figure 19.5.

The team must then decide the most appropriate headings under which the probable causes can be listed. In most cases there are four, and these are:

1. Manpower – the people doing the work (people, supervision, operator, etc.)
2. Machines – equipment or tooling used to do the work (equipment, apparatus, plant, etc.)
3. Methods – specifications or job instructions
4. Materials supplied or required to do the work

Occasionally others such as vendor, supplier, environment, office, etc., may be more applicable, or may be included in addition to those mentioned above.

These headings form the ends of further arrows pointing towards the main arrow already drawn on the sheet of paper (see Figure 19.6).

Once the diagram has been prepared the team is ready to commence the brainstorming process of identifying what it thinks are likely to be the most

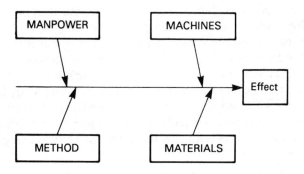

Fig. 19.6

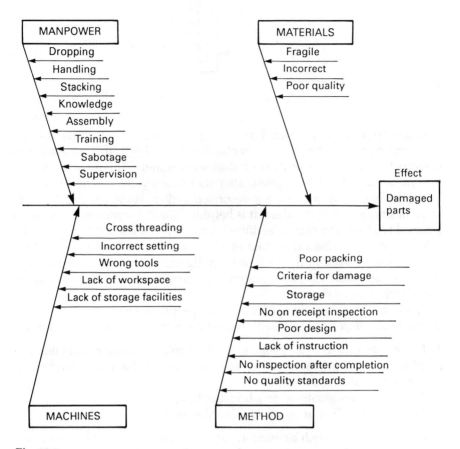

Fig. 19.7

probable causes. Someone is selected to act as leader, and to write the ideas on the diagram as they are suggested. It is frequently possible to write the ideas under more than one heading, for example 'Incorrect setting' could be either a manpower problem, or a method problem, depending on whether it is the method which is wrong or whether the person doing the job is using the wrong method; it is therefore necessary for the member to guide the brainstorming leader by prefixing his or her idea with 'under Method incorrect setting' or 'under Machines', and then stating the idea. Figure 19.7 shows such a cause classification diagram after completion.

As a general rule, it will usually take a group one meeting to complete a diagram similar to the one shown in Figure 19.7, and frequently this will take place during the same meeting in which the Pareto chart was roughly drawn and the problem selected. Normally, though, a team will deliberately make the completion of the cause and effect diagram span two meetings. This is for two important reasons:

1. Not all the best or most relevant ideas are thought of in the first brainstorming session, and the problem is only *selected* at that meeting. Members need time to mull over their ideas, think about the problem on their own, and make observations during their work. At the second session many new and important ideas may come to the surface.

2. It gives non-team members and opportunity to voice their opinions and to have their ideas included with the others which have been mentioned. In the case of Quality Circles and other voluntary group activities it is vitally important that other people in the section should see the Circle as 'their section's Circle'. Even with mandatory project teams this principle should be followed wherever possible. Circles should be encouraged to post their diagrams in the work area so that others can add their ideas at any time. (Obviously, a Circle would not do this if it were likely that graffiti would appear, and this may be a problem in the early stages of development.)

As with the basic brainstorming, now that the diagram is complete, it is necessary to evaluate the suggestions. This evaluation is carried out in much the same way as the initial brainstorming, except that this time the team is attempting to identify the most likely major causes from amongst the many potential causes that have been listed.

The team leader will take each idea in turn and ask the members whether they think the idea in question is likely to be a major cause of the problem. If the answer is no, then a mark is made against the item to signify that it has been evaluated, and the leader will then move on to the next idea, and so on. If the group, by consensus, believes that the idea may be a major cause, then the leader will circle that idea, and again move on to the next. This process continues until all the ideas have been evaluated. At this stage, it is likely that there will be a small number of ideas, usually between about one and four, that have been circled.

The next step will be to rank these ideas in order of priority, and again, the typical approach is to vote. Following this stage the cause classification diagram will probably look similar to that shown in Figure 19.8.

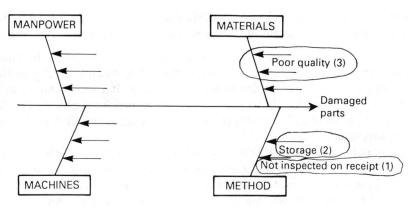

Fig. 19.8

In this example, the members of the group believed that 'not inspected on receipt' was the prime cause of their problem. They did not know this with certainty, so it was necessary for them to verify their opinion. The subjective assesment just described is really intended to save time and to home in quickly on the most plausible possible causes rather than to spread attention over the less likely.

The evaluation depends upon the nature of the cause. In the case described above, because the Circle members now know the number of occurrences of the problem from their data collection, they can find the proportion of parts that were damaged on receipt.

It is likely that they would have arranged for some form of goods inwards check to be carried out in order to validate their opinion. If they are proved right, they can proceed to develop some kind of incoming material control, possibly recommend some form of co-operation with the supplier and, if the Circle has been well trained, evaluate the costs and benefits of their improvement prior to making a management presentation.

But what if their data collection proves them wrong and shows that incoming parts were not faulty? Then they must go back to the cause classification diagram, and the second most likely cause will be evaluated and verified in the same way. Of course, different causes may require different methods of verification, and these may include histograms, drawings showing defect locations, polar diagrams, further Pareto diagrams, etc., and the team members should be trained in these techniques during the preliminary stages of its work. If they do not receive adequate training, then activities will be severely restricted and achievements relatively unimpressive.

This is proving to be a significant problem in Western organisations, and even in the more impressive ones, there is a marked difference between the relative thoroughness of Japanese and other problem-solving activities.

Cause analysis and process analysis

Some problems require a deeper analysis than that which is afforded by the cause classification diagram. In this case, three possible alternatives exist:

1. *Construct further cause classification diagrams*, this time on the cause that has been highlighted as a prime suspect. For example, in Figure 19.7 'poor packing' was identified as a possible cause. If it were thought to be the prime cause it would be useful to place this problem in the box on the right of the sheet and the team could conduct a cause classification session on that topic.
2. *Carry out cause analysis.* This only varies slightly from cause classification but involves the leader in asking questions of the group as a whole. In the previous example, had 'poor quality materials' been selected, the leader would ask, 'In what way are the materials of poor quality?'. Any member could answer and someone might say, 'variable hardness'. The leader

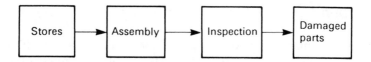

Fig. 19.9

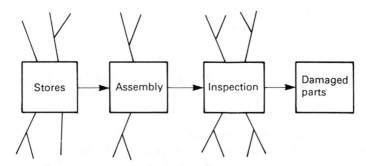

Fig. 19.10

would then say, 'Are there any other causes of poor quality?' and perhaps a suggestion might be that they were 'out of alignment'. This line of questioning would continue until all the ideas had been exhausted, and he would then return to the first idea and ask, 'Why is there variable hardness?', and so on. This process is an extremely penetrating method for getting down to the finest detail, and many problems are solved in this way.

3. *Process analysis.* This technique is essential for cross-functional group activities, and features in a high proportion of such projects. It is less relevant at the level of Quality Circles, who will be mainly concerned with very specific problems. So far, we have discussed problems that occur at only one stage or point in an operation, but sometimes they may occur over several stages. In this case, the teams may decide to use a further variant of the cause and effect analysis by preparing a 'process analysis' diagram. To do this, again, the name of the problem is written in a box, but this time, the names of the operations are written in sequence in adjacent boxes across the sheet, as shown in Figure 19.9.

At this stage, the team conducts a brainstorming session on each box in turn. The leader will ask, 'In what way can Stores cause damaged parts?'. As before, the ideas are recorded on the diagram. When those relating to Stores are exhausted, the leader will turn to Assembly, and finally to Inspection. At this point the diagram will probably look like Figure 19.10.

Such a diagram is an extremely useful way of highlighting common elements. Factors such as lack of job instructions, contamination, or lack of training, may be evident at each stage, indicating that there may be serious widespread problems.

Presentation

When the team members have completed their analysis and verified their solutions, it is likely that they will have carried out an extremely thorough piece of work. They will probably feel proud of their achievements and will have enjoyed working together as a team. They will be looking forward to presenting their ideas to whoever may be concerned with the solution or conclusion they have reached.

This presentation should be the highlight of all group activities. Throughout the project the teams should have been mindful of this, and so the presentation will be a climax to their activities. It is therefore extremely important that the management team does not in any way underestimate the importance of this occasion.

Project presentations fulfil the following goals:

1. give recognition to the team's achievements.
2. allow higher levels of management to judge for themselves the value of small group and, where appropriate, Quality Circle activities.
3. enable others, possibly less committed, to see how the improvement process works in order to gain wider acceptance.

There are also many other good reasons why teams may make their presentation on various occasions and in other circumstances, and these have been discussed in an earlier chapter. In view of the importance attached to project presentations it is vitally important that teams be given adequate training to make them in a professional way.

It must be emphasised again that management is under no obligation to accept a team's proposal if it does not wish to do so. It is the responsibility of the members to 'sell their idea in such a way that it appears attractive to the appropriate level of management'. They should be trained to speak the upper manager's language, in order to present their ideas in the context of measures which are uppermost in the minds of most managers, namely:

- cost improvements
- quality improvements
- scheduling or inventory improvements, etc.

Rejection of improvement team proposals is fortunately extremely rare. If it becomes obvious that a team is heading towards a totally unacceptable conclusion, there are usually many opportunities to warn them of this. If the members still insist on pursuing the idea, that is up to them, but the group will be encouraged to offer alternative ideas to give the decision-makers a choice when it comes to the presentation.

In the case of Quality Circles, following the presentation, and hopefully the acceptance of the proposal, the team will begin thinking about its next project. At this stage the members may wish to brainstorm all over again, or in many cases, take the next problem on the list.

It will be seen therefore that the brainstorming can be used as a work sheet. They will only conduct a further brainstorming when they begin to feel that the list needs topping up, or that many new problems have surfaced, or when they have noted problems relating to them on other Quality Circles' brainstorming lists. They may also add items retrieved from Quality Control defects analysis, customer complaints or suggestions from non-Circle members.

Occasionally, the company may decide to initiate a quality awareness campaign, and may invite Circles to participate in some activity, such as a poster competition, or the design of a novel product. Once Quality Circle have become established, there is an endless variety of activities in which they can participate. The two most important things to remember are that the one hour per week is 'the Circles' hour', and that self-control is the ultimate goal.

CHAPTER 20

PROJECT TEAM DATA GATHERING AND ANALYSIS

Learning the techniques

It is necessary for project teams and Quality Circles to acquire a basic under-standing of data: how data can be collected, analysed, and controlled. Two of the basic techniques for handling data – check sheets and Pareto analysis – were briefly reviewed in the previous chapter. In this chapter we shall look at data collection and analysis as it applies to small group activities in order to show the depth of training that should be given to new team members.

Types of data

Basically there are three kinds of data:

1. variable data, i.e. speed, temperature, time, volume, weight, length, voltage, resistance current, pressure, etc.;
2. countable data – or attributable – i.e. number of errors, right/wrong, is/is not, black/white, broken/not broken, etc.;
3. subjective data – this is subjective to the senses, i.e. taste, feel, sound, appearance, etc., and can be treated as countable in most cases.

The differences and similarities should be understood by all forms of group, and teams must be able to identify and to deal with each of these categories, all of which are likely to occur at various times and stages in project work at all levels.

100 per cent inspection versus sampling

Data collection can be both time-consuming and, often, tedious. The question of how much data to collect is always difficult to answer. Of course, a statis-tician will have no difficulty because he will know how to use formulae or sampling tables to give him his answer. Generally speaking, Quality Circles and, frequently, teams at other levels do not have this level of knowledge and fortunately for the majority of their activities, a fairly rough-and-ready result is all that is required. Nevertheless, the teams will need to have some guidance on this point.

Assuming a perfect inspector and perfect measurements, 100 per cent inspection will provide the answers we need. However, this is not always possible or practical. For example, 100 per cent inspection of one day's production of washers when output is in the order of tens of thousands per day could not be justified financially, unless of course it could be done automatically. Fortunately it is not usually necessary. Therefore, sampling of some kind must be considered. In any case, 100 per cent inspection is rarely perfect, and sampling is frequently more accurate – if it is carried out properly.

In the case of a continuous process, it will be necessary to agree on a representative period over which the observations will be made.

There are two basic risks which are always present in sampling:

1. the data indicates that something has changed, when in fact it has not,
2. the data indicates that it has not changed, when in fact it has.

Whilst these risks will always be present to some extent, they are in fact directly related to the size of the sample. The bigger the sample, the smaller the risk. The team must decide roughly how much risk it is prepared to take, or the degree of certainty it wishes to have to be reasonably confident that it is correct.

It is not necessary to bombard a newly formed group with deep statistical theory in order to be able to do this. Most people, in their everyday experience of life, with the addition of skilful teaching and guidance, are capable of developing a common-sense awareness of the limitations of the data they are collecting. There are several alternative ways in which this awareness can be achieved, depending upon the kind of data to be collected. One such method is described in the following example.

Example

With countable data, boxes of various coloured beads can be used for a simple demonstration. If one colour of bead is classified as a defect, and all the remainder are classified as good items, the following demonstration can be carried out.

Equipment

1. Box containing approximately 1,000 beads or other similar items, carefully mixed, with a fixed percentage nominally defective.
2. Chart papers ruled off into columns or rows with the rows marked 0, 1, 2, progressively.

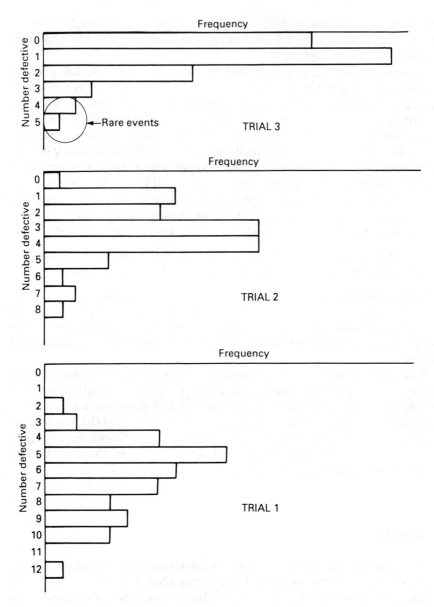

Fig. 20.1

Method

The trainees working as a group take a fixed-size sample from the box (100 items). The number of defective items in the sample is then recorded on the chart paper using the tally check method. This procedure is repeated approximately 50 times and the result recorded each time.

If the number defective in the population is then changed slightly the demonstration repeated, and then changed for a second time three separate sets of results will be obtained, as shown in Figure 20.1.

The frequency distribution diagram produced can be used to illustrate several points:

1. Chance variations normally produce a unique shape when recorded in this way.
2. By conducting the demonstration using different proportions of beads, the pattern will change, and this will demonstrate to team members that this method of recording data can be useful to detect changes.
3. It will show the members that they must not jump to conclusions when changes appear to have occurred in a process. It may only be a chance variation in the data similar to that observed in the demonstration.
4. They can also use the information they have collected as a basis for control.

Use of data for control

By observing the results shown in the diagram it will be noted that the bulk of the results centre about the mean value. This is to be expected, and more important to the team will be the less frequent events which occur at the extremes, shown circled in the diagram. These are relatively rare events. Of course, they do occur occasionally, as observed. Once this fact has been established by the data, the team now knows that these are rare events and it will watch out for them.

In the case of experiment 3, if on one occasion five defects occur, the members will say, 'Well, that is a rare event, and it has to occur once in a while!', but what if it occurs again fairly soon afterwards? Then the team will be suspicious because the members will have been taught that two similar rare events occurring consecutively are extremely unlikely. They will know that it is far more likely that something has changed, and will take action accordingly.

The same process can be used by a team to compare two different methods of processes. In this case, experiment 1 may represent the results from process line A and experiment 3 the results from line B. This will lead the team to attempt to discover why line B performs better. Now they are using the technique as a diagnostic tool, and whilst simple, it is yet proven to be extremely effective.

It can be seen that a team can make considerable use of this type of data without needing sophisticated training in statistical techniques. That doesn't mean to say that such training should not be given. The main reason why our society is less numerate than it might be is possibly because we usually try to teach too much too quickly. The greatest power of statistical techniques lies in their most elementary form. Considerable use can be made of basic statistics without any knowledge of the mathematics of probability theory, or even the standard deviation, but both of these will be very much more meaningful when the student can appreciate the value to him of learning these concepts. It teams are taught the basic ideas already outlined and begin to use them in their activities, it will not be long before the members will want to learn more when they are encouraged by their results.

Variable data

This type of data can be handled in much the some way as countable data, as, for example, if we want to record temperature variation at various intervals in a process.

It is first of all necessary to determine the maximum range over which the variations are expected, and their value, i.e. suppose we expect the extreme variation to be 30°, with a minimum of say 20°. We know then that we are very unlikely to record a value less than 20° or greater than 50°. These can be written on the vertical axis of the chart as shown in Figure 20.2.

The team will then have to decide the intervals of measure within which the various readings will be grouped. If we assume also that they believe 5° intervals are likely to be satisfactory, the chart will then look like Figure 20.3.

All recordings above 20 and up to 25 will be recorded in the 20 row, and so on. If the members were right in their estimate, the completed chart will probably look like Figure 20.4. It can readily be seen that this diagram is similar in many respects to that produced for countable data, and in many cases diagrams of this kind can be treated in similar fashion.

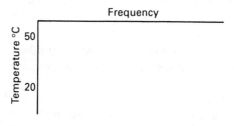

Fig. 20.2

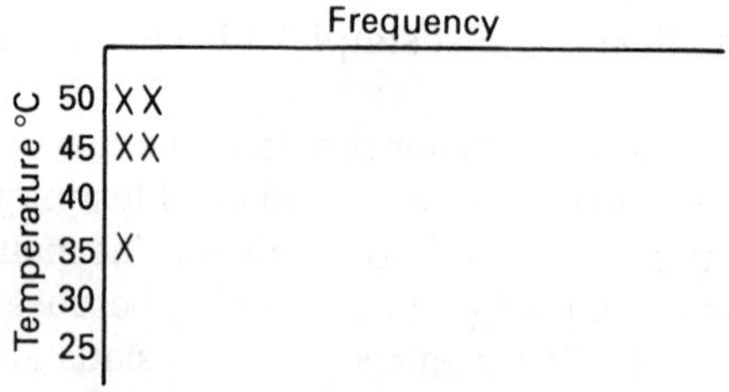

Fig. 20.3

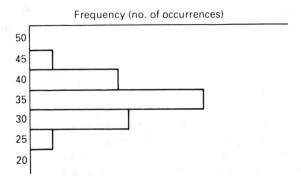

Fig. 20.4

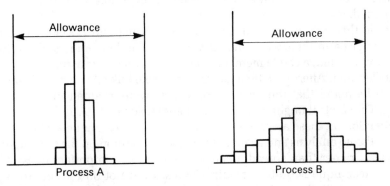

Fig. 20.5

For example: if two apparently identical processes are compared side by side, the diagram (Figure 20.5) may show process A is well able to keep within its allowance, whereas process B is in trouble at both extremes.

The techniques shown above are both extremely simple to use. Circles of cleaning staff, labourers, unskilled and semi-skilled workpeople have all been trained by DHA to use these techniques in a very short space of time without difficulty. More important, they are actually using them in their everyday work, and they also *like* using them.

The reason why a great majority of people shy away from mathematical concepts is not because they are not interested. It is usually because they lack confidence in themselves, and do not believe they can learn. Once they find that they can understand what they have been taught, and that the ideas are useful in their work, they become more interested and develop a desire to learn more. These techniques should be regarded as the basic building blocks upon which more sophisticated concepts can be built later.

It was this simple approach to statistics which formed the central theme in Dr Deming's lectures in Japan, 'Keep it simple'. He did not introduce statistics as is widely believed. Just as in the West, the Japanese were already aware of statistical techniques but, also like the West, found them difficult to apply. Dr Deming advised a more simple approach. Unlike the West, the Japanese accepted his advice.

Drawings showing defect locations

This remarkably simple technique is a great favourite among Quality circle members. It is used by Circles when they want to establish whether or not any pattern exists concerning the problem they are studying.

Consider an example from a group of workers in a garment factory. Their task was to perform several different operations, such as sewing together the various component parts of the garment, stitching hems, and so forth. They wished to discover whether more defects occur in one part of the garment than another.

To do this they made a drawing of the product and posted it in a convenient place in their work area accessible to Circle members. Each time a defect was noted, a Circle member made a mark on the drawing at the appropriate location. After some time the drawing looked like the one in Figure 20.6. It will be noted that the majority of defects were grouped in two distinct areas. The Circle thought there must be some reason for this, and concentrated its attention on these areas. It can be seen that this technique is similar in effect to Pareto analysis and again helps to focus attention on the few important problems rather than spread it across the many less important ones.

This technique is quite versatile. Circles use it not only to improve products but also in the design of forms and the location of errors. The design of a work area might be an example. For instance, in one place in the Potteries, a Circle made a drawing of its work area in an attempt to see where most breakages occured. After four weeks, a distinct pattern emerged and enabled the Circle to design a better layout. This greatly reduced the number of breakages.

Other groups' projects that have benefited from the technique have included: printed circuit board manufacture and assembly; injection moulding faults; and form design.

Fig. 20.6

Check lists

Many of the activities of project teams result in much more clearly defined work routines. Frequently there are several alternative ways of doing the same job and the team will design a check list to ensure that its proposals are properly implemented and maintained. Check lists include such items as:

- training routine for new employees in the work area;
- ensuring that all elements of a task have been completed, i.e. similar to the countdown of a rocket;
- essentials for the production of procedures manuals.

Graphs and charts

All forms of project team including Quality Circles should be taught to use pictures, charts, or graphs. Apart from the communication value of charts and graphs, teams enjoy using this approach to present their ideas. It is important that training is given in how to produce and use them. Basically there are six types of charts and graphs used in small group activities:

- line graphs
- scatter diagram graphs
- column or bar charts
- pie graphs
- pictographs
- organisational graphs

Again, the advantage to be gained from the use of such techniques is that it enables the teams to present their ideas in a way that is familiar to most managers. They give a good impression, and the results are far more likely to make an impact.

The techniques in perspective

To conclude this chapter let us look at the way in which these techniques would normally be applied.

1. A new project team or Circle, or perhaps an existing one which has exhausted its previous list, or one which feels that new and important problems have arisen in its area, will conduct a brainstorming session.
2. When the list is complete the team will segregate the ideas into
   - not team or group controllable
   - partially group controllable
   - totally group controllable
3. Several smaller problems easily dealt with will be given priority.

4. A Quality Circle type team will vote on a theme. Possible themes include:
    - waste materials
    - lost time
    - safety
    - energy
    - customer complaints
    - materials handling
    - housekeeping, etc.
5. Having selected a theme, the group will list the problems relating to it that were highlighted during brainstorming.
6. Next the members will produce a check sheet in order to determine the relative importance of each item.
7. From the check sheet they produce a Pareto diagram. This will highlight the few important problems and separate them from the many trivial.
8. The problem thus selected will be analysed using cause classification.
9. The cause classifications will be evaluated by using the job knowledge of the members to identify what they believe to be the most likely key causes.
10. The first potential key cause will be evaluated to determine whether or not it is the true cause.
11. This evaluation may involve the use of further cause classification relating to the cause now highlighted.
12. Alternatively it may call for cause analysis, process analysis, histograms, drawings, showing defect locations, check sheets, and Pareto analysis, depending upon the circumstances.
13. When the true cause has been established the team must seek a solution. This may involve either brainstorming or experimentation or both.
14. Alternative solutions may be evaluated in order to establish the best solution, or to offer management a choice.
15. Following the establishment of the 'best' solution, the team should prepare a management presentation.
16. The management presentation will involve all of the members of the team and sometimes two or three meetings will be required to prepared their materials and the method of presentation.
17. The management presentation will be made to the manager of the section together with others who may be affected by the suggestions.
18. When relevant, management should make a decision whether to accept, partially accept, or reject a team's proposal.
19. In the event of partial acceptance or rejection, it is important that management give the group clear reasons for its decision, which, if done tactfully, will normally be accepted, albeit reluctantly, by the team. Rejection can usually be avoided when it is expected by presenting management with a choice of two or more alternative solutions. These should, of course, be evaluated prior to the presentation.

In the case of Quality Circle type groups, this cycle takes place continuously (as shown in Figure 20.7).

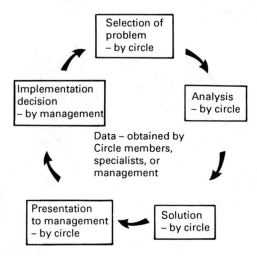

Fig. 20.7 The problem-solving process

Figure 20.8 (overleaf) shows the sequence of problem solving for Quality Circles.

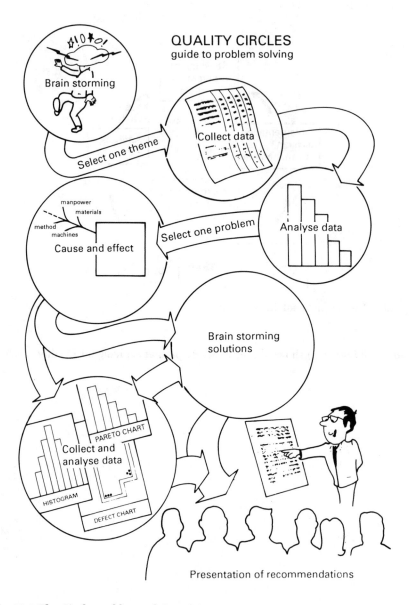

Fig. 20.8 The Circle problem-solving sequence

CONCLUSIONS

- Survival of Western businesses and industrial heritage depends upon the recreation of vision-led, market-orientated management.
- Market share must be the prime business measure affecting resource allocation and decision making.
- Success is dependent first on board room strategies and tactics.
- Total Quality provides the means by which strategies and tactics can be effectively and successfully achieved.
- Vision-led management means clear leadership from the top. This requires a visible, credible Chief Executive, with a fully supportive management team.
- Total Quality must be introduced from the top and cascade down layer by layer.
- The full power of Total Quality cannot be achieved until the voluntary improvement process has also been fully installed and related to policy deployment.
- Care should be taken to establish the elements of supportive structure ahead of introduction of the concepts.
- The power of the techniques should never be underestimated, and all training should be effectively carried out.
- Visit Japan and witness the state of the art!
- Introduce the 'Quality Month' concepts with national recognition for Total Quality, and create supportive activities such as Circles conventions, foremen's conventions, management and executives' conventions, preferably somewhere like the NEC in Birmingham in the UK, or other large and prestigious centres.
- Quality concepts should become part of the national curriculum at 6th-form level, and younger people should have the opportunity to visit factories and plant.
- The evening Institutes of the 1950s and 1960s should be re-introduced, and all employees encouraged to attend vocational courses.

EUROPEAN HISTORY OF QUALITY CIRCLES

The first awareness of Quality Circles came to Europe through the EOQC Conference held in Stockholm in 1966, when Dr Juran suggested that through Quality Circles, Japan would emerge as world leader in Quality. Unfortunately, whilst delegates were fascinated, no one did anything about it, and after this conference nothing much happened for several years. Those who were aware of the concept in those early times – including the author – did not consider it likely that anything which had been developed in Japan would be adaptable to European society.

For example, in 1969 Harry Drew, the then Director General of the Defence Quality Assurance Board, visited Japan with Frank Nixon, a Quality Director from Rolls Royce. Later he wrote to me and said that he returned to the UK full of enthusiasm for the Quality Circle concept but nobody would listen to him. Shortly afterwards Dr Brian Jenney of Birmingham University included Quality Circles in the management syllabus of the education requirements of the Institute of Quality Assurance.

In 1972 a Japanese book entitled *Japan's Quality Control Circles* was published in English by the Asian Productivity Organisation with an introduction by Frank Nixon of Rolls Royce Ltd. He wrote: 'Quality Control Circles represent something which is much bigger, much more fundamental to management, than Quality Control as it is understood in most Western countries. The Circles are, basically, an effective means by which the senior managements of a large sector of Japanese industry have succeeded in involving their employees in the aims and purpose of their enterprises. This involvement, and the special factors which have made the Quality Control movement possible, are underlying reasons for Japan's rapid rate of progress.'

I first introduced an appreciation of Quality Circles into my three-day 'Management of Quality Assurance' seminars in 1972. This was also the time when quality assurance was increasingly being demanded as a contractual requirement by large procurement organisations such as the Ministry of Defence, electronics companies, and the automative industry. At this time I became increasingly concerned that these developments, whilst important, appeared to concentrate almost entirely on systems and procedures, and lacked any appreciable attempt to involve people. It was at this point that I took a deeper look at Quality Circles, and it happened to coincide with a visit to the UK by a Japanese Quality specialist, Dr Kano. As secretary of one of the regional branches of the Institute of Quality Assurance, I was fortunate to become involved with some of the organisation of his UK tour. It was at this point that I began to realise that there was nothing inherently *Japanese* in Quality Circles; they represented as much as anything a better way of treating people.

I subsequently began to seek out all available information, and fortunately, in 1978, made the acquaintance of my now good friend Professor Naoto Sasaki, then of Sophia University, and now of the University of Tsukuba. When I told him my feelings he replied that he happened to be an acquaintance of Professor Ishikawa, the father figure of Quality Circles in Japan. He said that when he returned to Japan he would inform Professor Ishikawa of my interest.

I later received some correspondence from Professor Ishikawa in which he offered to come to the UK, to give a seminar on the topic. Included with his letter was some material on Quality Circles which gave me a much greater insight into the concept, and it was from this material that I understood clearly the reasons why Taylorism prevents the emergence of effective Circle programmes in our society. The effect of this realisation was electrifying, and from that moment my mind was flooded with the implications.

At that time, as a lecturer in a college of higher education, I had no platform from which to project these ideas with any impact, and the college was certainly not in a position to finance a speculative function involving an eminent Japanese expert. Such was my enthusiasm that, in co-operation with a private organisation with which I was involved, a conference was arranged in 1979 at the Institute of Directors, with Professor Ishikawa speaking on the first day. At that time I was totally unaware of developments in the United States or in Western Europe.

In order to do justice to such an eminent visitor, I contacted the Department of Trade, for suggestions as to who might be approached as supporting speakers. My contact then told me that Rolly Royce at Derby were operating a similar programme which they referred to as 'Quality Control Groups', and put me in contact with Jim Rooney at Derby who was responsible for the development of the programme.

Jim invited me up to Derby in June 1979. He showed me the training materials that they had prepared and which were based, to some extent, on a Japanese tape slide entitled 'Quality Control Circles for Foremen', and he gave me the opportunity to talk to group members, a shop steward, and several managers. I then asked Jim if he would like to participate in my conference. Not only did he agree, but he also offered to bring with him a shop steward, Tony Hunt, who was a keen member of one of the groups. Tony received a standing ovation for his presentation. I made subsequent visit to Rolls Royce at Derby with Jason Crispe of the *Financial Times*, after which an article appeared on 28 August 1979 entitled 'Rolls Royce Shares in the Secrets of Japan's Success'.

During 1978/79 I had worked with Stan Warboys, Quality Manager at

Eurotherm Ltd, Worthing, to develop a number of Circles in that factory. The Eurotherm work resulted from Stan's attendance at a Quality Seminar I had organised in 1977. This was followed by Stan asking me to give an one-day presentation to his supervisors in 1978, at a seafront hotel. These supervisors became extremely enthusiastic, and the seminars were followed by the establishment of the first Quality Circles. Stan Warboys was also invited to speak at the London conference, and so we were able to follow Professor Ishikawa's presentation of the concept by two real examples of success in British industry.

The object of this was to birdge the credibility gap and prove that the concept really can be made to work in our society.

The conference was a huge success, with over 120 delegates from a broad spectrum of industry. These included representatives from Brintons Carpets, British Leyland, British Aerospace, Ford Motor Company, Mullard Ltd, Marks & Spencer, Chloride Ltd, Linotype Ltd, Welworthy, and many other well-known companies. The conference was featured on World Service Radio, and given publicity in a large number of periodicals and newspapers.

Almost immediately after it, I made the acquaintance in London of Jeff Beardsley, the Quality Circle Consultant from the USA referred to earlier. We became instant friends and after long discussions about the concept, training, the pitfalls, and in fact every aspect of the subject, agreed to collaborate with each other. The effect of this was immediate, and the injection of Jeff's experience into my own knowledge gave me the background to offer what has become the backbone of both my and all other David Hutchins Associates training methods and advice. Following these discussions with Jeff Beardsley, at the end of 1979 I began the training of Brintons Carpets Ltd, introducing the ideas which I had learned. This was followed soon afterwards by a similar training programme which included participants from S R Gent Ltd, Peter Blond & Co Ltd, Sussman Ltd, and a Scottish company which did not subsequently take up the concept.

At the London conference Professor Ishikawa said: 'Do not expect too much. If you have managed to developed Circles in two companies in one year you will be doing well.' In the event, I had trained 15 companies, with between 6 and 12 Circles in each company. By 1983, and with Consultants Ted Jowett and Brian Tilley and then others joining me, the figure had risen to over 100 locations with active programmes.

During this time other consultants appeared on the scene, each with a different approach and varying levels of ability. Conferences have been organised by the National Economic Development Organisation (NEDO), the Work Research Unit of the Department of Industry, and many others.

David Hutchins Associates also developed a Circle Network, membership of which was automatic upon receipt of DHA Quality Circle training. This was supported by a regular news sheet entitled 'Circle Review'.

In 1982 a National Society of Quality Circles was formed, spearheaded mainly by Dick Fletcher of Wedgwood who became its first chairman and then President. Membership of the Society is open to organisations who have active Quality Circles, and its basic intention is to provide a forum for cross-fertilisation and increasing the awareness of others to the concept. It is not a training organisation.

I believe that Quality Circles in the UK and Europe generally are exposed to the same risks as in the USA: namely, that they will fail unless underpinned by Total Quality, and the external infrastructure. This infrastructure does not exist in our society and it was for this reason that Circle Network was formed. It enabled those companies that we had trained to obtain the relevant support to ensure the combined growth and development of their programmes. DHA now conducts network-style workshop on Total Quality which are increasingly well attended (over 100 in 1989).

The development of Circles on the continent of Europe originated in Sweden as a result of the activities of B. Orjan Alexanderson, a well-known speaker at EOQC Conferences.

Apart from Norway, where the awareness of Quality Circles was stimulated by Asbjørn Aune of Trondheim University, it is difficult to pinpoint any particular individual responsible for developments in other European countries. Most countries have some development, with origins mainly in one or other of the sources already mentioned.

We ourselves have worked in many non-English-speaking countries and our experience has further confirmed our conviction that there is nothing cultural in Total Quality. The concept will work anywhere where people work together and share common work experience. People want to be recognised for their knowledge and talent. If you treat them like human beings they will usually behave like them. Most of our problems stem from treating them otherwise.

In answer to the question 'Should we start Total Quality?' one might reply, 'What future do we have if we do not!'.

Highlights of the Quality Circle movement

Events worldwide

Apr	1962	*GEMBA TO QC* (*QC for the Foreman*) begins as a quarterly publication. Formation and registration of Quality Circles are solicited.
May	1962	The First Quality Circle is registered.
Nov	1962	The first Foreman QC Conference is held.
May	1963	The first Quality Circle Conference is held.
Jan	1964	*GEMBA TO QC* is changed into a monthly publication.
Sep	1964	Regional Chapters are organised.
May	1965	Reports on the Quality Circle activities in Japan are presented at the 19th ASQC Convention held in Los Angeles.
Nov	1965	FQC Award is established.

Jun	1966	Special session on Quality Circle activities is organised at the Joint Conference at EOQC and ASOC held in Stockholm.
Feb	1967	QC Basic Course for Foremen starts.
Apr	1968	The first Quality Circle Team (1FQCT) visits USA.
Oct	1969	Many reports on Quality Circle activities are presented at the International Conference on Quality Control (ICQC 1969 – Tokyo).
Nov	1970	*Fundamentals of the Quality Circle* is published by Japanese Union of Scientists and Engineers.
Nov	1970	QC correspondence course for foremen starts.
Aug	1971	The 200th Quality Circle Conference is held.
Nov	1971	Quality Circle Grand Prize is established. The first All Japan Quality Circle Conference is held.
Aug	1972	The number of Circles registered reaches 50,000.
Jan	1973	*GEMBA TO QC* is renamed *FQC*.
May	1973	The 300th Quality Circle Conference is held.
Nov	1973	The number of Circles registered reaches 60,000.
Oct	1974	The 400th Quality Circle Conference is held.
Oct	1975	First Quality Circle formed in the United States at the Lockheed Missiles and Space Company.

Highpoints relevant to the United Kingdom

Sep	1979	First UK Conference on Quality Circles entitled, 'The Japanese approach to Product Quality Management' attended by over 100 people. Organised by David Hutchins and held at the Institute of Directors in London.
Feb	1980	International Conference on Quality Circles organised by David Hutchins at Cavendish Conference Centre.
Sep	1980	World Convention on Quality Circles organised by David Hutchins and held at the Waldorf Hotel, London. Speakers from Japan, Norway, Sweden, Brazil, Germany, USA, Australia and UK.
Sep	1981	Second International Convention on Quality Circles, Tokyo. British party organised jointly by David Hutchins Associates and the Institute of Quality Assurance.
Oct	1981	*Circle Review* published by DHA. The first regular newsletter specifically for Quality Circles to be circulated in the UK.
May	1982	Inauguration of the National Society of Quality Circles.
June	1982	'If Japan can, so can we' – two-day conference with Quality Circles making presentations, Cavendish Conference Centre, London.
Oct	1982	First British/Japanese National Quality Circle Convention held at the Skyway Hotel, Heathrow, London.

Mar	1983	First Northern Convention of Network Circle Members Leaders and Facilitators in the UK held at the Post House, Manchester.
Mar	1983	First Southern Convention of Network Circle Members Leaders and Facilitators in the UK held at the Skyway Hotel, Heathrow, London.
May	1983	First National Society for Quality Circles Conference, London.
Mar	1984	First National Convention of Network Circle Members Leaders and Facilitators in the UK held at Stratford-upon-Avon.
May	1984	Second National Society for Quality Circles Conference, London.
Jun	1984	World Quality Congress, Brighton.
Sep	1984	First European Seminar on Quality Circles, Helsinki, Finland.

Highpoints relevant to the United States

June	1966	Dr J.M. Juran address at European Organisation for Quality Control (EOQC) Seminar in Stockholm, Sweden, predicts Japanese success due to Quality Control Circles.
Oct	1974	First US Quality Circles established at Lockheed Space Missile factory in California.
Late	1977	International Association of Quality Circles (IAQC) founded.
	1980	IAQC membership exceeds 1000.
Mar	1982	International Resource Development Inc. report indicates 12,424 Circles in US companies.
Mar	1982	IAQC National Conference attracts over 2000.
Oct	1982	IAQC holds first Regional Conference in Memphis.
	1982	New York Stock Exchange Survey shows that 75% of the large manufacturing companies (over 10 000 employees) have Quality Circles. 44% of the total companies with over 500 employees are using Quality Circles.
Apr	1983	IAQC National Convention attracts over 2000 participants.
	1984	Membership of IAQC over 6000 with more than 70 Chapters in US.

Examples of successfully applied Total Quality programmes

THE QUALITY REVOLUTION AT AMERSHAM INTERNATIONAL
PROGRESS WITHIN LIFE SCIENCES

(Source: *Quality Review*, June 1989)

Life Sciences

Amersham International is renowned world-wide for providing high-technology products which improve the quality of life by helping to diagnose disease, by advancing the understanding of processes of life and by enhancing manufacturing efficiency. One of the four major business units is Life Sciences (formerly Research Products) which concentrates on supplying innovative reagents and instrument systems to the life science market.

Life Sciences
- Sales: over £64 million (1987/88)
- Employees: over 500
- Sites at Cardiff and Amersham
- 90% of business is outside the UK, serving 150 countries
- 2000 products, 80% of which are radioactive
- More than 95% of order shipped within 24 hours of receipt.

Awakening to Quality
Despite the success already achieved by Life Sciences, the senior managers realised that even greater efforts would be needed to remain competitive in the future. Exposure to the Quality message through seminars and the DTI initiative led them to belive that Total Quality Management was the way forward, and would result in the culture change that they desired.

Mobilisation to action on Quality began over a year ago when the General Manager of Life Sciences, Dr Sandy Primrose, launched the Quality Improvement Programme at the time the new business unit was formed:
- A new post of Quality Improvement Manager was created, with the responsibility to drive the programme forward on a day-to-day basis.
- A Quality Council of senior managers was set up to lead the programme through its early stages.
- The General Manager chaired the Quality Council.

The Policy
The key task of the Quality Council has been to publish the Quality Policy needed to meet the long term mission of the business:

Life Science Quality Policy
Life Sciences will be seen by its competitors and customers as a World Class leader in Quality.
- We will make Quality and Safety key priorities in everything we do.
- We will fully understand the needs of our internal and external customers, and supply products and services that meet or exceed their expectations.
- We will use everyone's skills and enthusiasm to achieve our Quality Policy.
- We will set ourselves annual, ongoing targets for Quality Improvement, based on the principle of 'Get it right first time'. This message was circulated to all members of Life Sciences.

The Four Stages of Quality
To help in planning the programme, the Quality Council asked each major function in Life Sciences to defined the milestones which would point the way to World Class status. These milestones were then combined into our four stages of quality which plot the path we will take through the Stages of Innocence. Awakening, Commitment/ Implementation to World Class Leadership in Quality.

- World Class Quality is to be achieved in three years.
- 'Right First Time' with 'zero defects' are to be the standards for World Class Quality.

The Programme
Our tactics have been to seek out the best ideas available in Quality Improvement and adapt them for our use. Key to our current campaign are the teachings and philosophy of Dr Joseph Juran, but we have also adapted other ideas from Crosby and Deming as well as those from other companies.

Cornerstones of the programme at present are:
- raising the awareness of Quality
- training in the Problem Solving Process
- project-by-project approach to improvement.

Quality Awareness
Quality Awareness talks have been held for staff of both sites to:
- introduce the concept of quality
- explain the aims of the programme
- make everyone aware of the role they can play.

This is followed up with progress reports through our monthly Team Briefings, and is supported by a regular poster campaign to advertise the success of project teams.

Training in Problem Solving
We have committed significant resources to training senior staff in the Juran problem-solving process. Through David Hutchins Associates we have bought sets of Juran Video-tapes and assistance with our initial training, but we have now developed our own two-day in-house training programme tailored to the needs of Life Sciences. So far:
- 48 senior staff have been trained
- 60% of these are or have been involved in projects.

Project-by-Project Approach
We have set up Quality Improvement Projects which will attack the 'vital few' chronic Quality problems. Often there is the same key problem affecting both our sites and, because of the nature of the work, each will require different diagnostic and remedial journeys. So we use the opportunity to set up parallel projects on each site, and encourage liaison to maximise any benefits.

Already we have:
- completed two projects
- eight more underway, two 'stand-alones' at Cardiff with three others which have parallel undertakings at Amersham.

All are individually approved and monitored by the Quality Council.

The Results So Far
This revolution in Life Sciences has given us some notable successes:
- 90% improvement in meeting due dates for one group at Amersham.
- 48% reduction in scrapped products at Cardiff.
- 24% reduction in finished stock, with no reduction in service levels.
- 90% saving in the cost of certain components.

The Future

After approximately one year, the Quality revolution has begun and is going well. Persistence and hard work have certainly been essential in getting us this far, and will be needed for some time yet before the process is self-sustaining.

The next phase of the revolution includes the introduction of Quality Circles throughout Life Sciences. Eventually we aim to have all managers and supervisors visibly involved in Quality Improvement, with most staff actively taking part in Quality Circles.

We aim to make this revolution unstoppable!

A Hodgson, Quality Improvement Manager, Life Sciences
Amersham International plc

QUALITY IMPROVEMENT IN SHORT BROTHERS PLC

(Source: *Quality Review*, January 1989)

Background

Short Brothers PLC is located in Belfast where it employs 7600 personnel in the design and manufacture of Commuter Aircraft, Aerostructure Components and Guided Weapon Systems. The Company was founded in 1901 and since then has maintained an enviable record for the innovation and quality of its products. The high quality of their aerostructure products has been confirmed by winning seven of the coveted 'Pride in Excellence' awards from the Boeing Commercial Airplane Company, the seventh being the only award to a European supplier this year.

Shorts have a highly developed Quality Control System and hold both Civil Aviation Authority and AQAPI certification in respect of their civil and military products. In common with all aerospace companies worldwide Shorts has employed comprehensive inspection procedures to ensure the quality of their finished goods. These procedures are highly formal and operated by Quality Control personnel who are thus seen to have sole responsibility for product quality. The workforce tend to feel little responsibility for quality under these conditions but until recently this was regarded as an inevitable consequence of the rigid control system.

However, during 1986 the Company Management was attracted by the 'Total Quality' concepts which were being widely publicised at that time. This interest led to an industrial tour of Japan and the USA by the Company Quality Manager, and his report, coupled with increasing competition in all sectors of our business, generated a powerful 'awareness of the need' for Quality Improvement within Shorts.

Planning for Quality Improvement

It was conceded at the onset that the Company would need the assistance of Quality Improvement Consultants during the design and introduction of the programme. Considerable emphasis was placed on the need for a Company-wide Quality Improvement programme which was relevant to all areas of the Company, and not just to manufacturing areas. The Juran approach, supported by David Hutchins staff was chosen for this reason and joint planning of the programme took place during the Summer of 1987.

A three-tier organisation was developed to manage the Quality Improvement activities. The top tier is the Company Quality Council, which is chaired by the Managing Director and has a membership of Company Executive Directors. Their role is to define overall policy and to support Quality Improvement activities affecting Corporate matters.

The second tier consists of two Divisional Quality Councils covering Quality Improvement activities in the Aircraft and Missiles Divisions respectively. These two councils are chaired by Divisional Directors and have a membership of Senior Managers representing most of the functional groups within each Division.

The third and final tier of this Quality Improvemet 'management' structure consists of 18 Functional Quality Teams each responsible for awarding priorities and resources to the Quality Improvement activities within their department or functional areas.

Making a Start

The first major step in the Quality Improvement programme was to train the members of the Quality Councils and Functional Quality Teams and to form them into dynamic groups who would identify and action the key Quality Improvement opportunities within their areas of responsibility. Training each group took the form of consultant-led three-day workshops, starting with the members of the Company Quality Council whose workshop took place during October 1987. Subsequent workshops were organised to train the Divisional Quality Councils and Functional Quality Teams. The task was completed by June 1988 with all teams meeting weekly for Quality Improvement planning and continuation training in the 'Juran' process.

The creation of an initial pool of project Team Leaders was also given high priority. The personnel were chosen for their ability and for the probability of Quality Improvement projects being nominated in their area. Several consultant-led, four-day Team Leader training courses were run during the first months to satisfy the expected need as projects were identified.

A permanent Quality Improvement Centre was also established. Its primary role has been the co-ordination of Quality Improvement training and the support of the Quality Council and Functional Quality Team meetings. The Centre staff are seconded for one to two years from a wide range of Company functions and rapidly become proficient in the teaching and application of Quality Improvement techniques. The Quality Improvement Centre provides administration, training, support and publicity facilities within its splendid new base at our Queen's Island complex. The building was originally the airfield fire station which is strangely appropriate since the Centre's objective is to minimise the 'fire-fighting' approach to problems used at present.

One Year On

The Short's Quality Improvement Programme is just over one year old. A total of 750 senior personnel have now received Quality Improvement training. Approximately 300 have attended consultant-led three- and four-day training courses and 450 have attended in-house one-day Quality Improvement awarenes courses.

Eight Quality Improvement projects have been completed and over 60 more have been nominated and are under way. The completed projects have produced significant benefits such as a three week reduction in engineering drawing cycle time in one case, and a saving of £30,000 per year through streamlining one aspect of design procedure in another. The larger projects are still in progress and are expected to generate substantial savings as their remedies are implemented.

As might be expected Quality Improvement activities have not developed uniformly across the Company. In some areas enthusiasm is high, with many projects being nominated and supported, whereas other areas display a much lower level of involvement while waiting to see if these new ideas really work. The uneven take-up of Quality Improvement is not unusual: it was evident during a recent visit to a large US aircraft company who were almost three years into their programme. However, the performance difference between the 'Quality Improvers' and the 'non-believers' had become so obvious that most were now making serious efforts to catch up.

The Quality Improvement activities have also generated improved teamwork and understanding between the various groups involved in project work. The concept of the 'internal' customer and supplier is beginning to be recognised with a resultant improvement in the overall effectiveness of some of our complex tasks and procedures.

It was very interesting to compare Short's progress into Quality Improvement with that of the delegates and speakers at the recent 'Impro 88' conference in Chicago. Our progress would appear to be on, or just above, average in spite of our long history and highly traditional working practies.

The occasion also allowed the author to present Dr Juran with a specially woven bow tie to thank him for his 'Good Luck' message when our Quality Improvement Centre was opened recently. The bow tie depicts the 'Wright Flyer' aircraft in commemoration of Short Brothers first aircraft contract, which was to build six 'Wright Flyers' for the famous Wright Brothers in 1909. Dr Juran was also presented with a copy of the Company history, 'Pioneers of the Skies' since his philosophy on Quality Improvement is likely to have a profound effect on the contents of our 'next chapter'.

Future Plans

During 1989 the 'top-down' Quality Improvement training will be extended to senior technical and administrative staff and to the shop-floor supervisors. The training will proceed at an accelerated rate and with greater effectiveness through the extensive use of local Managers who have already received training.

The 1989 programme also includes a Company-wide publicity campaign to explain the role of the Quality Improvement programme to all personnel. It was considered untimely to start this publicity before a 'critical mass' of senior staff was available to provide a visible role for their staff. However, this is now in place and any further delay will cause unnecessary suspicion and fear of Quality Improvement amongst the workforce.

It is expected that about 150 projects will be nominated during 1989. These projects are expected to include a higher proportion of cross-functional projects than was the case in 1988 when many teams were wary of tackling the bigger projects until they had increased their confidence in their new found skills.

The immediate future of Short's contains many new challenges including privatisation and the further development of the brilliant new FJX Aircraft project. However, no-one is in any doubt about the need to continue our progress into Quality Improvement as a vital aspect of retaining our position as a world class supplier of aerospace products and this programme has our total commitment.

William Morris
Manager, Quality Improvement Centre
Short Brothers PLC

ANSWERS TO THE 152 QUESTIONS MOST FREQUENTLY ASKED ABOUT QUALITY CIRCLES

During the early years of involvement in consultancy and training involving the implementation of Quality Circles, David Hutchins Associates began recording and collating the questions most frequently asked at seminars and in training sessions. The answers are designed to help those concerned with the development of Circles in their own companies. Many of the answers summarise points in the earlier chapters and can be used as quick references to important points. To reduce excessive repetition, reference is sometimes given to the appropriate pages or chapters in the text as an alternative to giving a direct answer in this appendix.

Because it is difficult to list the questions in alphabetical order, they have been grouped into the following categories.

Questions relating to:

Origins of Quality Circles

1. Q. *What is a Quality Circle?*

A. A Quality Circle is a small group of between 3 and 12 people who do the same, or similar, work voluntarily, meeting regularly for about one hour per week, in paid time, usually under the leadership of their own supervisor, to identify, analyse, and solve some of the problems in their work, presenting recommendations to management and, where possible, implementing the solutions themselves.

2. Q. *How much Japanese culture is involved?*

A. None. The philosophy of Quality Circles transcends all cultures and has been convincingly proven in widely differing cultures worldwide. The concept originated in Japan rather than elsewhere as a result of very special circumstances in the years following the war.

3. Q. *Why 'Quality' Circles?*

A. Quality Circles are part, and only part, of Total Quality. 'Quality' means more than just defects, as explained in Chapter 3.

4. Q. *Why is Britain slow in adopting Quality Circles?*

A. The most likely reason for the original delay is that it is the first concept to be introduced into worldwide management that was not originally developed in one of the formerly recognised industrial nations. Also, the link between Quality Circles and Total Quality has proved difficult for companies to grasp.

5. Q. *What is the growth rate around the world?*

A. It is difficult to estimate an accurate answer to this question. It appears that the growth rate in any country, or indeed in any individual organisation, if introduced correctly, is approximately exponential. The data which exists supports this observation in Japan, Korea, Brazil and the United States. In 1979 it was claimed that there were over 1,000,000 Circles in Japan, 300,000 in Korea, and 30,000 in Brazil.

At that time Circles were relatively new in the United States, and it was estimated that about 150 companies were developing the concept. Since then, the growth has been phenomenal, and in 1982 a figure of 5,000 companies was quoted. However, concern has been expressed that the Circle developments in the USA are somewhat divorced from Total Quality and there are some fears as to their long-term survival under these circumstances.

6. Q. *Will QCs help non-Japanese countries to compete?*

   A. Yes. That is the main point of the exercise. However, this will only be possible if the entire philosophy is properly understood. See Chapters 3 and 4.

7. Q. *Are there differences between large and small companies?*

   A. Only in the selection of the facilitator (see Chapter 11). Apart from that, the only other difference will be the ultimate number of Circles.

8. Q. *Will we just go round in Circles?*

   A. No. Quality Circles result in very positive improvements. Whilst Circles are not just concerned with cost reduction problems, nevertheless they will resolve a sufficient number of such problems to more than justify the programme.

9. Q. *Are Quality Circles a voluntary form of scientific management?*

   A. Quality Circles represent a voluntary form of participative management leading to self-control. Scientific management will continue to operate the overall systems within which the Circles will operate.

10. Q. *Will it work short-term or long-term?*

    A. Quality Circles are part of a totally new concept of management. They are therefore neither long- nor short-term but represent a permanent feature of this form of management.

11. Q. *What is the long-term track record of Circles?*

    A. Circles originated in Japan in 1962 and their development is continuing. Even those companies which pioneered the concept are continuing to develop new ideas to increase the effectiveness of the concept. Although Circles have a much shorter history elsewhere, there is no evidence anywhere of a properly introduced and developed programme subsequently resulting in failure. Many of the earliest programmes in the UK, the United States, and elsewhere, are continuing to flourish and develop.

12. Q. *Is the Circle idea likely to go away like so many other ideas?*

A. It is inconceivable that an organisation would want to suspend Circle activities once the full benefits have been realised. It is equally inconceivable that employees would ever want to go back to the old style of working once they had felt the full flavour of Quality Circle style management. Even when programmes have failed due to lack of management support, the enthusiasm has been readily awakened when restimulated.

Nippon Steel has claimed that this style of management is estimated to be responsible for around 25% of their profits. It is unlikely that they would want to abandon a concept which had such proven potential.

13. Q. *What if other nations (and other competitors) start Circles?*

A. This is what competition is all about. Either we equal or better the achievements of competitors or we fail. Until a better approach to management appears on the scene, the best protection available is to apply vigorously all the concepts of management that are currently available and offer potential for improvement. Hopefully, this book will make some contribution to that for those who are prepared to accept the Circle concept.

14. Q. *Have Quality Circles come too late?*

A. Better late than never. Theoretically it is quicker to develop an idea after someone else has done the pioneering work, and so ultimately it may even prove to be an advantage. Unfortunately, however, there is little evidence that Western Companies are even developing as fast as Japan, let alone faster.

15. Q. *Are there any Quality Circles in white-collar areas?*

A. Yes. Quality Circles work anywhere people work together and share common problems. Circles exist in accounts departments, wages, field sales, design, warehousing, distribution, supervision, management, together with traditional production operations.

16. Q. *Can Circles operate in areas of rapidly changing technology?*

A. They can and do. In fact there have proved to be additional advantages resulting from the involvement of operators and others in the development of new methods of workings.

17. Q. *Will Circles work with part-time workers?*

A. The main difficulties here include:
- difficulty in reducing even further the 'on-job' hours
- part-timers are sometimes less committed to the organisation.

However, they also have capabilities worth tapping, and, given the opportunity; many would like to make a greater contribution to the organisation. By giving part-time workers this opportunity, they are likely to exhibit greater loyalty in the execution of their tasks.

18. Q. *Are there any 'no-go' areas for Quality Circles?*

A. Yes, there are principally two;
   - Circles must never tackle projects relating to pay; conditions, and terms of work
   - They must not criticise individuals or departments. Circles tackle problems, not people.

Preparation

19. Q. *How and where do you start a Quality Circle programme?*

A. First of all do nothing, and involved no one, until certain that thorough, sound advice is available from a well-experienced source.

   Second, it is essential to ensure the total commitment of top level management prior to any other activity. Then, introduce Total Quality from the top and get this well established.

   Only then is it time to commence discussions with others, such as senior management, middle management, trade unions, etc., prior to the introduction of a pilot programme of Quality Circles.

20. Q. *How much does it cost to implement a programme?*

A. Despite the unfortunate experiences of some companies, there is no reason whatsoever why the start-up costs at an individual location should be excessive. The cost of top quality consultancy and support should not be much more than a year's salary of a typist.

   The other cost considerations will be:
   - facilitator's salary
   - members attending meetings
   - time spent by the steering committee
   - meeting room facilities and equipment
   See Chapter 12.

21. Q. *How important is management commitment?*

A. It is essential. Without the total commitment of the most senior management team, failure is certain. See Chapters 12 and 13.

22. Q. *Why should workpeople trust management's motives?*

A. This is a chicken and egg problem, particularly in companies with a poor industrial relations record. The opportunity for worker representatives to join the steering committee is the best way to overcome such problems.

23. Q. *How long does it take to set up a Circle programme?*

A. This will vary greatly from one organisation to another, depending upon circumstances. As a rule of thumb, it is unlikely that an organisation will be able to form the first Circles in less than three months from the date of the original decision to go ahead, and it will probably be nearer six months for most. For some it will be a year. Speed is not the important factor. The benefits to be gained from a well-prepared programme will far outweigh any advantage gained by jumping too many fences at once. In fact the impatience of some managers has often resulted in some very serious problems. A gardening adage is very relevant at this point: 'Prepare the ground before planting the seed.'

24. Q. *Who gives the tuition?*

A. As soon as the facilitator and initial Circle leaders have been trained, usually by a consultant, they will conduct the subsequent training of the Circle members themselves.

It is not a good idea to use a consultant or training specialist to train Circle members. This should be done by the Circle leader with the help of the facilitator as part of their own development. However, the initial training of the facilitator, first Circle leaders, and steering committee by a *fully experienced specialist with a good track record is essential to success.*

25. Q. *At what levels of the hierarchy do Circles apply?*

A. Quality Circles, as opposed to other voluntary improvement teams, can only exist at direct employee level, and include people doing similar work, by definition.

26. Q. *Is there an optimum company size?*

A. No. Circle have been proved to be beneficial in companies ranging from a mere handful of employees up to the international giants. The mode of operation is identical, and the benefits comparable.

The only problem which is likely to trouble the small company is the difficulty in finding groups larger than three people who do similar work.

27. Q. *Do Circles lose momentum?*

A. They can, and often do, but they should not. They sometimes do in situations where management or the facilitator is taking insufficient interest in the group and it begins to lose confidence. The members may hit a snag which they cannot resolve by themselves, and will become demoralised. It is very much the facilitator's job to help them over such crises. This aspect is fully covered in Chapter 11.

28. Q. *Will Quality Circles have teeth?*

A. Quality Circles are not an alternative power force in the organisation. They are formed to make more effective use of the existing organisation and must work with all other groups.

Of course, if they find it difficult to have their ideas implemented or accepted, they will soon lose heart. This is why management commitment is so important. This is the only way in which the Circle actually has 'teeth'. 'Circle power' is really generated from the enthusiasm of the activists which usually proves irresistible.

29. Q. *How do you control a Circle?*

A. A Circle should not need controlling if its members have been trained properly. It is all a question of trust, and given clear guide-lines it is very unlikely that such trust will ever be betrayed.

30. Q. *How do you 'sell' Quality Circles to the shop floor?*

A. It is not really so much a question of selling the concept as of telling the story well. Provided that the concept is clearly described there is usually sufficient support forthcoming to be able to make a start. This is even true in the most unlikely situations where there has previously been considerable hostility to management proposals.

31. Q. *Is there any point in starting Circles if good communications already exist?*

A. Basically yes. Such areas are normally the best ones to start in because it should be easy to get the Circles established there. There will then serve as models for others.

32. Q. *Do Circles cause interdepartmental communications problems in the early stages?*

A. Circles should only tackle problems in their own work area, not look over the fence into the affairs of other departments.

33. Q. *Will it work in a class-based society?*

A. Yes, but obviously the most visible manifestations of class within an organisation are always a source of friction. It is difficult to engender loyalty when people are treated differently and made to feel inferior.

Hopefully, such organisations will use Quality Circles as a means of reducing these differences and create a better society in the future.

34. Q. *What will Circles mean to our company in the long term?*

A. They will help it to survive, make it more profitable and a better place to work in.

Consultants

35. Q. *Why should we use a consultant?*

A. It is difficult to answer any question in this section without appearing biased, but that would be equally true for non-consultants too.

The advantage of a consultant is that his reputation depends upon doing a good job. That assumes, of course, that the client takes the trouble to check the consultants' claims.

A good consultant is an expert. His life, his work, depend upon his success, and it is a hard road to the top. Quality Circles are a complex topic, and whilst a superficial knowledge of the concept is easily acquired, there are many pitfalls, the solutions to which lie beyond the scope of a single text. An experienced consultant will probably have confronted the same problems before. As has been stated many times in this text, the potential of Circles is such that it would be foolish to risk failure by pennypinching, particularly when good advice need not be expensive.

36. Q. *How do we find the best consultant?*

A. In the field of consultancy, the best is not necessarily the most expensive in terms of total cost, nor necessarily the cheapest either.

The track record of the consulting organisations is the most important consideration. Ask for a list of satisfied clients, contact as many of them as possible, and compare their comments with those of the clients of other consultants. Under no circumstances should a consultant organisation be selected as a result of its reputation in other fields, or because of its size.

37. Q. *Does our management see Quality Circles the same way as the consultant?*

A. This is another reason why and initial presentation to top management is important. Everyone should have the confidence that they are being told the same story.

38. Q. *It is necessary for the consultant to be experienced in our particular industry?*

A. No, but obviously it helps if the consultant is familiar with work-related jargon or terminology. All DHA consultants make themselves familiar with the processes and cultures of the organisations they are working in during the training process.

39. Q. *What is the total role of the consultant?*

A. In a sense the consultancy required to assist in the introduction of Quality Circles is not consultancy in its purest sense. It is primarily a training service with consultancy support. A good consultant will train a company to run its own programme rather than come in and do it for them. This should be fully supported with comprehensive training materials for the company's own internal use.

The Consultant should then be contracted to make regular audit visits to review the developments to date and give advice for future development.

Senior management

40. Q. *How do you make managers listen?*

A. You cannot. But provided there is management commitment at the top, and there is sufficient support amongst some of the middle managers to get the programme started, others will come around to the idea later. Rome was not built in a day, and some people will take time to become accustomed to the reality of such a revolutionary change. There may be some who will never accept the concept, and this is a problem which senior management will eventually have to face up to. Fortunately it is unlikely to involve more than one or two managers at the most, even in large organisations.

41. Q. *Do Circle programme pose a threat to management?*

A. Just the opposite. Quality Circles are totally supportive of management. In fact Circles do not pose a threat to anyone. They attack problems in their own work and do not become involved in critising the activities of others.

42. Q. *Can Quality Circles lead to a change in management attitudes?*

A. Yes, leading to a far more participative style. This is one of the aims of a Circle programme.

43. Q. *Is management too remote from direct employees?*

A. In some cases yes, but Quality Circles can help to close the gap. This is first achieved through the presentations by the Circles, but later on a closer involvement will develop.

44. Q. *How do you maintain management commitment?*

A. Top management must do this for itself. It Circles are achieving results, this is hardly likely to present a problem, particularly if the steering committee is doing its job and keeping management informed of achievements.

45. Q. *Are Quality Circles only an extension of good management?*

A. Quality Circles do not stand on their own, they are part of Total Quality. Quality-Circles-style management constitutes a new way of thinking. It is consistent with good management, and provided that managers can accept the concept of 'self-control' there is unlikely to be any conflict with other management approaches.

46. Q. *Are Quality Circles 'just another management confidence trick'?*

A. Another? It must be remembered that everything relating to Quality Circles is voluntary and completely open and above board. If people feel that they are being manipulated in any way whatsoever they can always opt out. The fact that this rarely happens shows the trust which develops through a Circle programme.

47. Q. *Does management receive training in Quality Circles?*

A. Yes, but normally only appreciation training, except of course where Total Quality project teams are also being introduced. The training in depth is usually concentrated on the steering committee, the facilitator, Circle leaders, and Circle members in that order.

48. Q. *Will management support Quality Circles?*

A. It must if the programme is to be successful. Circles should not be started in a work area if the support of its manager is in any doubt.

49. Q. *How does management participate?*

A. By ensuring that the facilities are available, that training takes place, that speedy action is taken to implement Circle suggestions, by taking an interest in Circle activities, and by learning more about the concept through reading and discussion. Management can be most supportive by deliberately feeding information to the Circles in its area.

50. Q. *Are Circles consisting only of direct employees good enough to solve complex problems, particularly if the members are only semi-literate?*

A. It is surprising to many just how sophisticated Quality Circles can be, even when comprised of the least skilled employees. However, what is more impressive is the fact that many of the most dramatic improvements originate from initially very simple projects.

One fact which has emerged dramatically from Quality Circles is that everyone can benefit from training and everyone, no matter who they are, can make a contribution because in their job they are experts.

51. Q. *Are we solving management's problems?*

A. In a way, yes, but such a question stems from Taylorism (see Chapter 4). In reality, if everyone is to become involved in the organisation, then the problems are everyone's. Management can only solve problems at management level. With Quality Circles everyone becomes a manager at his or her own level.

52. Q. *Do Quality Circles by-pass managers to achieve results?*

A. No. Quality Circles are taught to work within the system, not to create an alternative.

53. Q. *What can Circles do about a manager who is holding a section back?*

A. If this becomes a serious problem, the Circle should discuss it with the facilitator who may be able to deal with it himself. If not, and it is impeding the programme, the facilitator will raise the matter at a steering committee meeting. If it cannot be resolved here, then it becomes a problem for top plant management. See Chapter 11.

54. Q. *Can you have management Circles? To whom do they report?*

A. In a sense, yes, however, these are really voluntary improvement teams. It is an excellent idea to form teams of managers although these are usually referred to as project teams. Apart from the fact that they are often extremely effective, there is the added advantage that such managers become even more familiar with the spirit of the voluntary concept and can be more helpful to their own Circles.

Such management teams would normally report to the next most senior manager. If possible the groups should be formed from managers who have a common direct report.

Middle management

55. Q. *Why should we want Quality Circles?*

A. Because it will help to improve the overall performance of the section.

56. Q. *How are Circles any different from 'good supervision'?*

A. This question is a hardy annual. The first Circles will usually be formed by good supervisors. Many managers have subsequently commented that one of the most impressive benefits they have gained from Quality Circles is that their supervisors are now talking like managers. No matter how good a supervisor may be, he or she is always capable of further improvement, and Circles afford a good opportunity for this.

57. Q. *Does a successful Circle programme affect the role of middle managers?*

A. It will affect their role because they will develop a different relationship with their people, but this is a positive factor.

58. Q. *Will Quality Circles improve supervisor/management communication?*

A. This again is one of the great benefits of Quality Circle programmes.

59. Q. *What if there is more than one supervisor in the department?*

A. This does not present a problem. Presumably it is a large work area, and in such cases there is no reason why all supervisors should not have the opportunity of leading a Circle if they wish.

60. Q. *How do you prevent some supervisors from feeling inadequate?*

A. This is a problem which can arise after the initial programme has matured. The first Circle leaders will have been selected from amongst the more confident, but of course that means that eventually the last supervisors to be approached will be the least confident. Added to this will be the fear that they cannot match the achievements of the more mature groups. The only real solution is to devise supervisory training to increase the self-assurance of such supervisors prior to inviting their participation in Quality Circle activities.

Specialists (see Chapter 15)

61. Q. *How do Quality Circles relate to specialist functions?*

A. Circles must be trained to work with the specialists and the specialists must be shown how Quality Circles work. Eventually, the specialists are likely to rank amongst the greatest enthusiasts for the concept, but only if they are involved. See Chapter 17.

62. Q. *How does a Quality Circle programme affect the quality control department?*

A. One of the signs of maturity in a Circle programme is when the quality control department begins to realise that Quality Circles are actually helping to achieve the results they want. It is only when this form of interaction becomes established that an organisation can even begin to think that it is moving towards Total Quality. See Chapter 4.

63. Q. *Will Quality Circles cause conflicts between departments or with specialists?*

A. The training of Quality Circles should ensure that such conflicts will never arise. Circles must work with others, not against them. There is no point in Quality Circles making a presentation of an idea to management if there is no chance of its acceptance by another key group. The Circle must obtain such support prior to its presentation.

64. Q. *How relevant are Circles to service industries?*

A. Again, Circles will work anywhere where people work together and solve common problems. There are Circles in the gas industry, in electricity, public transport, health and welfare, and in the finance industries.

65. Q. *Should a Quality Control Inspector be in the Circle?*

A. There is nothing wrong in the idea of forming Circles of inspectors or any other kind of employee. The inspector would not normally be a permanent member of other Circles unless invited to do so by the homogeneous group.

Trade unions

All the usual questions relating to trade unions have been dealt with in some detail in Chapter 16 which is devoted to that topic. Given the nature of the questions normally raised and the structure of Chapter 16, it was felt that to answer them again here would be unnecessarily repetitive.

Steering committees

The following questions relating to the steering committee are all covered in some detail in Chapter 17 which is devoted specially to this topic. These questions, which will not be covered again here, are:

What is the role of the steering committee?
What is the role of the steering committee's chairman?
Are steering committee members volunteers?

Other questions about steering committees include the following:

66. Q. *Who guides or controls Quality Circles?*

A. Circles may be guided, but not controlled as such. Within the constraints of the overall programme, Circles should have complete freedom of choice for their activities. Guidance may be given by the steering committee, facilitator, manager, or others when requested by the group. Of course, policy deployment will enable Circles to align their projects with company goals and targets.

67. Q. *Do steering committee members receive training?*

A. As awareness of the importance of steering committees has grown, so has the realisation of the importance of steering committee training Such training will make a significant difference to the effectiveness of steering committees.

The facilitator

As with the trade union questions and those relating to the steering committee the majority of questions raised under this heading have been adequately covered in the text of Chapter 11. Questions which require further amplification include the following:

68. Q. *To whom does the facilitator answer?*

A. Normally to the chief executive. It is definitely an advantage to remove the facilitator from the political arena, which would not be the case if he reported at a lower level.

69. Q. *Does everything 'go through' the facilitator?*

A. Certainly the facilitator should be involved in all major issues, but his role is supportive rather than line functional. It would be wrong to keep information relating to Circles from the facilitator. Therefore, he should at least be informed of all developments.

70. Q. *Who makes sure that Circles stay on course?*

A. Primarily the Circle leader. The facilitator only becomes involved if asked to by the Circle.

71. Q. *How do you prevent duplication of effort in a Circle programme?*

A. The facilitator can be effective in such matters by making sure that everyone is informed of all related activities.

Circle leaders

72. Q. *Does each Circle have its own leader?*

A. Yes. The leader is usually the supervisor or next level up from the Circle members. Occasionally, a Circle may elect its own leader but only in exceptional circumstances. As has been emphasised earlier, Circles are concerned with making better use of the existing organis-ation, not with creating an alternative. The supervisor is the appointed leader and should therefore at least have first refusal to lead the group. Should the supervisor not want to do so, and there are no objections to the group finding its own leader, the supervisor must be given every opportunity to be involved and also to attend management presentations. He should never be by-passed.

73. Q. *How do you select Circle leaders?*

A. All leaders must be volunteers, although they may have been invited. The first leaders should be those who already have a good relation-ship with their workpeople.

74. Q. *What is the role of the Circle leader?*

A. Refer to Chapter 14.

75. Q. *Is it the supervisor's Circle?*

A. No. It is a team, and the Circle leader's role is to co-ordinate activities and keep the group together. When the group is in the meeting room, everyone has one vote and no one's opinion is any more or less important than anyone else's.

76. Q. *Can leaders help choose the problems for Circles to tackle?*

A. As members, yes. But again they have no more influence on the choice of problem than any other member of the team. As policy deployment develops, the circles will find the selection of problems much easier.

77. Q. *What sort of problems face a leader?*

A. The biggest problems are likely to be the occasional personality clashes which can occur in any group activity. However, experience has shown these to be somewhat rare in Quality Circles, mainly due to the method of working.

Members

78. Q. *Should Circles comprise single or multi-disciplines within a department?*

A. Whilst multi-discipline Circles do exist and some are successful, such groups also account for a high proportion of Circle failures, due to difficulty in finding problems which are relevant to all members. Wherever possible homogeneous groups should be the aim.

79. Q. *How are Circle members selected?*

A. Selection is not a good word. Members are volunteers. That is not to say that some may not be invited to join. In the event that more people wish to join a Circle than can be accommodated, the alternatives are either to form more than one Circle or to reduce the member by some form of lottery. Deliberate selection is likely to bring accusations of favouritism which will, of course, be very unhelpful.

It is most important to ensure that all Circle and non-Circle members are made fully aware that it is their section's Circle and that all will have the opportunity to become involved if they wish.

80. Q. *What happens if there are insufficient volunteers in a given work area?*

A. Then it is impossible to start a Circle there straight away. Better to start somewhere else but make sure that the employees in the first work area have an opportunity to see what is going on. Perhaps it might be an idea to let them see a presentation by an existing Circle or even invite someone from another organisation to come and talk to them. It is rare for people to remain permanently unmoved if they have the opportunity to see the enthusiasm of other groups.

81. Q. *What happens if someone wants to leave a Circle?*

A. There should never be any pressure on anyone to remain in a group if they do not wish to. People should be free to join a free to leave. However, someone leaving a Circle should be regarded as a warning sign that all might not be well, and that it would be worth making one or two discreet enquiries.

82. Q. *Are manual workers capable of understanding the techniques used?*

A. Such a question is a sad reflection on the attitudes of a few managers towards their direct employees. When asked to reflect on the hobbies and pastimes of such employees many such managers finally agree that a job does not necessarily relate to intelligence, and in fact Circles made up of totally unskilled members, such as clening staff and labourers, have achieved incredible results and have had no difficulty whatsoever in learning and using the techniques. The level of education of most direct employees is more a reflection on our eduational system than it is on the intelligence of the people concerned.

83. Q. *What about the time lost during Circle meetings?*

A. The enthusiasm, greater care, and the projects of the Circles themselves will more than compensate for the loss of time. Employees will almost always produce more in the one-hour-shorter week, with Circles, than they did previously.

84. Q. *What about fast-moving process work?*

A. Of course, it would not be justifiable to stop a fast-moving process in order to hold Quality Circle meetings. Management knows this and so do the potiential Circle members. In such situations the Circle members will often propose meetings during the lunch break, after shift time, or during a break between operations. If people want to participate, it is surprising how enterprising they can be. People can usually find time for a meeting if they really want to.

85. Q. *Are there problems with mixed ethnic groups?*

A. Quite the contrary. Quality Circles tend to reduce such problems. The author has experience of many such Circles. One calls itself 'Ebony and Ivory' and another, the 'Black and White Minstrels'.

86. Q. *Are there problems with labour turnover in Quality Cicles?*

A. Yes. There can be no doubt that stability is a valuable ingredient. Some labour turnover is inevitable, and in such cases it is worthwhile training the new members to Circle independently from the group prior to their introduction.

87. Q. *In a large area should membership be rotated?*

A. Definitely no. It is much better to start another Circle. There is no limit to the number of Circles which can be formed, and 100% involvement is the number to aim for.

Non-members

88. Q. *Do Quality Circles split up workforces?*

A. Not if the programme has been properly developed and the Circle properly trained with a good facilitator.

The problem has occurred, and when it has, the most common cause has been pressure from management attempting to force a Circle to select a problem of its choice. This has caused non-Circle members to react, unfavourably to the Circles.

Generally speaking, Quality Circles tend to build bridges rather than destroy them.

89. Q. *What reaction can be expected from those who do not volunteer initially?*

A. Extremely varied, and it depends upon the historical industrial relations climate. Initial hostility is relatively rare but does exist. Provided that such hostility is not sufficient to discourage the volunteers, it should die away quickly and usually does. There are several cases where hostility has been reversed to the extent that requests have been made to start another Circle in only a matter of two or three weeks after the first Circle has started.

90. Q. *Do non-Circle members accept the recommendations of the Circle?*

A. Yes, if they are given the opportunity to contribute their own ideas and are kept informed of progress by the Circle. In most cases non-Circle members are very co-operative.

91. Q. *Will non-Circle members cover the work during Circle meetings?*

A. Invariably, if they are approached in the right manner. This is particularly true when some Circle projects have proved to make life better at the workplace.

Organisation

92. Q. *How long before a Circle becomes effective?*

A. It depends how effectiveness is being measured. If enthusiasm and morale are considered to be important then the answer is 'immediately'. Usually, the first project is selected within 2 to 4 weeks from commencement and the training constitutes guided experience. This project may be completed within 6 to 8 weeks from the first Circle meeting or it may take 6 months. This is not really important. The most important factor is whether people are enjoying Circle activities and look forward to meetings. If enthusiasm can be maintained the results will show soon enough. As far as the techniques are concerned, it is unlikely that many Circles will be fully skilled in the use of all the techniques is less than six months, and the facilitator should always be available to give guidance when required.

93. Q. *How do we overcome the time problem if some members are absent?*

A. Absenteeism from Circles is always a nuisance when it occurs. If it is due to lack of interest then something is fundamentally wrong. Some Circles have deliberately suspended their meetings for 3 to 4 weeks during the peak holiday period. This is not to be recommended as a general solution. It is better to suspend the project, but use the meeting time for some related activity. Suspending meetings can become a habit.

94. Q. *How do Circles relate to one another?*

A. Usually extremely well. Circles assisting one another in the collection of data is one sign of a healthy programme.

Meetings

95. Q. *Will Circles just lead to even more unproductive meetings?*

A. No. Circles are extremely productive. In fact, the techniques and the manner in which they are used give every meeting a purpose, and that is to progress towards the eventual solution of the problem. Circles do not keep minutes in the usual way, and do not follow the formal agenda sequence of committee meetings. Therefore, they do not waste a lot of time going through minutes of the last meeting, matters arising, and so forth.

96. Q. *Where do Circles meet?*

A. Facilities must be made available and this can become a problem with a rapidly growing programme. Meeting rooms should be free from distractions and noise, and members should be able to keep their materials in a safe place.

97. Q. *What happens if management does not allow a Circle to meet?*

A. Occasionally there will be situations and crises where Circle meetings become inconvenient. Usually the Circle will be aware of the circumstances and if the problem is discussed with its members, they may even decide to hold the meeting outside company time. If a meeting is suspended without adequate explanation, or it happens frequently, the Circle will interpret this is a lack of management support and may discontinue its activities. The steering committee must formulate a policy covering this situation, and should be referred to before any Circle meetings are suspended.

98. Q. *Is one hour per week long enough?*

A. Surprisingly yes. It is amazing how much a Circle can actually achieve in a single hour. Very occasionally, a Circle may need longer for a special reason, but if so it must sell the idea to its manager who will make the final decision.

99. Q. *What problems exist in multi-shift operations?*

A. The Circle concept can be quite flexible in shift work. There are many cases where each shift has its own Circle, there are others where Circles span shifts. Obviously, in the latter case, some agreement must be reached about payment if some Circle members are meeting outside their own shift time, but this is usually reached.

100. Q. *How can you release people for Circle meetings?*

A. Circle meetings usually take place at the least disruptive time in the week. Friday afternoons are often quiet times in some operations. In others, the meetings may take place during the break between operations.

Problem selection

101. Q. *There are so many problems – how can Circles help?*

A. Although a Quality Circle only tackles one problem at a time, there are a great many problems which are only caused by carelessness resulting from a lack of job interest. Many of these problems will simply diasppear when Circles are formed. David Hutchins Associates usually refer to this as the 'sprinkling of magic dust'!

102. Q. *How does a Circle select its problems?*

A. It is important that the Circles choose their own problems. That does not mean that problems may not be suggested by others. See Chapter 19.

103. Q. *Who decides if the project is accepted?*

A. If a Circle tackles a project which is known by its managers or others to be undesirable for some reason, the Circle will accept this provided that the reasons are explained to its members. Of course, if this happens frequently they will put a different interpretation on the rejections.

104. Q. *What kind of problems do they select?*

A. Anything which relates to their work and which they believe they can tackle and solve. Waste, delays, incorrect equipment, losses, are all common items. See Chapter 19.

105. Q. *Do Circles solve problems of any importance?*

A. All problems are important if they frustrate the people involved, even though they may sometimes appear trivial to others. Although many projects may save very considerable sums, these must be regarded as a bonus. It must be remembered that the main purpose of Quality Circles is to create a better work environment through which management benefits from a more co-operative workforce. The one hour per week is the Circles' hour which may or may not produce benefits for management. Management's pay-off comes in the other 38 or 39 hours or the working week.

106. Q. *How do Circles tackle problems which have outside causes?*

A. They cannot directly, but if they can gain the co-operation of others, they may work together for a mutually acceptable improvement.

107. Q. *Should a time limit be set on problems?*

A. This question shows a fundamental lack of understanding of the concept. It is really no concern of management how long the project takes. See also Question 105.

108. Q. *What if the Circle cannot solve the problem?*

A. Fortunately this is quite rare. Circles can be very resourceful. If failure seems likely, the Circle may abandon the project, but more usually, the facilitator will suggest that an outside specialist join the group to work with them. In one case a university professor joined a Circle and stayed with it until the presentation.

109. Q. *Can Circles work in a fast-changing jobbing situation?*

A. See also Question 16. Yes. Whilst the product may vary, usually the work locations, procedures, tooling, etc., are standardised and there are many problems relating to these. Such work environments frequently offer many opportunities for housekeeping improvements.

110. Q. *What if a change of design affects a patent or outside contractual requirement?*

A. These situations will frequently cause considerable delays in the implementation of accepted suggestions. The reasons for this should be clearly given to the Circle, and these will usually be accepted.

111. Q. *Can Circles affect manning levels?*

A. It is possible but unlikely. It is not unusual for a Quality Circle to work on a project which ultimately results in a reduction in man-hours, but obviously, if management were to take advantage of this, it is almost certain that the Circle programme would come to an abrupt end. Management knows this and so do the workpeople. Additionally, it must be remembered that the job concerned would be those of the Circle members themselves and they would be unlikely to present a suggestion if they feared that management would take that kind of advantage. Normally, if a Circle were to arrive at a solution of that nature, the members would discuss it fully with all their colleagues, and if relevant, with the union, and their presentation to management would almost certainly include a suggestion as to how the saved time could be effectively utilised.

It must also be remembered that a Circle programme is intended to make a company more competitive and it would be hoped that an effective programme would be more likely to create jobs than to abolish them.

One British company has claimed that it does not believe it would have survived the recession in 1980–2 if it had not been for the activities of its extensive Quality Circle programme.

112. Q. *What happens when they have solved all the problems?*

A. Surprisingly this question is asked seriously and frequently. What an incredible world it would be if there were no problems left to solve! Even if it were possible, it should not interfere with the Circle's activities because by that time the Circle would have progressed from problem solving to problem prevention and on to improvement and developmental activities. There is always something that a Circle can be doing to make improvements.

Presentations

113. Q. *How are presentations made to management?*

A. The Circle presentation is usually made at the completion of a project after the members have verified the validity of their solution. Sometimes, however, an interim presentation may be made, if the project is likely to take a long time, or if the Circle needs a management decision before some aspect of the problem can be studied. The presentation should always be made to the Circle's own manager, although sometimes others may be invited. Subsequently, selected presentations may be repeated to other groups such as the steering committee, other departments, or at Circle conventions.

114. Q. *Who gets the recognition?*

A. All the members of the group and anyone who may have contributed ideas or assisted the Circle. All Circle members should be encouraged to participate in the presentation, and ideally those others who have helped should be invited to attend.

115. Q. *Is the presentation the end-product of the project?*

A. Solving the problem and successfully implementing the improvement is the end-product, although, to hold the gains, some remedies may require subsequent monitoring. The presentation is intended as a means by which management can show its support of the Circle by listening to its story, and giving thanks to Circle members for their efforts. The value of the presentation to the members comes from the natural human need to talk about achievement. Presentations should be fun, and the highlight of Circle activities.

116. Q. *Would the recommendations be written?*

A. Yes. It is always a good idea for all projects to be recorded. This does not require volumes of written explanation.

117. Q. *Will too much time be spent on the presentation as opposed to the problem?*

A. The more polished the presentation the better. It makes a good impression and will increase the commitment of all. Bearing in mind that the one hour per week is 'the Circles' hour', it is up to them to judge how much time to allow for their preparation.

118. Q. *Can an individual present his or her own problem or solution to management?*

A. A Quality Circle is a group or team, and it is strongly recommended that all members are encouraged to participate in presentations. Even the most shy members will gain confidence by being encouraged to take an active part.

119. Q. *What happens if the recommendations cost money?*

A. Management has the right to reject a recommendation if it so wishes. Having said that, rejection is quite rare because Circles are usually very thorough in their work and generally produce extremely persuasive arguments in their recommendations.

120. Q. *How much does cost affect the likelihood of management's acceptance of solutions?*

261

A. Obviously such factors as cost and resources must be evaluated by management in the light of economic circumstances and other plans. If these factors outweigh the benefits from the Circle's project, the recommendations may be rejected. As stated earlier, in such situations it is important that management gives an acceptable explanation for rejecting a project. Fortunately, such rejections are rare.

121. Q. *Will Circles have authority to make changes?*

A. Circles do not have any authority as such. It is up to them to sell an idea to management in their presentation.

122. Q. *Is there an anticlimax after a successful presentation?*

A. Yes. The more successful the project, the more the Circle will be likely to crash afterwards. This particularly true with new Circles. Usually, however, a little support from the facilitator in the next one or two meetings will carry the Circle into its next project. Momentum will then be restored.

Measurement

123. Q. *How do you measure the results of a Quality Circle programme?*

A. It depends which factors are uppermost in the minds of managers. These include: cost reduction, quality and productivity improvements, waste and energy reductions, increased pride, loyalty and trust, and improvements in morale and general attitudes. See Chapters 12 and 13.

124. Q. *Do Quality Circles require appraisal/monitoring meetings?*

A. This is part of the function of the steering committee. Of course, some Circles will be better organised than others, and it is important to develop a mechanism whereby mutual cross-fertilisation between Cirles becomes possible.

125. Q. *How cost-effective are Quality Circles?*

A. Some Circles may never make tangible savings. Others will. On balance, the tangible benefits from the cost-saving projects of a number of Circles will more than justify the programme. A minimum of 3:1 benefit to cost is likely in the first year, rising to an average of 8 or 10:1 for a more established programme. *Individual Circles should never be compared on the basis of how much they have saved.*

126. Q. *Will Quality Circles influence the cost of the end product?*

A. This must be one of the ultimate objectives. One of the main at-
tractions of Circles to their members is the fact that they have the
opportunity to help make their organisation more successful.

127. Q. *Do monetary savings ever cause problems?*

A. No, but it is important to read Chapter 7 carefully to understand
why.

128. Q. *How do you cover implementation costs?*

A. Apart from the facilitator's salary, the costs of initiating a Circle programme should not be high, and this includes the cost of consultancy.
On the basis that you only get what you pay for, consultancy will
not be free if it has any value, but at the same time it should not be
expensive either. Check the claims of any would-be experts before
accepting their services, and be suspicious of anyone who has
conducted less than 10–20 complete programmes and is unwilling
to invite you to check this with his clients. Your company and your
people are too important for you to take chances.

A badly implemented programme may be impossible to resurrect
and in the end will cost far more than good advice in the first
instance.

129. Q. *How long to break even after initial set up costs have been measured?*

A. It is impossible to say. In some cases the total costs of the first two
years might be saved even before the first leaders have completed
their training. In others it will take longer, but will usually be less
than six months from the initial outlay.

130. Q. *What is the failure rate of Quality Circles?*

A. It depends whether they were properly trained. If the rules of this
book are carefully followed and a well-experienced consultant or
trainer is used failures should be very few indeed. In such cases, the
total collapse of a programme will be caused by factors outside the
influence of the programme. Even the best-trained organisations
should expect the occasional loss of an individual Circle, again due
to external influences. It would be surprising if such failures amounted
to more than one Circle in twenty.

Failures due to badly implemented programmes resulting from bad
advice are believed to be almost 100%. Very few self-help programmes
have survived for more than one year in the UK.

131. Q. *What are the potential causes of failure?*

A. The most likely causes in order of importance are:

1 Ill-conceived advice
2 Lack of management commitment
3 Deliberate obstruction from within the organisation
4 Poor choice of facilitator
5 Inadequate steering committee
6 Not part of Total Quality programme
7 Entrenchment of Taylorism

132. Q. *If Circles fail, who is to blame?*

A. The possible reasons are many, varied, and potentially complex. It is better to seek a review of the programme by an expert and take his advice than start recriminations which will only lead to more entrenched attitudes and a worse situation.

133. Q. *What would be the results of failure?*

A. Of course it depends on how and why the programme failed. Failure can range from sudden and catastrophic failure, due to the withdrawal of support by a key group, to the gentle sinking back into the sand, resulting from lack of interest or support. Either way, there is always the likelihood of loss of face by someone and the need to re-establish the credibility of the concept.

The possibility of failure underlines the importance of sound advice in the early stages.

134. Q. *Do Circles work best in labour-intensive industries?*

A. There may be more difficulties is getting people together for a meeting in some situations, but there is no evidence to suggest that any one industry is either better or worse than any other.

135. Q. *How do Circles ensure that problems do not recur?*

A. This is one of the advantages that Circles have over other forms of problem solving. Because the problems relate to their own work, they have complete control of the situation. Problem prevention is one of the most powerful signs of maturity in a developing Quality Circle.

Motivation and reward

This was regarded as such an important topic that it was covered almost exhaustively in Chapter 7 and it is recommended that the points highlighted in that chapter are thoroughly digested before a Circle programme is introduced.

One or two questions which were not covered in the chapter include:

136. Q. *Is it possible to create the right environment before implementing Circles?*

A. Difficulty here will depend upon the industrial history of the organisation. It is essential that all levels of employee involved have a clear idea of what to expect before the programme is commenced. An atmosphere of trust is essential and the formation of a steering committee along the lines described in Chapter 17 will help considerably.

137. Q. *How do you get people interested?*

A. Only by presenting the concept in an attractive way and by answering all questions openly and honestly. Whilst 'Rome was not built in one day', it is likely that there will be sufficient volunteers to get started, provided the concept is well explained.

138. Q. *What happens if the project reduces the work content when payment by results schemes are in operation?*

A. It is important to the smooth running of such schemes that equality of earning power is maintained in the incentive scheme, and that standards of performance are maintained after the introduction of Quality Circles. This is an area for negotiation, but Circles must accept some re-evaluation if the work content of a task is reduced. How such savings are subsequently appropriated is, of course, a topic for consideration by the steering committee.

139. Q. *Would it save money if we stopped piecework?*

A. Whilst direct payment by results schemes are still predominant in some industries such as the clothing and textile industries, they are generally regarded as less than satisfactory and are being replaced in most others.

It is the belief of the author that eventually Quality Circles will produce higher levels of productivity than can ever be achieved by direct payment schemes.

140. Q. *Will Quality Circles work in a piecework environment?*

A. Surprisingly, yes. In the early part of the author's involvement with Quality Circle training it was expected that it might be difficult to implement them here. However, problems have proved to be almost non-existent.

Other group activities

141. Q. *Why Quality Circles rather than other small group activties?*

A. Strictly speaking, although an individual Circle might be described as a 'small group activity', this is not true of the concept as a whole.

Chapters 2, 3 & 4 show how Quality Circles are an integral part of a totally new philosophy of management and do not stand on their own. They therefore cannot be compared with other types of small group activities.

142. Q. *How do Quality Circles differ from 'Briefing Groups', 'Communication Groups', 'Action-Centred Leadership', 'Task Forces', 'Project Groups', 'Job Enlargement and Job Enrichment', etc.?*

A. *1. Briefing Groups*   These are not concerned with solving problems, only with passing down information. The process is also referred to as cascade briefing.

2. Communication Groups   Superficially, they may seem similar to Quality Circles but they are only concerned with highlighting problems and not with solving them. They are also referred to as 'grumble shops', 'bitching meetings', 'canteen committees', and so on. These groups are more likely to use the meetings to criticise others than to highlight problems in their own work.

3. Action-Centred Leadership, Task Forces, Project Groups, etc. Whilst these groups may be involved in problem-solving activities, they differ fundamentally from Quality Circles in several ways.
- Management usually selects the membership of these groups which, unlike true Circles, consist of people from different disciplines. Indeed it is the variety of the disciplines represented that constitutes the main usefulness of such groups.
- The problem is selected by management, not by the group, as occurs with Circles.
- The group usually disperses after the successful completion of the project although members may be re-formed into different group for the analysis of other problems.

  Circles, on the other hand, are a permanent grouping or team.

4. Job Enlargement and Job Enrichment These activities do not represent an alternative to Circles. They can take place alongside or within the groups. A certain amount of J.E. will take place as a result of Circles being in existence.

It must be emphasised that none of these activities is in conflict with Quality Circles, and all may exist side by side in the same company. This can lead to an extremely powerful form of organisational development.

General problems

143. Q. *How do we break down 'them and us' attitudes?*

A. Such attitudes may lead to some suspicions when the concept is being presented but since Circles build bridges, their introduction should produce a dramatic improvement in relationships. A properly constructed steering committee will also help to do this. See also Question 33.

144. Q. *Is it necessary to introduce single status canteens, etc., before commencing Circles?*

A. The divisions created by selective facilities for refreshments, toilets, car parking, etc., and other conditions of employment far outweigh any conceivable advantages and are best eliminated, whether Circles are to be introduced or not. However, Circles do operate in even the most extreme cases of such environments.

145. Q. *What restriction do strict customer specifications have on Circle activities?*

A. In industries such as defence where tight contractual control in exercised in specification requirements, there will inevitably be some added constraints on the activities of Quality Circles. Provided that the reasons for such restrictions are clearly explained this should not lead to problems. It will also mean that the recommendations of some projects may not be implemented immediately, and again it will be necessary to ensure that Circle members are aware of the reasons for this.

146. Q. *Do the needs of productivity/quality ever give rise to conflicts?*

A. Not if the true meaning of quality is properly understood. From a study of Chapter 2 & 3 it will be appreciated that hold-ups, delays, wastage, losses, rework and scrap are all quality problems. If everyone is concentrating on these items, productivity will take care of itself. There is no point in making twice as many items if half of them are rubbish. Much better to make a few more good ones for the same effort. Quality Circle activities make this possible.

147. Q. *How much power does a Circle have?*

A. None save management's desire to show its support by accepting the Circle's idea. 'Circle Power' is a manifestation of the power of enthusiasm, and that is a very persuasive force. See also Questions 28, 90, 97, 102, 103, 119.

148. Q. *How do you prevent 'over-design' with Circle-type activities?*

A. The facilitator can help to prevent such a situation occurring. There is no value either to the Circle or to management if they re-invent the wheel'.

149. Q. *Can Quality Circles work where poor industrial relations exist?*

A. Yes, but this is where failures are most likely to occur. In such situations, the appointment of a high-calibre facilitator is essential. This, together with the construction of a truly representative steering committee with union representation, and the services of a consultant experienced in these situations are also essential if success is to be achieved. Hopefully, the establishment of a good pilot programme will lead to a general improvement in industrial relations, and this would be one of the key objectives in introducing the programme.

Total Quality

150. Q. *Do Circles work in isolation or as an integral part of company activities?*

A. Initially, Circle members will tend to work on projects confined to their own work and will only involve others to a limited extent. As the Circle begins to mature, it will begin to tackle larger projects and will require help and informations from others.

This is the essence of Total Quality. Circles should be involved in the achievement of corporate goals in line with the definition given in Chapter 3. The steering committee can play an important part in the development of this objective.

151. Q. *How can Circles be integrated with Quality Control?*

A. To some extent this will happen naturally. The process can be advanced considerably by involving Quality Control in the initial training programme.

152. Q. *How do Quality Circles relate to suppliers and customers?*

A. Circles can often get suppliers to do things that buyers and quality assurance personnel have found to be impossible. It is surprising how much effect the actual users of the materials can have on a recalcitrant supplier.

If a company has introduced a successful Quality Circle programme, why should it not publicise this fact as a means of impressing its market? This is consistent with the overall objective of being more competitive. Why not also impress upon suppliers the virtues of the concept in order to encourage them to follow suit? One must add that care must be taken *not* to use undue influence in this respect. A Circle programme can only be successful if people want to participate, not if they are forced to. This is just as true at senior management level as it is amongst direct employees.

OBITUARY FOR PROFESSOR KAORU ISHIKAWA (1915–1989)

(from: *Quality Review*, June 1989)

Kaoru Ishikawa was the originator of the worker involvement concept of Quality Circles which revolutionised post-war Japanese worker-management relationships.

After leaving university, Ishikawa followed in his father's footsteps to become an eminent authority in Management Science. His two main claims to fame are the Ishikawa diagram, a problem-solving technique, and the now world-famous Quality Circles formed by teams of workers.

The Quality Circle, one of the principal phenomena of Japan's post-war success, is a small group of people trained to identify, analyse and solve work-related problems and present their solutions to management. Since Japan's emergence as a major industrial power, much has been written about Quality Circles, and more recently it has been estimated that Quality Circles have been formed in over 50 of the world's leading industrial countries.

Ishikawa first identified the philosophy which led to the development of Quality Circles in the late 1950s, when it became apparent that American-style management was not working well in Japanese companies. He recognised that the American system whereby 'management manages and people do' was alien to Japanese culture, and recommended that a blend of management techniques combining the best of American concepts with the best of Japanese and European experience might provide the most desirable option. These thoughts were first published in 1960 in a prominent Japanese magazine entitled *GEMBA to QA*.

Ishikawa's ideas led to a fusion of traditional European craftsmanship with American flowline production. He believed that it should be possible to bring craftsmanship back to groups rather than individuals.

The Ishikawa or 'fishbone' diagram is probably the best known of all problem-solving tools. Ishikawa invented this system in 1943, principally as a management problem-solving tool, but it was quickly adopted by Quality Circles, and is now regarded as one of the most powerful problem-solving techniques available. It can be used to identify the potential causes of any kind of problem.

Ishikawa's Quality Circles were first tested in Japan in 1962 at the Nippon Telegraph and Cable Company. After that, the concept swept through Japan until in 1978 it involved over an estimated 1 million Quality Circles and 10 million of the Japanese workforce. Currently there are 2 million Japanese Quality Circles involving 20 million workers, the later development being mainly in the service industries.

Kaoru Ishikawaa will go down in history as the pioneer of a new and more humanised industrial culture – possibly the architect of a social industrial revolution. He is probably the first Japanese to achieve world status as a guru of management science and it is significant contribution to the creation of a society where self-respect and respect for others is one of the better features of the post-war era.

INDEX